£5·95 N+

KW-222-354

CHINA: POLITICS AND GOVERNMENT

Tony Saich

WITHDRAWN
FROM STOCK

M

© Tony Saich 1981

All rights reserved. No part of this publication
may be reproduced or transmitted, in any form
or by any means, without permission.

First published 1981 by
THE MACMILLAN PRESS LTD
London and Basingstoke
Companies and representatives throughout the world

Typeset in 11/12pt Baskerville by
STYLESET LIMITED
Salisbury, Wiltshire

Printed in Hong Kong

ISBN 0 333 28742 8 (cased)
ISBN 0 333 28743 6 (paperback)

TO MY MOTHER

Coláiste
Mhuire Gan Smal
Luimneach
Class No. 320.951 /SAI
Acc. No. 74.052

The paperback edition of this book is sold subject to the condition
that it shall not, by way of trade or otherwise, be lent, resold,
hired out, or otherwise circulated without the publisher's prior
consent in any form of binding other than that in which
it is published and without a similar condition including this
condition being imposed on the subsequent purchaser.

Contents

CHINA IN FOCUS

Coláiste Oideachais Mhuire Gan Smal
Luimneach

Macmillan International College Editions will bring to university, college, school and professional students, authoritative paperback books covering the history and cultures of the developing world, and the special aspects of its scientific, medical, technical, social and economic development. The International College programme contains many distinguished series in a wide range of disciplines, some titles being regionally biassed, others being more international. Library editions will usually be published simultaneously with the paperback editions. For full details of this list, please contact the publishers.

China in Focus series

S. Aziz: Rural Development — Learning from China
H. Baker: Chinese Family and Kinship
M. Yahuda: The End of Isolationism — China's Foreign Policy after Mao
J. Gardner: Chinese Politics and the Succession Problem
G. White & P. Nolan: Equality & Development in the Peoples' Republic of China
H. Baker: Chinese Culture & Society

Related titles

J. van der Kroef: Communism in South-east Asia
D. Albright: Africa and International Communism

Preface

The aim of this book is to provide an up-to-date introduction to the politics and government of the People's Republic of China. Since the dramatic events of 1976 when Mao Zedong, Zhou Enlai and Zhu De died and the Gang of Four were arrested there have been major changes in both policies and personnel. Particularly since the Third plenum of the Eleventh Central Committee (December 1978) the degree of experimentation and change has meant that almost daily new information about the Chinese political system has been released. Obviously this makes the proposed objective a difficult task but it appears that the basic pattern for the future is set. Although prediction is a dangerous exercise, particularly in the field of Chinese politics, it does seem that China is set for a relatively calm period in the near future. The problem of succession, in terms of both people and policies, has been solved. This problem has provided a sharp focus of debate throughout the seventies. The policies and personnel associated with the Cultural Revolution have been rejected, Mao's personalisation of politics attacked and the way paved for a collective leadership to assume power. However, this does not mean that there is no potential for future conflict. The programme of the four modernisations will entail a sharp competition for scarce resources while those left behind in the race to modernise may seek redress. The promises of the new leadership to raise living standards may lead to mass discontent should the promises not be fulfilled.

In some respects the book has been a race to keep abreast of the new developments. Even while the preface was being written, it was announced that the National People's Congress is to meet. The meeting is to make several important announcements worthy of mention. For example, Xu Xiangqian is to be replaced as Minister of Defence, Song Zhengming is to resign as Minister of Petroleum and Wu Bo is to be replaced by Wang Bingqian as Finance Minister. The head of the

State Planning Commission, Yu Qiuli, is to become the head of a new State Energy Commission. His place is to be taken by Yao Yilin. At the meeting new laws are to be discussed governing Chinese citizenship, income tax for joint ventures and marriage. The more open approach the Chinese are taking is shown by the fact that, for the first time in twenty years, four of the sessions will be open to foreign correspondents. Although further such announcements about personnel changes and so on will render parts of the book out of date by the time it is published the general trends dealt with in the book are sufficiently well set to ensure that the vast majority of the text will remain relevant for the foreseeable future. It is to be hoped that these do not prove to be 'famous last words'.

Although the book concerns the People's Republic of China I felt it necessary to devote chapter 1 to the period before 1949. Most students reading this book will be unfamiliar with the history of this period. A consideration of this period demonstrates the large-scale changes China has undergone in the twentieth century. More importantly, it shows the effect the struggle for liberation has had on the developmental strategy and institutions employed in China since 1949.

I have profited from the advice of many people while writing this book and from the many detailed studies from which I have drawn general observations. In particular I would like to thank Dr James Cotton for his valuable advice on some of the earlier chapters of the book. I am grateful to Dr Martin Harrop for his suggestions concerning the first two chapters. The book as a whole has benefited from the careful proofreading, suggestions and companionship of Heather Stewart. I am indebted to David Chambers for providing the general map of China and to Mrs Oxley for her excellent typing of the manuscript. Finally I would like to thank David S. G. Goodman for the incalculable debt I owe to him. First as teacher and later as a colleague and friend, he has provided a constant source of stimulating ideas about the nature of Chinese politics. The final product owes much to his expert advice. The responsibility for any errors and shortcomings in the book lies entirely with myself.

A. S.

Abbreviations

APC	Agricultural Producers' Co-operative
BR	*Beijing Review*[1]
CC	Central Committee
CCP	Chinese Communist Party
COMINTERN	Communist Third International
CPPCC	Chinese People's Political Consultative Conference
CQ	*China Quarterly*
GHQ	General Headquarters of the People's Liberation Army
GMD	Guomindang
GMRB	*Guangming Ribao* (*Guangming Daily*)
MAC	Military Affairs Commission
NCNA	New China News Agency
NPC	National People's Congress
PC	Party Congress
PLA	People's Liberation Army
Politburo	Political Bureau
PR	*Peking Review*[1]
PRC	People's Republic of China
RMRB	*Renmin Ribao* (*People's Daily*)
SWB FE	Summary of World Broadcasts: the Far East

[1] *Beijing Review* and *Peking Review* are the same journal. The first edition of 1979 adopted the Pinyin system of romanisation and consequently the name changed from *Peking* to *Beijing Review*.

Chinese measures

mu   Measure for land equal to one-sixth of an acre. Often spelt mou.

yuan   Chinese currency unit. Obviously the precise value of this against the English pound varies, but there are approximately 3.3 yuan to £1.00 sterling.

Romanisation

The system of romanisation for Chinese characters used in this book is the Pinyin system. This system is used by the People's Republic of China and is increasingly used by scholars in the West. However, some people still use the Wade—Giles system of romanisation and students will come across this system in most of the books written before 1979. Also, there are numerous names with familiar spellings in English which belong to neither of these two systems. Two names have been used throughout the text in their more familiar spelling — China and Sun Yat-sen. Given below are some of the more frequently occurring names in both Pinyin and their more common English spelling.

Pinyin	*Familiar spelling*
Beijing	Peking
Changjiang	Yangtse River
Deng Xiaoping	Teng Hsiao-p'ing
Dongbei	Manchuria
Guangdong	Kwangtung
Guangzhou	Canton
Guomindang	Kuomintang
Hua Guofeng	Hua Kuo-feng
Jiang Jieshi	Chiang Kai-shek
Jiang Qing	Chiang Ch'ing
Liu Shaoqi	Liu Shao-ch'i
Lugouqiao	Marco Polo Bridge
Mao Zedong	Mao Tse-tung
Nanjing	Nanking
Nei Menggu	Inner Mongolia
Shaanxi	Shenxi
Sichuan	Szechwan
Sun Zhongshan	Sun Yat-sen
Tianjin	Tientsin

Xian	Sian
Xinjiang	Sinkiang
Xizang	Tibet
Yanan	Yenan
Ye Jianying	Yeh Chien-ying
Zhang Chunqiao	Chang Ch'un-ch'iao
Zhao Ziyang	Chao Tsu-yang
Zhejiang	Chekiang
Zhou Enlai	Chou Enlai
Zunyi	Tsunyi

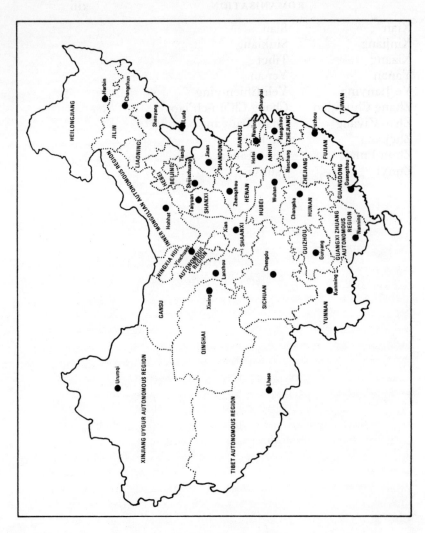

Map 1. China provinces

1

From revolution to liberation: the emergence and triumph of the Chinese Communist Party

On 10 October 1911 the Qing dynasty, which had ruled China since 1644, collapsed as a result of the seemingly innocuous Wuchang Uprising. The boy emperor, Puyi, abdicated, leaving behing him a power vacuum. The next four decades were characterised by successive attempts to fill this vacuum culminating in the inauguration of a communist regime in Beijing in October 1949. At the turn of the century such an outcome would have seemed impossible as, on the surface at least, the political system had appeared relatively stable. Yet the imperial regime was to find itself confronting several problems which were eventually to sweep it away. Three interrelated reasons combined to bring about the collapse of the system: first, the incredible stability of the political system had produced a rigidity incapable of adapting to new factors. Secondly, pressures on the internal economic system had increased. Thirdly, the system had been shaken by the effects of Western intervention both directly, through invasion, and indirectly, through the infiltration of new ideas.

The collapse of the dynasty

With a few notable exceptions traditional Chinese society was relatively isolated from outside influence. In large part this derived from the temper of China's intellectual heritage, a heritage which produced a self-perpetuating continuity and which both defined and limited the parameters within which meaningful change could occur. The foundation of this heritage was confucianism, a doctrine which preached obedience to the sage-kings, filial piety, and instilled the notion that virtue equalled education — thus ensuring 'good and stable' government. At the pinnacle of the confucian system stood the emperor, who ruled by virtue of the 'mandate of heaven'. This granted the emperor the right to rule by heavenly decree. Should this mandate be removed it was considered right for the people to rebel; the removal of the mandate was signalled by a series of natural disasters. In practice, however, the only indication of the correctness of rebellion was whether the rebellion succeeded. Although the earth might tremor and the plains might flood the emperor would retain the mandate until replaced. Particular dynasties might be replaced but the continuity of the system was ensured. Thus the Manchus, who swept down from the north-east as 'barbarian invaders' and founded the Qing dynasty, were forced to adapt to Chinese culture, adopt traditional Chinese agents of legitimisation and use conventional social structures to maintain effective control. In consequence, there developed an insular attitude towards alternative modes of thought and an ethnocentrism which the Chinese felt was justified by the heritage of which they were the unique heirs. This insularity is reflected by the name of China itself, Zhongguo, which literally means the middle or 'central' kingdom.

The stability of the system was reinforced by an education system which severely limited the opportunity to reach elite positions. In fact the reform of the examination system played a key part in the collapse of the empire because it enabled a greater proportion of the population to attain literacy, providing them with greater access to positions of power. Academic success, in turn, was integrally connected to landed property through family connections and class. The landed families provided the imperial servants, and in return a strong, central government worked to protect their livelihood.

Although there was stability in the political order, there were disturbances in the social order such as frequent rebellions against landlords. The work of Balazs and Elvin has recently questioned the idea of the unchanging nature of

Chinese society.[1] Elvin feels that the success of peasant rebellions undermined serfdom and that the independence of the serfs and tenants increased in the sixteenth and seventeenth centuries. The disappearance of serfdom led to greater social and geographical mobility and provided a new power structure at the grass-roots level. From this perspective nineteenth- and twentieth-century China is seen as the most fluid agricultural society in the world, with many people rising quickly from hired labourer to rich peasant. As long as the elite remained united the system continued and functioned well. This unity was to fall apart as economic disaster and Western influences undermined the system.

Droughts and famines had, of course, occurred prior to the nineteenth century; but what increased their impact in the latter half of the eighteenth century was the unprecedented population explosion. Before this time over-population had not been a problem — indeed there had on occasion been labour shortages. During the eighteenth century, however, health-care improvements, agricultural improvements and a period of peace meant that the population more than doubled from 150 million to 313 million. According to Professor Ho Ping-ti's calculations the maximum economic welfare for the population was produced between the years 1750 and 1775.[2] After this time any population increase inevitably caused severe problems for the economy. The situation might not have been so damaging if it had been accompanied by technical innovation and scientific discovery in industrial and agricultural production. Between the thirteenth and nineteenth centuries China had passed from a position of scientific advance to scientific backwardness. According to Balazs, the main reason for this was that the bureaucracy stifled innovation; Elvin, on the other hand, concludes that China moved into a 'high-level equilibrium trap', having gone as far as was possible with traditional techniques. The scholar-gentry felt that there was no need for change and so there was no search for new techniques and capital to build up industry. In fact, population growth meant that there was no stimulus to adopt machinery and labour-saving devices since a ready supply of cheap labour was always available.

The consequence of population growth in a period of economic stagnation was a progressive lowering of the standard of living as the rich became poor and the poorest died of starvation. Population growth created land starvation; the figure of 3.86 mu *per capita* in the mid-eighteenth century had declined to 1.86 mu *per capita* in 1833.[3] There was a growth in tenancy, a phenomenon which previously had been confined to the south of China. This all posed severe problems for both the local officials and for the Qing government, problems which were accentuated by the rising prices of land and food. The increasing vulnerability of the authorities was shown by an increase in the number of rebellions. These rebellions further aggravated the economic crisis, causing economic dislocation, a drain on funds and an increase in taxes to equip the armies needed to put down the rebellions.

In the first decade of the nineteenth century China was shaken from her isolation by Russian expansion towards the Pacific. Subsequently, the West began to look towards China for new markets and raw materials. The first reaction of the Chinese to this clash of cultures was incredulity at the reluctance of the 'barbarians' to accept the superiority of the Chinese intellectual tradition. Inevitably, conflict occurred. Opium smuggling by the British and Americans, together with other activities of the foreign firms in Guangzhou (Canton), created a crisis of authority that challenged the state's ability to rule. Also, the growth of smuggling and the consumption of opium led to a shortage of silver which had a debilitating effect on the monetary system. The Opium Wars (1839–42, 1856–60) led to a series of unequal treaties in favour of the imperial powers. The foreign powers were able to open up 'treaty ports', areas which eventually totalled 4 million square miles. The unrestricted commercial and industrial activities of the foreign powers, permitted by the treaties, hampered native enterprises. Domestic products lost their market as imports flooded in. In the face of military defeat and economic subordination, the Chinese response to foreign influence began to alter direction and seek accommodation.

Internal repercussions were substantial. The Taiping Rebellion (1850—64) was partially a consequence of Western economic and intellectual intervention. Levenson has shown the fundamental challenge the rebellion presented to confucianism and how it adopted elements foreign to the traditional order of peasant rebellions, many of which foreshadowed the intellectual revolution of the twentieth century.[4] These events convinced some of the necessity of reform and the remainder of the century saw attempts at reform within the system and the emergence of groups which saw the system itself as the root cause of China's difficulties.

The first attempts at reform consisted of a mechanical borrowing of certain features of Western progress and were not intended to introduce new cultural values. In particular, China recognised the military superiority of the West and the need to learn from Western techniques and equipment. This policy of selective adaptation proved short-sighted. The Chinese did not comprehend the interrelated nature of Western societies and failed to see that Western technology could not easily be disentangled from the social and cultural matrix in which it was embedded. During the last decade of the nineteenth century intellectual opinion took a more radical turn. This can be attributed to China's defeat in the Sino-Japanese War (1894—5) which, according to Schwartz, 'produced an almost traumatic change in the climate of literati opinion'.[5] It became apparent that attempts to regenerate China by grafting pieces on to the confucian frameword were doomed to failure. The focus of enquiry therefore shifted to the confucian ethic itself. This was now seen as the centre from which all China's failures radiated. Perhaps the best representative of this viewpoint was Yan Fu. He realised that Western strength lay ultimately with its ideas and values and although he was not an 'all-out Westerniser' he did express profound disillusionment with his intellectual heritage.[6]

Western intervention revealed the inability of confucian orthodoxy to cope effectively with the emerging challenges. The inadequacies of confucianism created a gap in the intellectual sphere which other belief systems sought to fill. A period of intellectual ferment and discussion culminated in the May Fourth Movement (1919). With the erosion of its legitimacy, the Chinese political system became increasingly unstable and the ineptitude of the imperial authorities more apparent.

This situation produced the second group of people who sought change. These were the revolutionaries who, under the leadership of Sun Yat-sen, organised the Alliance Society (Tong meng hui) in Tokyo in 1905.[7] The society rejected the notion of an emperor, who was the apex of both the political and cultural systems in traditional China, and proposed republicanism in its place. In autumn 1911 their first objective was achieved when the the Wuchang Uprising led to the collapse of the old political and cultural order. However, the initial impetus of the revolution came more from opposition to the Qing rule than from a desire to create a republic. But once the emperor had been removed the logic of the situation demanded a republic for the simple reason that there was no obvious candidate to found a new dynasty. It was under these circumstances that Yuan Shikai became the President of the Republic.[8] Initially, he followed the demands placed upon the leadership but he gradually acquired more and more power until by 1915 his power was equivalent to that of an emperor. Yuan used this power and his own prestige to launch an attempt to revive the imperial system; an attempt which met with widespread opposition. Notwithstanding his subsequent retreat, the problem was not resolved until his death in 1916.

The May Fourth Movement

During the second decade of the twentieth century a wide-ranging attack was launched against the 'old confucian shop', a term used to designate the undesirable features of the old system. However, the attack was not a united one and much confusion surrounded the question of what should be put in its place. The May Fourth Movement, which incorporated these attacks, was strengthened by the strong nationalist feelings created by Japan's pursuit of her expansionist ambitions. These ambitions were pursued under the smoke-screen of the First World War. Early in 1915 the Japanese presented their twenty-one demands to Yuan Shikai, demands calling for Japanese control of substantial parts of China. The final spark which ignited the May Fourth Incident, from which the more general movement takes its name, was the Versailles Treaty of 1919. China had joined the allies during the war and felt entitled to presume that the German concession of Shandong would be returned to its control. But Japan demanded control of the concession at the Versailles conference and it was revealed that Britain, France and Italy had secretly agreed to this during the war. The indignation which this aroused led to a 3000-strong demonstration on the streets of Beijing (Peking) on 4 May 1919. The demonstration began peacefully but ended with the arrest of 32 demonstrators.

Related developments proved more important than the incident itself. The movement represented the culmination of the attack on traditional Chinese culture developed in the previous century. Instrumental in promoting this attack was the magazine *New Youth*, set up in 1915 and edited by Chen Duxiu, which contained regular contributions from liberals such as Hu Shi as well as marxists such as Li Dazho and Chen himself. These writers sought to replace the principles of confucianism with political and social practices to bring China into line with the modern world. The two essential features of this transformation were believed to be democracy and science. The Chinese intellectuals and people were exhorted to learn from 'Mr Democracy' and 'Mr Science'. Initially, many intellectuals were influenced by liberalism and particularly by the ideas of Hu Shi. When combined with a nascent nationalism, this liberalism became a powerful force for mobilisation but it must be noted that liberalism in the Chinese context differed from liberalism in the West. In China the unleashing of an individual's energies had as its objective the restoration of the power of the Chinese nation. As the May Fourth Movement progressed it became apparent that, in addition to criticism of the past, directions for the future were required. It was at this point that liberalism was found to be sadly lacking.

The fundamental problem remained that of political power. Many felt that the pragmatic liberalism of Hu Shi could not solve this problem. A new factor in the situation was the 1917 Bolshevik Revolution which had demonstrated the possibilities for radical change in the context of underdevelop-

ment. While Chen and Li reacted favourably to the revolution
Hu did not. In 1919 he published 'More Study of Problems,
Less Talk of Isms'. This work rejected any doctrine offering
an all-embracing and fundamental solution to China's problems. Hu felt such an approach would hinder the solution of
particular problems because it suggested a common cause to
problems which in fact had diverse origins. The formulation
of a doctrine, Hu stated, should be based on, and should
grow from, the study of specific practical problems. Li
Dazhao replied that such a study of individual problems was
not necessarily incompatible with a belief in a certain doctrine
but he stressed that a basic political transformation was a
prerequisite for any effective solution to the social problems
confronting China.

The crux of this debate, as Meisner has shown, was whether
China's problems should be solved by political revolution or
by slow, evolutionary change.[9] Certainly, time was running
out for the reformers as the political situation made any hope
of reform by 'inches and drops', as Hu Shi proposed, more
and more difficult. The political situation attracted people to
the total solution of revolution. After the failure of liberalism, marxism and neo-traditionalism were to vie for supremacy over the next three decades.

The birth of communism

Initially, marxism was one of many ideologies disseminated
during the May Fourth Movement. Yet by the time of the
Japanese invasion (1937) marxism had taken a firm grip on
the country's intelligentsia. Liberalism never recovered the
influence it had exerted during the May Fourth Movement
and neo-traditionalism, its successor in the form of nationalism,
was discredited by the practice of nationalist rule between
1927 and 1937. Before marxism could be fully accepted,
however, it had to be adapted to contemporary conditions in
China, a feat accomplished by Mao Zedong. From the caves
of Yanan, Mao summed up the theory and practice of the
Chinese revolution and outlined the operational code for
the future.

Apart from its intellectual appeal the influence of marxism

was increased by three factors.[10] First, there was the growing prestige of the newly founded Soviet Union. This was boosted by the Karakhan Declaration of 1919 which renounced the privileges formerly held by Tsarist Russia in China, breaking the tradition of foreign powers profiting from the unequal treaties. Secondly, as marxist ideology was assimilated an increasing interest was taken in the workers' movement. Thirdly, and most importantly, it was recognised that if revolution was to be carried through a party was needed to guide it.

The First Congress of the Chinese Communist Party (CCP) was held in the French concession of Shanghai during July 1921. The gathering represented a wide range of views, from those of the 'democratic wing', which included Li Hanqun, Chen Gongbo and Zhou Fuhai, to those of the group around Zhang Guotao. The former group proposed that the advantages of Western democracy and bolshevism should be investigated and then compared. Li Hanqun suggested that the 'brand of marxism' being promoted in Germany also merited research. The latter group, which comprised the majority of delegates, advocated an independent line of non-collaboration with other parties, ignoring Lenin's proposal of collaboration with bourgeois nationalists, and proposed that the Party should strive to set up the dictatorship of the proletariat.

These isolationist views with their hostility to an alliance with any other party were soon eroded and following Moscow's promptings an alliance was struck with the Nationalist Party, the Guomindang (GMD, Kuomintang, KMT). Adopted by the CCP's Third Congress (July 1922), the development of this alliance was facilitated by the reorganisation of the GMD under Sun Yat-sen's guidance, along bolshevik lines. The move towards an alliance was confirmed by the publication of the Sun–Joffe Declaration (January 1923). The Declaration acknowledged that communism was not yet viable and that the struggle for reunification of the nation, then controlled by a number of warlords, and full independence were paramount. Soviet support for this position was instrumental in causing the nascent CCP to accept an alliance based on such principles. In 1924 the alliance was established at the Congress for the Reorganisation of the Guomindang.

This united front, as it was termed, was only to last three years. The right wing of the GMD was to gain contol and turn on its communist allies.

The communists formed a 'bloc within' the alliance. This was a system of dual party membership under which a communist could, as an individual, enter the GMD, retaining his communist affiliation. Leadership of the movement was to reside with the GMD. Initially, the alliance proved to be a success; the Northern Expedition, a military exercise designed to unify the country, began to sweep all before it and the communists grew in strength and influence. Between January 1924 and May 1926 communist influence in the GMD grew steadily and CCP members occupied approximately one-fifth of the seats on the Central Executive Committee and one-third of the seats on the Standing Committee. In addition, the Organisation and Propaganda Departments were run by CCP members while the peasant movement was run by Mao Zedong. The communists saw the alliance as a 'Trojan horse' which would enable them eventually to control the movement, while Stalin and Maring[11] saw the GMD as a coalition of classes — the bourgeoisie, the proletariat, the petty bourgeoisie and the peasantry — rather than as the party of the bourgeoisie exclusively. Stalin, in fact, thought of the GMD as a lemon which could be squeezed dry and flung aside. The fact that leadership rested with the GMD, the success of the movement itself and Stalin's analysis all helped cause the debacle for the CCP. As the number of strikes increased and as foreign enterprises came under attack the GMD began to reconsider its alliance with the communists. This coincided with the increase in power of the right wing within the GMD, a right wing which envisaged a total realignment of the forces in China. The growth of revolutionary activity in the rural areas worried the GMD because it was to a large extent still tied to the traditional power stucture in the countryside. The Comintern and Stalin ignored the revolutionary potential of the peasantry and insisted on commitment to an urban, proletarian revolution in a country where over eighty per cent of the population were peasants. This insistence contributed further to the failure of the CCP.

The swing to the right in the GMD was aided by the death

of Sun Yat-sen (March 1925), after which power passed into the hands of Jiang Jieshi (Chiang Kai-shek). Although the break did not become complete until the spring of 1927, when the communists and their supporters were crushed in Shanghai, there had been warning signs. Jiang had obviously made his decision to break with the communists when, during the Northern Expedition, he decided not to march on Beijing when a military victory was within his grasp. Instead he turned eastwards to Nanjing (Nanking) and Shanghai in order to quell the workers' movement and make himself independent of Soviet arms by gaining the support of the Shanghai bourgeoisie. The workers, under the direction of the communists, had taken control of Shanghai on 22 March 1927 and, remaining faithful to the alliance, they awaited Jinag's arrival. But when Jiang arrived on the night of 12 April 1927 he ordered his troops to enter the town and take it by force if necessary. The result was the arrest and slaughter of many Communist Party members.

Surprisingly, this was not the end of the alliance. With Stalin's approval, the CCP formed a somewhat belated alliance with the left wing of the GMD in Wuhan. The Wuhan government, under the leadership of Wang Jingwei, regarded itself as the legitimate successor to Sun Yat-sen. The desire to keep the alliance alive posed a dilemma for the communists who were forced to play down and even oppose the workers' strikes and the radical activities of the peasantry. Tension was increased further because the basis of support for the left wing government did not in fact differ greatly from that for the right wing. On 15 July 1927 Wang Jingwei ordered the expulsion of the communists from the GMD, thus driving them underground.

The strategy lay in ruins. Stalin had completely underestimated the power of Jiang Jieshi and the revolutionary potential of the proletariat. Clearly the time was ripe for a rethink of strategy. Stalin, however, continued to promote the policy of a proletarian uprising leading to a nationwide victory. A series of uprisings was organised for the major cities and on 1 August 1927 an uprising took place in Nanchang. The leader of this uprising was Zhou Enlai, supported by He Long, Ye Ting and Zhu De. The uprising was a complete fiasco and only lasted four days but it is still celebrated in China as the birth of the Red Army. Parallel to this movement, and in many ways in oppostion to it, Mao began to organise the peasantry. The years 1927—34 saw a competition for supremacy between these two tendencies within the communist movement.

The failure of the Guomindang

Before looking at these two tendencies in detail it is worth considering why the GMD failed to form an effective government between the years 1927—37. This, in turn, will help to answer the question, why did the communists win? The defeat of the communists in 1927 left the GMD nominally in charge of the whole country. In fact, the party proved incapable of establishing an effective government. One of the major problems facing the GMD, Eastman suggests, arose precisely from its victory.[12] The purge of the communists by Jiang meant that the GMD was cut off from its mass base, causing a change of character in the party. The badly needed radical reforms could not be carried out because such reforms were identified with the communists while those who remained in control of the GMD were either advocates of reaction or supporters of the status quo.[13]

Jiang recognised the need for drastic measures but this took the form of flirting with fascism through the New Life Movement and the creation of the Blueshirts. The New Life Movement was launched in 1934 and was designed to bring about a 'rural reconstruction' built on a conjunction of neo-confucianism and fascism. At a Blueshirt meeting in 1935 Jiang had made it quite clear that he saw fascism as the medicine to cure China's maladies.[14]

Apologists for the GMD regime, and the GMD themselves, have attributed their failure to the lack of any settled period during their rule. Internally, there was the continued threat from the communist forces which Jiang was pledged to destroy. Within his own party Jiang had to deal with threats from Hu Hanmin, on the right, and Wang Jingwei, on the left. In addition, the GMD had to contend with the military leaders in the regions and the remaining warlords. Externally, there was the threat posed by the Japanese. From 1931 Japan began to occupy the entire north-east of China, setting up Puyi as their 'puppet emperor' in 1932. Although these factors undoubtedly form part of the explanation for the failure of the GMD, they do not tell the complete story.

Three additional reasons can be deduced for the failure of the GMD. First, the bureaucracy through which the GMD ruled was corrupt and inefficient. It operated with a system of commands passing down with little opportunity for ideas or reports on the effectiveness of policies at grass-roots level to filter upwards. The bureaucracy became an end in itself rather than a mechanism for implementing government policy. As Alitto has observed, in an attempt to create a modernised nation-state the GMD equated modernisation with bureaucratism.[15] Secondly, Jiang's fear of the CCP meant that he gave priority to their eradication rather than to resisting Japan. He believed that the external threat could be met only after the internal one had been removed. This belief was reinforced by Jiang's opinion that the USA would in time remove the Japanese threat. As a result, Jiang found it impossible to place himself at the head of the national defence effort when the time did come to resist Japan. Thirdly, the GMD was unwilling to address itself to the most crucial problem of all — land distribution. The party could not pursue the policies necessary because by so doing it would alienate the basis of its support. After 1927 the landowners offered the GMD strong support. Many landowners became party members and a strong link was forged between the GMD leadership and the landlords.

From the city to the countryside

Before we can provide a satisfactory answer to the question of why the communists won, we must consider the origins of a new approach which the Communist Party adopted to the problem of revolution. After the debacle of the First United Front the CCP found itself in the strange predicament of lacking a proletariat which might provide it with a basis of support. After the failure at Nanchang the CCP attempted another uprising with Stalin's express support in the latter

part of 1927. This time the uprising took place in Guangzhou
(Canton) but it too ended in defeat.

Before Guangzhou, another uprising had been staged under
communist leadership in Hunan province. Although it failed
it did provide the seeds of a new strategy on which Mao
Zedong was to elaborate. The uprising, known as the Autumn
Harvest Uprising (1927), used the peasantry as the basis of
its support. Mao was placed in charge of the uprising because
of his familiarity with the particular area and the peasantry in
general. After the defeat Mao led remnants of his troops to
the Jinggangshan where he was joined by Zhu De and together
they later established the Jiangxi Soviet. Although this was
not the first red base area[16] it was to become the most important because it was here that Mao began to develop the
ideas which were to reach fruition in Yanan a decade later.
The communist movement now contained two polar positions:
one insisting that the CCP find its support amongst the
working classes in the cities, the other emphasising the crucial
role of the peasantry in the revolution and favouring a policy
of surrounding the cities from the countryside.

The former position was supported by the Soviet Union.
The Sixth Congress of the CCP, held in Moscow from July to
September 1928, concentrated on the need to reorganise
the Party in the cities. The peasantry was seen as the back-up
force which could be used to help bring about victory in the
cities. Naturally enough the new leadership of the Party
reflected this point of view and set about turning the resolutions into practice. The most important figure here was Li
Lisan.[17] Li advocated breaking down the army into small
groups to protect them from the enemy while they were
awaiting the upsurge of revolutionary activity in the cities.

In 1930 the GMD remained divided and Jiang's forces
were engaged in the suppression of warlord forces in the
north. This give Li Lisan the chance to promote his policy. In
the wake of a series of strikes, the Red Army was detailed to
capture the three cities of Changsha, Nanchang and Wuhan.
But again the strategy failed. Organisation of the workers was
neither as strong nor as solid as Li had hoped; the communist
forces were ill equipped and the GMD was willing to forget
its internal squabbles when faced by an outside threat. In

the event only Changsha was taken and even here the communist forces, under Peng Dehuai's leadership, were forced to withdraw after ten days. Moscow was quick to denounce Li and the Third plenum of the Sixth Central Committee (CC) (September 1930) removed him from the leadership and cancelled the strategy. The initial criticisms of Li were quite mild but at the instigation of the Comintern much harsher criticisms were levelled at the Fourth plenum (January 1931). This plenum saw the inauguration of a Moscow-trained leadership (termed the 'twenty-eight bolsheviks'). Though highly critical of Li and his policies, they still did not acknowledge the importance of the peasantry and saw the future struggle as remaining with the workers in the cities.

Mao Zedong, however, had already turned to embrace the peasantry and in January 1927 he had stressed the importance of their role as a revolutionary force.[18] To Mao it was apparent that the struggle would necessarily be an armed one of long duration. He envisaged the soviets gradually expanding their power and influence, ignoring the urban proletariat. These two positions were debated at the First Congress of the Chinese Soviets (November 1931). The 'twenty-eight bolsheviks' had been forced to leave Shanghai after the Party's Fourth plenum and had taken refuge in the Jiangxi Soviet. The congress ended in stalemate and a compromise was reached between the two positions. Despite this, political differences remained over such questions as how the rich peasants should be dealt with and in January 1934 Mao was excluded from the leadership. This internal division weakened the ability of the CCP to resist external threats and between the end of 1930 and 1934 the GMD launched five 'encirclement and annihilation' campaigns against the red base area. These campaigns included an economic blockade as well as military attack. Although the first four were repulsed the fifth campaign of encirclement began to bite into the red base area. By the summer of 1934 the Jiangxi Soviet had been reduced to about 15 per cent of its 1932 size. Though the communists had not been annihilated by the campaign it was obvious that their position was extremely tenuous and so in autumn 1934 the decision was taken to break through the enemy lines and regroup elsewhere.

From Jiangxi to Yanan

The Long March is interesting to study for two main reasons. First, the march was in itself an epic struggle for survival. After the communists broke out of the GMD blockade they covered 6000 miles in 368 days with only 44 rest days. Throughout the journey the communists were harassed both by Jiang's troops and by troops under the command of local warlords. Of the 100 000 who set out only 5 to 10 per cent arrived in Yanan. Secondly, during some of the rest days the Zunyi Conference (January 1935) was held. This marked an important change in the CCP's military and political strategy. The conference condemned previous policies and charged the leadership with 'left deviationism'. It criticised the tactics of positional warfare adopted during the final suppression campaign and the way in which the Long March had been conducted to date. The Party and military commission leadership were overturned and Mao Zedong assumed effective leadership of the Party and army.

Although Mao's ideas had won out and he presided over a relatively united Party, his power was not supreme. Moscow continued to favour Wang Ming (one of the 'twenty-eight bolsheviks') rather than the leadership endorsed at Zunyi. Another challenge to Mao's leadership was posed by Zhang Guotao, who did not accept the decisions of the Zunyi Conference which he had not attended. Zhang objected to the proposed move to the north-west to continue the guerrilla warfare. He proposed instead that the armies should march to Xinjiang (Sinkiang) where the Russians would be able to provide support. This idea was discussed at the inconclusive Maoergai Conference (June 1935), after which the armies divided again, some following Mao north and others following Zhang Guotao.

The Second United Front

When the Red Army eventually arrived in North Shaanxi its numbers had been decimated. This and the renewed activities of the Japanese forces convinced the CCP of the need to form a united front to oppose Japan. The CCP had learnt from its previous experiences and this was reflected in the content of the Second United Front (1937–45). In the early 1930s the CCP and the GMD had shared the same idea: that the internal threat must be eliminated first. By 1933, however, the CCP had begun to adopt a more flexible approach and was willing to undertake an agreement with any armed force in China with the exception of Jiang's. This change of line found support in Moscow, for in 1934 the Comintern was moving away from its 1928 position of class against class to the idea of a united front. This trend culminated at the Seventh Congress of the Comintern (July–August 1935) which called for the adoption of a united front policy under communist hegemony.

In August 1935 the CCP issued the Maoergai Declaration. This called on 'all fellow countrymen' to unite together in the fight against Japan regardless of political differences. This time, the appeal extended to Jiang. A certain amount of controversy surrounds this declaration and Benton has shown that it was drafted by Wang Ming in Moscow and issued there rather than during the Long March.[19] The anti-Jiang slogans were dropped by the CCP in May 1936, when a telegram was sent to the GMD calling for the cessation of war. The new slogan was 'force Jiang to oppose Japan' (bi Jiang kang ri). On 25 August 1936 an open letter was sent to the GMD suggesting the formation of a united front, setting down strict conditions for the unification of the soviet areas with the Nanjing (GMD) government.

These appeals found support among various sections of the Chinese population, in particular students and intellectuals, but they found no favour with Jiang himself. At the beginning of December 1936 he arrived in Xian (Sian) to conduct a new anti-communist campaign with Zhang Xueliang's and Yang Hucheng's troops.[20] Zhang and Yang were more amenable to the proposals for a united front and had already established contact with the CCP. Their stance was given a further boost at the time of Jiang's arrival by the Japanese invasion of Suiyuan. Zhang suggested that they oppose the invaders. Jiang again rejected the idea but Zhang was not to be thwarted; he had Jiang arrested and published a Manifesto for the Nation reiterating the united front programme. Ironically, it was a communist, Zhou Enlai, who argued for Jiang's release, insisting that he was essential to the nation's cause. Such a course of action by the communists gave them good publicity by showing how far the CCP was prepared to go in giving primacy to the interests of national salvation.

As a result of these actions in February 1937 the CCP again called for an end to the 'civil war' and the launching of preparations to resist Japan. The GMD replied by affirming the need to completely eradicate the communist threat but did acknowledge that reconciliation was possible given certain assurances. The CCP was to abolish the Red Army and the soviet government, accept the Three Principles of the People,[21] call a halt to class struggle and cease urging sovietisation. In September 1937, two months after the incident at Lugouqiao (the Marco Polo Bridge near Beijing) which provided the pretext for the Japanese invasion of the remainder of China, agreement on the Second United Front was made public. The alliance survived until 1945 but it was subject to continual tensions. From 1938 the GMD carried out anti-communist measures, the most serious of which occurred in Anhui province in 1941 where troops of the communists' New Fourth Army were surrounded by Jiang's and many were killed or arrested. In fact these actions backfired on Jiang as the communists refused to retaliate and continued to direct their actions towards national salvation, thus providing a counterpoint to the apparent inactivity of the GMD.

The Yanan experience

It was in Yanan[22] that Mao became the undisputed leader of the Party. Here, he was able to evolve a strategy which was not only to bring victory in 1949 but which was also to provide a blueprint for the post-1949 society. For the communists Yanan had two distinct advantages. First, it was relatively isolated and secure, allowing the tired and harassed troops the chance to recuperate and develop the base area within which experimentation with policies and techniques could be carried out. Secondly, it was adjacent to the Japanese-held areas. This afforded a degree of protection from the GMD forces but, more importantly, helped the CCP promote its nationalistic image. The CCP had come in behind the enemy lines to fill the space left by the retreating GMD and it came to be accepted as the focal point for those patriotic Chinese who wanted to fight the Japanese.

In Yanan the 'sinification of marxism' was completed. A coherent social structure was created and independence from the Soviet Union asserted. This was the final product of the move away from the cities into the countryside. But the success of the communists created problems of its own. The strong patriotic appeal of the Party meant that many intellectuals came to Yanan to wage war against Japan rather than because they were attracted by communism. According to Mao, Party membership was 40 000 in 1937; by 1938, according to Nym Wales, it had risen to 200 000 while three years after the beginning of the anti-Japanese war membership had risen further to about 800 000. Not surprisingly the majority of these new recruits were not well versed in the tenets of marxism-leninism. Also, there were problems with some of the veteran Party members who were deemed incapable of applying marxism-leninism correctly. It became clear that if the CCP was to remain a coherent, fighting unit a certain degree of ideological orthodoxy was necessary.

To build a unified Party out of these heterodox elements a rectification (zhengfeng) campaign was launched (1942–4); the methods used still lie at the heart of Chinese politics. The campaign showed that the CCP was determined to plan and organise its own revolutionary activities rather than be dictated to from outside. The first major task of the campaign was to eradicate all dogmas, an element directed at the ape-like imitation of the Soviet experience. The 'guilty' men here were Wang Ming and the 'twenty-eight bolsheviks', who still exerted a great deal of authority within the Party because of their close connections with the Soviet leadership. In practice these men had sought greater accommodation with the GMD and were accused of deflecting attention away from the urgent problems needing solution. Crucial to this attack was the need to define a basic corpus of marxist texts, which, as interpreted by Mao, could be applied by the cadres to resolve actual problems in their own work. The 'arrow of marxism-leninism' was to be firmly directed at the 'target of the Chinese revolution'.[23] A body of thought was required which was 'marxist in principle but wholly Chinese in content'. This process of adopting the basic tenets of marxism-leninism to solve the problems encountered by the Chinese revolution is commonly referred to as the 'sinification of marxism'.

The final objective of the campaign was to define the correct relationship between leaders and led. It was essential to bring about a closer relationship between the Party and army members and the people if guerrilla warfare was to succeed. This objective was summed up in the expression 'the mass-line', which proposed that correct leadership should come 'from the masses' and return 'to the masses'.[24] This reconstruction of the Party's orientation was carried out by a process of re-education rather than by a series of bloody purges, as in the Soviet Union. This relatively peaceful transformation resulted in part from the contemporary situation in which human resources were scarce and all 'positive factors' had to be mobilised to defeat Japan. In addition, it is derived from Mao's own epistemological formula and his belief in the malleability of people. Mao believed that education (embracing both theory and practice) could change the character of individuals from different social classes. This transformation was to be carried out by a process of criticism and self-criticism to change people's views.

These principles were not only used for Party reform but also for social reforms carried out in a series of campaigns.[25] The army was essential to this process. Though poorly equipped, the army was highly disciplined and to many was a more tangible representative of communism than the CCP. The army was far more than just a military force. It was important as a mobilising body, carrying out educational functions, raising literacy levels and working as a productive force to help the peasantry achieve self-sufficiency.

What did the campaign achieve? Its basic achievement was to create a stable and unified leadership, something which is essential for a vanguard leninist party. This unity was no longer based on an abstract theory but on one suited to Chinese realities and which could provide a guide to action. It provided a system capable of maintaining central control combined with sufficient flexibility to encourage the local initiative essential for the guerrilla campaign. In addition, the campaign left Mao with unprecedented power. This was reflected in the Seventh Party Congress (April 1945), the congress which planted the seeds of the Mao-cult.

Seizure of power

This rectification campaign left the CCP well equipped to deal with the GMD in the civil war (1946–9) which followed the Japanese surrender of 1945. Initially attempts were made to form a coalition government but, despite the communists' desire for a political solution, the two movements could not be reconciled. Although the GMD retained some support, legitimacy had passed to the CCP. The period between Japan's surrender and the outbreak of civil war in the spring of 1946 gave the GMD a chance to demonstrate its ability to rule but the period was marked by inflation, corruption and speculation. The American aid which was given to the GMD simply resulted in greater corruption. The aid took the form of finance, for example through the extension of lend-lease agreements, and military supplies. The US gave the GMD 900 million dollars' worth of supplies taken from the Pacific islands. Although these supplies were declared 'civilain' a large proportion was designed for military use. Even though the GMD received this support from the Americans tensions and differences still existed between them. Similarly, differences existed between the CCP and their external supporter – the Soviet Union. In accordance with the terms of the Potsdam agreement the Soviet Union occupied the north-east of China on 9 August 1945, yet only five days later they signed a treaty of friendship with the GMD.

   When civil war finally broke out the initial successes went to the GMD. They made considerable gains in territory but they killed relatively few of the communist troops. As time progressed, flaws in the GMD military machine became apparent. Although their forces greatly outnumbered the opposition they were overstretched, demoralised and lacked extensive popular support. Resentment built up at the

increasing role of the United States and large student demon-
strations were staged in protest. Finally, the economy began
to collapse with all the attendant ills of unemployment,
inflation and so on. The CCP forces, in contrast, grew in
strength. By the end of 1948 they controlled the whole of
the north-east and on 31 January 1949 Fu Zuoyi (the GMD
commander in Beijing) surrendered, Nanjing was taken in
May, Shanghai in June and, on 1 October 1949, Mao Zedong
announced to the assembled crowds in Tiananmen Square,
Beijing, that 'the Chinese people had stood up'.

Why did the communists win?

For Hu Shi the answer was simple: it was the result of Soviet
intrigues and Stalin's grand strategy. Obviously the answer is
not that straightforward, not least because Comintern policy
often ran counter to the CCP's interests. Johnson brings us
closer to the truth in his impressive work on peasant nationalism in China.[26] Johnson suggests that the communists
triumphed not because they were good communists but
because they were good nationalists. Japan's aggression provided the CCP with the opportunity to develop mass support
by allowing it to portray itself as a patriotic party. Yet if the
answer revolves so much around the issue of nationalism,
why did the GMD, the self-professed nationalist party, not
win? One would have to conclude that though the GMD were
nationalists they were not very good ones. Johnson's thesis
helps explain much but it does not and cannot provide the
total answer. As we have seen, an important reason for the
GMD's failure lies in its inability to carry through the necessary social revolution. Bianco is correct when he writes that
'it was the national problem, not the social problem, that
acted as a catalyst' but he adds the important rider that 'at
the very heart of the decisive "national" stage of revolution
lay the social problem'.[27] The communists after their retreat
from the cities came to understand the problems of the
countryside and developed policies that suited the genuine
needs of the people. This, when combined with their vigorous
promotion of opposition to Japan, produced a powerful combination of forces which swept them to victory.

The legacy of the struggle

The legacy of the Yanan period has already been dealt with but it is worth reconsidering these points in the light of the liberation struggle as a whole. The mass-line has proved to be an important organisational principle which seeks to incorporate the ideas of the masses with those of the leadership. This has given rise to the stress on mobilisation of the masses as a means to achieve an objective. Mass mobilisation has been a common feature of post-liberation politics as demonstrated, for example, in the problems of land reform and communisation. However, a continual reliance on mobilisation as a means of bringing about change has in some instances become ritualistic rather than effective. The leadership has found it necessary to demonstrate mass support for its policies. Particularly in the years since the Cultural Revolution was launched (1966), this has resulted in the devaluation of the effectiveness of the method through over-use or through direction of the movements toward spurious targets. On occasions 'mass movements' have been initiated by one section of the leadership as a means of putting pressure on its opponents, thus reducing the masses to a kind of political football to be kicked around by the leadership. The stress placed on education and the dictum of 'save the patient by curing the sickness' have remained important. This approach to the resolution of leadership differences has saved those members of the leadership who have disagreed with the Party line from a bloody end. Until the end of the fifties when Party discipline began to break down it also gave them the opportunity of continuing work even if they had aired their disagreement with the policies being implemented.

The positive role which can be played by the army not only in the sphere of military policy formulation but also in the whole sphere of domestic politics has proved to be an important legacy. Before 1949 Party and military leaders were often interchangeable and since liberation many leaders have concurrently held Party and military positions. Many other people in important Party posts were military commanders during the pre-liberation years. The army itself has often been held up as an example of revolutionary purity to

24   CHINA: POLITICS AND GOVERNMENT

be studied by the whole of society. Individual soldiers have, on occasion, been put forward as models for emulation because of their embodiment of the communist spirit. Closely related to this is the notion of institutional overlap. As a result of the guerrilla heritage not only have individuals held concurrent posts in different institutions but also the divisions between the institutions themselves have often been blurred, no more so than during the Cultural Revolution. This tendency has varied in intensity over time and the present leadership is committed to ensuring that a clear distinction exists, in practice, between the differing roles of the institutions. Ensuring that individuals, as far as is possible, do not occupy top leadership positions in more than one institution will help to achieve this aim.

It is important here to recognise the indigenous nature of the Chinese revolution. Mao made it quite clear that the CCP was not fighting a war of liberation in order to become the 'slaves of Moscow'. Obviously the influence of marxism-leninism as an ideology and the practical help of the Soviet Union cannot be denied but the end product of Mao Zedong's Thought was a distinctive approach geared to and influenced by Chinese realities. The CCP was willing to ignore Soviet advice when it ran counter to national interests and to abandon the Soviet approach to development once its internal inadequacies and its inapplicability to the Chinese situation became apparent.

The experience of appealing to a broad section of the population during the years of resistance to Japan contributed to the notion of the People's Democratic Dictatorship. On assuming power the communists did not declare the dictatorship of the proletariat but continued the united front approach, declaring the Chinese state to be under the People's Democratic Dictatorship. This was a coalition of four classes: the national bourgeoisie, the petty bourgeoisie, the proletariat and the peasantry under the leadership of the CCP.

The continuation of this legacy has presented the leadership of the People's Republic with problems. There is a natural tendency to continue with a successful formula but what happens when reality changes and new problems require solution? There has been criticism of excessive reliance on old methods to solve new problems. It has been stressed that China must reject certain parts of its legacy and find new ways to deal with the problems facing the country. This view was put forward by Deng Xiaoping in January 1980 when he said:

> In the past we spent rather a long time mechanically copying the experiences of the army during the years of war. . . . Things are different now. . . . Even the army is different today. In the past the army was a matter of millet plus rifles and you could go to battle if you knew how to fire your gun, use the bayonet and throw a grenade . . . the area of knowledge required (now) is much broader. Today's army cannot get by using its past experiences, which is precisely the problem we must strive to solve.[28]

Although Deng refers explicitly to the army his words are more generally applicable in that one of the most important problems facing contemporary China is the need to find a post-Yanan leadership generation.

Finally, there is a profound ambiguity about a party which represents the vanguard of the proletariat taking power in a predominantly agrarian country with a relatively small and scattered proletariat. There is an even greater ambiguity about the coming to power of a proletarian party which had had no effective contact with the working class for twenty-two years. Whose interests was the party to represent: those who had brought it to power or those in whose name it was brought to power?

2

The first seventeen years: revolutionary consolidation or revisionist restoration ?

In 1949 when Mao Zedong announced that the Chinese people had stood up[1] they had stood up to face a country which was economically backward, predominantly agrarian and within which there remained substantial opposition to communist rule. This chapter considers the way in which the leadership set about solving these problems and the divisions that arose among the leadership as a result of the policies devised to cope with a changing situation. Initially the leadership was relatively united but as China moved from consolidation and socialist transformation to socialist construction differences of opinion began to appear within the leadership. The major problem concerned the attempt to find the correct Chinese path to socialism. This has remained one of the major issues dividing the leadership since the mid-fifties when China abandoned the Soviet model of development. Although there has been and still is agreement about what the final goal should be, there has been and still is bitter debate about the means by which it should be achieved.

1949–55 : Economic recovery and leaning to one side

The main aims of the Chinese Communist Party in 1949 were to revive the war-torn economy and to eliminate the remaining domestic opposition. If differences remained within the leadership they were hidden beneath a façade of unity. Although far-reaching reforms were envisaged they were aimed at the removal of the more obvious inequities of the old system thus ensuring support for the regime's policies among the vast majority of 'patriotic' Chinese. Full emphasis was given to the minimum programme subsumed under the name of 'New Democracy'. As was noted in chapter 1, the experiences of the communists during the liberation struggle had convinced them of the usefulness of the united front approach and this strategy was continued during the years of national recovery following liberation. The new state, as defined by Mao, was to be a 'People's Republic' under the 'People's Democratic Dictatorship'. Important practical considerations favoured the adoption of a relatively 'moderate' policy. On coming to power the communists suffered from a shortage of properly trained administrative, managerial and technical personnel. Since priority was given to economic recovery it was necessary to ensure that such scarce resources as were available were not wasted. This meant that there was no question of the immediate introduction of socialism. The 'moderate' mood was summed up in the slogan 'three years of recovery and ten years of development'. The reforms carried out were to be beneficial not only to the workers and peasants but also to the petty bourgeoisie and the national capitalists. The forces to be opposed and eradicated were the landlords, industrialists and foreign economic interests and their Chinese representatives who were connected with the Guomindang.

The first major economic problem facing the new regime was the need to 'stabilise commodity prices' and eradicate the speculation and massive inflation which had accompanied political instability. The money printed could not keep pace with the rapid circulation of money but early in 1950 the unified administration of the whole country's finance and economy was realised. This facilitated the introduction of methods, such as balancing revenue and expenditure, currency administration and the issuing of government bonds, aimed at contracting the currency circulating in the market. National capitalists were allowed to develop their industries as a prime requisite for the development of a modern economic structure which would then be ripe for socialist transformation. Although this meant the maintenance of a mixed economy only the state was capable of providing any real co-ordination. Also the state gained control over both ends of the production process. It both provided the industrial enterprises with their raw materials through the national ministries and placed orders with the private enterprises for processed and manufactured goods. The state was therefore able to control what went in and what came out. Once privately owned enterprises were tied up in this way, the CCP began to promote the creation of joint state—private enterprises. This made sense for many of the privately owned enterprises which found it difficult to compete with the state-run enterprises and which lacked the necessary capital to replace outdated machinery. This movement reached a peak in 1954 and was gradually extended into a programme to 'buy-off' the private owners who were paid interest on their shares in the enterprise at a rate determined by the state. This gradualist policy proved to be very successful for the communists and as early as 1952 industrial production was restored to its highest pre-liberation levels.

In contrast to this gradualist policy towards the industrialists, more sweeping policies were introduced for the rural sector. Even these were not as 'radical' as one might have expected. Although landlords were to be eradicated as a class and property relations in the countryside transformed, the Agrarian Law, introduced on 30 June 1950, was a moderate one. The need to increase production meant that the communists sought to mobilise all those groups in the countryside who might support their policies. By 1952 agricultural production exceeded pre-liberation levels but the small-scale farming methods employed set immediate limits to the amount by which production could be increased.[2] In the social sphere, the most important legislation was the promulgation of the Marriage Law in 1950. This aimed at improving the position of women in Chinese society by according them equality and freedom in their choice of marriage partner. The law also outlawed infanticide and the sale of children.

The period until 1952 was characterised by a series of campaigns to suppress 'counter-revolutionaries' and to eradicate certain malpractices. The actions of the Chinese government against the counter-revolutionaries were given added impetus by China's involvement in the Korean War. Before this, the communists had little to fear in terms of organised resistance but war increased the communists' fears while at the same time enabling them to mobilise the patriotic support that had initially helped them to power under the slogan 'Resist America and Aid Korea'. This fear that external threat might lead to internal revolt led to the 'Campaign for the Suppression of Counter-Revolutionaries' which was ruthlessly pursued throughout 1951 until the war reached a stalemate. Two other major campaigns were launched during the early fifties: the Three-Anti Campaign (August 1951–June 1952) which aimed at the abuse of official position to practise corruption, waste and bureaucratism, and Five-Anti Campaign (January–June 1952) which sought to curb the violation of official regulations by private businessmen.[3]

Although the emphasis on the need for reconstruction meant that attention was focused on the solution of immediate problems, one decision was taken which had implications for the longer-term developmental strategy chosen by China. In his article 'On the People's Democratic Dictatorship' (June 1949) Mao outlined the policy of 'leaning to one side' which entailed the necessity of learning from the Soviet Union.[4] Initially, the attempt to copy the Soviet model was not the dominant feature of the period; in 1949 Soviet credits were very small and until November 1952 the Soviet model was not the prime model for organisational affairs. Towards the end of 1952 the Chinese began to move from rehabilitation of the economy to development of the economy. This generated a need for greater centralisation and for the conscious application of Soviet developmental techniques. This adoption of the Soviet model of development entailed the adoption of certain measures which were contrary to the Chinese experience of revolution.

In particular, the heavy urban bias of the Soviet model caused a reversal of the urban–rural relationship which had been built up by the CCP's 'years in the wilderness'. The Soviet model of development, as it evolved under Stalin's leadership, attempted to build up the heavy industry sector by a planned concentration of resource and investment allocation on it. This process required a high degree of centralisation. The stress on high-level industrial development meant that a good deal of power and prestige passed to the technocrats and managers on whose skills the success of the plans depended. With the benefit of hindsight one can point to the inherent problems of applying such a strategy to China's situation. At the time, however, the difficulties were not so apparent. In the early fifties the model was the only socialist model for modernising an economically backward country and as far as the Chinese were concerned it had already demonstrated its success. Practical considerations also guided the adoption of the Soviet model. To carry out the industrialisation programme China needed a considerable quantity of financial and technical aid. Given the contemporary climate of world opinion it was obvious that such aid would not be forthcoming from the West. This meant that the Soviet Union was the only source of supply. However, as the reformers had discovered during the nineteenth century, importing foreign technology also involves the import of forms of organisation and management appropriate to the level of development of that technology.

By the end of 1952 the economy had recovered. In October 1953 the government launched the 'general programme for the transition to socialism' of which the First Five-Year Plan (1953—7) was the concrete embodiment. The base from which the Chinese attempted to transform their economy was considerably weaker than that of the Soviet Union in 1927 when their First Five-Year Plan was launched. In 1927 Soviet output *per capita* was about four times that of China in 1952; in agriculture, Chinese output was about one-fifth of that of the Soviet Union. This meant that fewer funds were available for extraction from the countryside to finance the programme of heavy industrialisation. To solve the problem meant increasing agricultural production but this was 'fettered' by the small-scale nature of Chinese farming units and the political pressure to push ahead with the socialisation of agriculture increased. Although the plan was not officially promulgated until early 1955 it also covered the temporary economic programmes of 1953–4. The plan concentrated on industrial development with 88 per cent of the state's capital investment going to heavy industry. Six hundred and ninety-four major industrial enterprises were to be built, of which 472 were to be set up in the interior regions — 156 of the total were be be constructed using Soviet advice and equipment.

The plan proved a success. Industrial production grew at 18 per cent per annum, compared to a target of 14.7 per cent. Heavy industry grew at 15.4 per cent per annum and light industry at 12.9 per cent. However, agricultural production lagged behind with a growth rate of only 4.5 per cent per annum.[5] Despite these considerable successes the strategy came in for increasing criticism and the leadership began to evolve its own developmental strategy.

As was noted earlier, the leadership was relatively united in this period but in 1954 the purge of Gao Gang and Rao Shushi occurred.[6] A variety of reasons have been put forward to explain the purge of these two men. These range from accusations that they had set up 'independent kingdoms' to accusations that Gao had maintained excessively close relations with the Soviet Union. In February 1954 the Central Committee charged Gao with having attempted to set up an 'independent Kingdom' in the north-east and with having tried to organise the seizure of state power. The case still remains unclear but it seems most likely that what lay at the root of the differences were Gao's close ties with the Russians and his continued support for the Soviet developmental strategy, support based on the fact that such a strategy benefited the industrialised north-east over which he presided. The purge of Gao showed the Chinese leadership's desire to limit Soviet influence in the north-east. It was followed by a more general debate on the feasibility of the Soviet developmental model for Chinese conditions. In March 1955 the Sufan campaign (the Campaign to Wipe Out Hidden Counter-Revolutionaries) was launched to weed out Gao and Rao's supporters and to restore Party control over the economic and political bureaucracies which had gained power with the launching of the First Five-Year Plan.

1955–60 : The origins of the Chinese path of socialism

Although it was not until 1958 that the Chinese made a radical break with the previous economic practice there had been earlier signs of disillusionment. In April 1956 Mao Zedong

had proposed his own blueprint for China's future development in his talk 'On the Ten Major Relationships'.[7] Despite
the relative success of the First Five-Year Plan problems became increasingly apparent and the Second Five-Year Plan
was abandoned in favour of the more radical policies of the
Great Leap Forward. The Soviet model had contradicted the
previous experience of the Chinese revolution because the
large-scale, forced savings required from agriculture went
against the interests of the peasantry. As was shown in Chapter 1, it was the peasantry that provided the basis of Party
support and the majority of its membership, even though
concerted efforts were made to recruit workers in the years
immediately following liberation. Yet the interests of the
peasants were sacrificed to help build up heavy industry. The
systemic faults of the Soviet model, with its emphasis on
urbanisation and decentralisation, for a country where over
eighty per cent of the population were peasants soon became
apparent. New inequalities began to arise as a result of the
strategy. The richer areas got relatively richer and the poorer
areas poorer. Since a premium was placed on those with
managerial and technical skills, this was reflected in the
greater rewards made available to these people. In particular
the gap between the cities and the countryside widened as
the rural areas began to lag even further behind the cities in
their ability to offer wefare, education and cultural facilities.
The excessive centralisation which such an approach to development required when applied to a country as vast and diverse
as China meant that local shortages and bottlenecks appeared
in the economic system.

   These economic problems were aggravated by the political
problems resulting from Stalin's death. On 25 February 1956
Krushchev delivered his 'secret speech' which denounced
Stalin's crimes and attributed them to the cult of the individual, an assessment that could be interpreted as reflecting
adversely on Mao, who had himself defied the Party with his
proposal for collectivisation in 1955. Not surprisingly Mao
was unwilling to go as far as the Soviets in his denunciation
of Stalin. He reaffirmed his belief in Stalin's progressive role
while acknowledging that he had indeed made mistakes. Mao
outlined his own methods regarding correct leadership in the

Ten Major Relationships. He suggested here that a balance be drawn between democracy and centralism and argued that the mass-line would prevent the leaders from becoming divorced from the led. This theoretical position, together with Mao's reaction to the events in Hungary (1956) and his desire to shake up a Party apparatus which was becoming increasingly conservative, led to the launching of the Hundred Flowers Campaign. Mao felt that the uprising in Hungary occurred, in part, because the regime had mechanically copied the experiences of the Soviet Union. Although Mao considered the reaction in Hungary to be 'rightist' in nature he was concerned that the mechanical copying of the Soviet Union might also lead to problems in China. The solution to this problem, Mao felt, was to operate properly the mass-line. What was needed was not the repression of complaints, but the encouragement of open criticism of the Party apparatus.

The Hundred Flowers Campaign was launched in May 1956 and tried to generate greater discussion and debate by widening the forum of those who could engage in criticism of the Party. As a result writers were encouraged to produce works containing more than received stereotypes. The movement was opposed by those sections of the leadership favouring a more orderly and limited form of criticism. For a while, the campaign was shelved or at least scaled down. In February 1957 the campaign was revived by Mao and given a more radical twist with his speech 'On the Correct Handling of Contradictions Among the People'.[8] Mao used the campaign to challenge the Party leadership which was at that time at odds with his economic policies. The speech invited intellectuals to raise criticisms and suggested that the Party was not above criticism from those outside it. Such criticism, Mao suggested, could help prevent the leaders from becoming divorced from the led. By May 1957 Party opposition to the campaign had been circumvented and criticism reached a peak. The range of criticism was wide, from the airing of personal grievances to indictments of the whole political system. These indictments came not only from opponents to the communist regime but also from people who assessed the system on its own terms and found it wanting. Some writers have seen the Hundred Flowers

Campaign as a clever trick designed by Mao to draw out the regime's opponents and then to punish them but it appears that the leadership, including Mao, was genuinely surprised at the extent of the criticism. On 8 June 1957 the movement was brought to a close when the *People's Daily* published an editorial denouncing the 'rightists' who had abused their freedom to attack the Party and socialism. For the remainder of the year and indeed through to 1959 the 'Anti-Rightist Campaign' was waged and hundreds of thousands of intellectuals were investigated as China abandoned the democratic experiment. The present Chinese view of this period maintains that it was correct and necessary to counter the attacks of the 'rightists' but that the mistake was made of widening the scope of the attack so that many innocent people were unnecessarily harassed. The 'Anti-Rightist Campaign' is now seen as the first of the 'leftist errors' which have characterised Chinese politics since socialist transformation was completed and socialist construction began.[9]

In the economic sphere the main debates concerned the speed of development, the relationship of socialisation to technical transformation and the question of whether the economic process should be decentralised. Mao's view concerning agricultural transformation was signalled in his July 1955 speech in which he rejected the view that collectivisation should be subordinated to mechanisation. Mao felt that China's conditions meant that technical transformation would take longer than social transformation and in 1956 he put forward his Twelve-Year Plan for Agriculture which saw socialisation as the necessary prerequisite for a rapid increase in production. It was a while, however, before Mao's economic thinking gained the support of a majority within the leadership and his plan was shelved in 1956 with the more moderate climate only to be revived again in 1957.

The Eighth Party Congress (September 1956) acknowledged the success of the First Five-Year Plan and approved Zhou Enlai's proposals for the second plan to start in 1958. This second plan again gave agriculture the lowest priority for the allocation of funds but more emphasis was placed on light industry to meet consumer demand. Some decentralisation was also introduced to curb the power of the central ministries. Despite these modifications the plan lay within the orbit of Soviet development strategy and assumed that socialist transformation required a developed industrial base, an assumption which ran counter to Mao's thinking as embodied in his views on agricultural development. These views were ignored by the congress and it is clear that a serious divergence of opinion emerged. Apart from differences over development strategy in general there was particular debate about decentralisation of the economic system, a debate which was resolved at the Third plenum of the Eighth CC (September–October 1957).

To move away from the centralisation of the Soviet system in economic decision-making two possible solutions were put forward.[10] The proposal put forward by Chen Yun, a Vice-Premier of the State Council and the Minister of Commerce, and supported by the economist Xue Muqiao was to enlarge the power of initiative for individual enterprises, making them into 'genuinely independent accounting units' as in Yugoslavia. The second proposal was to decentralise power only to the local areas. The first approach would facilitate the use of material incentives as a stimulant for orderly economic growth but was opposed on the grounds that it would lead to units producing for self-gain according to the dictates of the market rather than according to the plan. In fact Chen Yun's advocation of 'big plans, small freedoms' at the First plenum relied on economic measures to stimulate production. Also, the first approach would lead to a decrease in the influence of the Party, a crucial factor if mobilisation techniques rather than material incentives were to be used as the main stimulant for economic growth. Decentralisation to the regions would allow greater flexibility but it would not permit the growth of 'spontaneous capitalist tendencies' and would ensure continued Party control and conformity with central planning.

This issue was one of the major items discussed at the Third plenum of the Eighth CC, which adopted the radical measures paving the way for the Great Leap Forward. The type of decentralisation eventually introduced was essentially that which Schurmann termed decentralisation 2, or decentralisation to the regions, but with modifications which meant that some decentralisation of power was also to be carried out within the individual units.[11] A revised version of Mao's Twelve-Year Agricultural Plan was adopted but it is clear that there was opposition to the radical measures. Mao's plan was 'basically' rather than completely adopted and Chen Yun's report on proposed changes in the system of economic administration and Zhou Enlai's report on wages and welfare were never published.

The Great Leap Forward which was launched in 1958 signified a radical break with the Soviet model. Although the Second Five-Year Plan was never officially revoked it was completely ignored. In recent years with the return of Chen Yun and Xue Muqiao to positions of power the 'hot-headed-ness' of 1958 has been severely denounced and the correctness of the original plan restated.[12] The Second Five-Year Plan proposed that national income should increase by about 50 per cent by 1962. Industrial output was to double and agricultural output to increase by about 35 per cent. These relatively cautious projections were cast aside by the euphoric predictions accompanying the Great Leap Forward.

The Great Leap Forward represented a return to the mobilisation techniques of the Yanan period. It was based on the premise that the enthusiasm of the masses could be harnessed and used for economic growth and industrialisation. Following the general line of 'going all out and aiming high to achieve greater, quicker, better and more economical results in building socialism', an express aim of the movement was to overtake Britain's output of major industrial products within fifteen years.[13] It was hoped that agricultural production could be boosted since this, in turn, would increase the amount of capital which could be accumulated. The strategy rejected the notion that high-level development of the productive forces was a necessary prerequisite for socialist transformation; its theoretical foundations lay rather in Mao's notion of 'permanent revolution'.[14] The Great Leap strategy was outlined in Mao's speech to the Supreme State Conference (28 January 1958) and in the draft directive 'Sixty Points on Working Methods' (31 January 1958).[15] Significantly, the planning system was to combine central control with the advantages of local initiative, such as the innovation and improvement of basic agricultural implements.

An integral part of the strategy was the method known as 'walking on two legs' (rang liang tiaotui zoulu). This promoted the dual use of modern, large-scale, capital intensive methods of production and traditional small-scale methods. It was hoped that this combination would tap the huge reservoir of hitherto unexploited resources in the rural areas so that they would be capable of providing their own industrial goods, manure and agricultural tools. The most notorious result of this approach was the 'backyard steel furnaces' which produced a huge volume of steel, much of it useless. Other more successful small-scale projects were the creation of small electric-power generators and chemical fertiliser plants. This use of intermediate technology remains the greatest legacy of the Great Leap Forward. Hand in hand with the Great Leap strategy went the programme of communisation which was an attempt to create much larger collective units through the amalgamation of higher-stage agricultural producer co-operatives.

The Great Leap Forward was not quite the wild act of voluntarism which it has often been portrayed as in the West. Economic justifications for the policy have indeed been presented by Western writers.[16] Despite the occasional reference to 'guerrilla habits' and the debate which had taken place prior to the adoption of the Great Leap strategy, it received the support of the leadership once the decision to launch it had been taken. Even now, it is acknowledged that the Great Leap Forward was a 'joint mistake'.[17] While the leadership was united about its launching, its subsequent progress sharpened the previous differences of opinion and created new ones. Initially the programme had appeared successful. By the end of 1959 many of the projections of the Second Five-Year Plan had been fulfilled (according to the plan these targets would not have been met until the end of 1962) but this apparent success obscured the real limitations of the strategy.

The Great Leap Forward rendered centralised planning a virtual impossibility. Local variations and changes would have required the continual revision of plans. The imbalance within the structure of the national economy, combined with inevitable bottlenecks, meant that stoppages in production occurred and many enterprises over-extended their productive capacity. The enthusiasm for production resulted in the return of falsified figures which contributed to setting incorrect targets in future plans. It is clear that although many people doubted the more excessive claims for production increases, they were reluctant to speak up for fear of being criticised. In particular the plans for 1959 were based on false estimates of agricultural output for 1958, although it had, in fact, been a good year. The original estimate for 1958 was 375 million tons, double the 1957 production figure, but later this had to be revised down to 270 million tons.

The communisation programme also encountered problems. Many peasants resented communal living and the confiscation of private plots. Other problems arose from the unwieldy size of the communes and the lack of competent personnel to administer them. Two other major setbacks occurred which helped to undermine the Great Leap strategy and plunge China into economic crisis. First, during the summer of 1960 the Russians withdrew their aid. This caused problems in the industrial sector. Secondly, floods and droughts in 1959 and 1960 increased the problems in the agricultural sector. The severity of the natural disasters has been used in the past by the Chinese to excuse the disastrous effects on production of the Great Leap Forward. Seventy per cent of the blame was put down to the natural calamities and only 30 per cent to the strategy and its mismanagement. The present Chinese leadership's view of the catastrophe is, however, less charitable. They see the most important problem as the stirring up of a 'communist wind' and the exaggeration of production figures, a view shared by many Western writers.

From 1959 production in all sectors began to fall. In industry the situation was made worse by the fact that much of what was produced fell below basic quality requirements. Food shortages and famine occurred and it became obvious that a strategy had to be found which could restore production and, in particular, assure food supply for the population.

1960–65 : Economic recovery and the origins of the Cultural Revolution

Serious opposition to the Great Leap Forward first became apparent at the Lushan plenum which was held in July and August 1959. The main critic at the plenum was the Defence Minister, Peng Dehuai, who attacked Mao and the Great Leap strategy over a wide range of issues. Essentially Peng disagreed with Mao's view of the relationship between the political and the economic and he set out his criticisms in his 'Letter of Opinion'.[18] Peng criticised the speed with which the programme had been implemented, the exaggeration of figures which made planning impossible and also condemned the communisation programme. Additionally Peng criticised Party practice, claiming that democracy in the Party and the Party's relations with the masses were being severely hampered by the 'petty-bourgeois fanaticism' characteristic of the Great Leap. The following year the strategy was abandoned but, at Lushan, Peng found himself isolated by the extent of his criticisms. He was denounced as the leader of an 'anti-Party clique' and was replaced as Defence Minister by Lin Biao. However, Mao did accept some blame for the excesses of the Great Leap Forward; in particular he blamed himself for the backyard steel furnaces and the speed of communisation.[19] He was not prepared to see the entire strategy abandoned and virtually asked the Party to choose between himself and Peng, stating that he would go back to the peasants and lead them to overthrow the government if his ideas were rejected. He continued: 'If those of you in the Liberation Army won't follow me, then I will go and find a Red Army, and organise another Liberation Army. But I think the Liberation Army would follow me.'[20] Lushan proved a hollow victory for Mao. He found himself increasingly unable to influence policy-making and by the end of 1959 he reluctantly acknowledged the need to dismantle the Great Leap strategy. The plenum, in accordance with a prior agreement, replaced Mao as President of the Republic by Liu Shaoqi to whom powers of policy implementation increasingly passed.

The Lushan plenum proved an important turning point in

the People's Republic. It is now seen as marking the start of the disappearance of democracy in the Party. Mao's position is criticised and Peng's 'Letter of Opinion' was used as study material in Beijing University in October 1978.[21] The Third plenum of the Eleventh CC (December 1978) posthumously rehabilitated Peng and an article by Lu Dingyi in March 1979 moved closer to denouncing Mao by name for his role at the Lushan plenum. Lu accused the plenum of committing a leftist error by attacking Peng's 'correct ideas' rather than dealing with the plenum's original objective to investigate shortcomings in the Party's work. According to Lu, this leftist error developed into a line which was not rectified until the Gang of Four were arrested in October 1976. In pointing the finger of accusation at Mao, Lu wrote, 'Now it is perfectly clear that Peng Debuai in his "Letter of Opinion" at the Lushan plenum of 1959 was correct. It was not Peng Dehuai who was mistaken but the man who opposed him.'[22]

After the failure of the Great Leap Forward the leadership concentrated on achieving economic recovery. The policies implemented provided correctives to and reversals of those of the Great Leap and the period is often referred to in the literature as one of liberalisation. The policies promoted during this period provided the basis for the conflicts which occurred during the Cultural Revolution.

The most pressing problem was how to revive agricultural production. The policies of adjustment, worked out at the Beidaihe Conference (July and August 1960), were adopted at the Ninth plenum of the Eighth CC in January 1961. The order of priority for economic development was changed, with agriculture taking priority over light industry and with the formerly favoured sector of heavy industry placed last. This meant that in rejecting the Great Leap strategy the Chinese did not resurrect the Soviet developmental strategy and a lower growth rate for industry was anticipated than was put forward in either the First Five-Year Plan or the Great Leap Forward. In the countryside the policy of 'three freedoms and one guarantee' (sanzi yibao) was introduced under which the private plots abolished during the communisation programme were returned to the peasants. Peasants were again allowed to sell their goods in rural markets. Also, the number of small enterprises assuming responsibility for their own profits and lossses was increased. This placed a greater emphasis on the role of the market than had previously been the case. Finally, the quotas for output were removed from the collective units, the brigades and teams, and were fixed on the household. Once again, this made the family the most important economic unit. The communes were not abolished but they were greatly reduced in size. Though they remained political entities, the socio-economic functions they had acquired during the Great Leap were reduced.[23]

In the industrial sector a policy of financial retrenchment was introduced to help rationalise production. The scope of capital construction was reduced and work stopped on over 1000 construction projects. In 1962 it was proposed that investment for capital construction be lowered by 80 per cent and over 10 000 projects were stopped or scrapped. The workforce was greatly reduced as the 20 million or so peasants who had joined the industrial workforce during the Great Leap were returned to the countryside under the Hui Xiang (Return to the Villages) programme. These policies were accompanied by an emphasis on material incentives as the main stimulant for increasing production and by a greater freedom for managers in determining policy in their own enterprises.

The recovery programme was an impressive success. By 1964 some people put forward the view that the work of economic readjustment was complete. While there were undeniable economic gains, they were brought about by increasing the rural–urban differences and by increasing the differentials between various groups in society. This process had proved especially advantageous to skilled workers and technocrats and the social and political problems that resulted caused some to question the wisdom of continuing with these policies. The new priority given to agriculture was not disputed but there were differences over the substance of specific policies. The main source for disagreement stemmed from the continued debate over the Great Leap Forward. Nobody proposed a complete return to these policies and Mao acknowledged that a more cautious approach to planning was necessary. Even so, Mao was not willing to see all the Great Leap policies abandoned in favour of policies which were less concerned about the means through which economic development was to be achieved.

In the early sixties Mao found himself unable to direct the policy-making process and referred to himself as a 'dead ancestor'. His attempts to preserve something of the Great Leap experiment were thwarted but his speech in January 1962 signalled his intention to return from the political wilderness.[24] In this speech, Mao criticised the practice of Party life since the Great Leap Forward. Like Liu Shaoqi, Mao stressed the importance of the principle of democratic centralism though unlike Liu he spoke at great length of the importance of democracy and the continued use of the mass-line. He felt that these policies had been abandoned during the years of economic retrenchment. Crucially for later developments he put forward the idea that class struggle did not gradually die out in socialist society but continued to exist.

These views were reiterated at the Tenth plenum of the Eighth CC in September 1962. Mao's speech at this plenum represented the culmination of two months of discussion among the leadership. Answering his own question as to whether classes and class struggle existed in socialist countries, Mao stated, 'We can now affirm that classes do exist in socialist countries and that class struggle undoubtedly exists'.[25] With reference to the Yugoslav example, Mao claimed that it was possible for a socialist country to change its nature and become revisionist. Mao's insistence at this time on the continuation of class struggle did not predict the great upheavals of the mid-sixties. He made it clear that class struggle should not interfere with work but should proceed simultaneously. It was made clear that mistakes made by the rural cadres should be treated as 'contradictions among the people'. A movement along the lines of the 1942–4 Rectification Campaign in Yanan was proposed and out of the plenum grew the Socialist Education Movement (1962–5).

Following a slow and limited start the movement was launched in earnest across the country in May 1963 with the publication of the 'Early Ten Points'. The movement sought to remove the 'spontaneous tendencies towards capitalism' which had arisen because of the policies of economic retrenchment and to counter the increasing bureau-cratisation of the Party which had led to a high level of cadre corruption. Poor and lower-middle peasant organisations were formed to investigate cadre corruption and the collusion of rich peasants and Party cadres in the countryside. Accompanying the creation of these organisations was a rectification campaign aimed at eliminating the corrupt practices. The process of 'self-education' was also revived. During this movement the model held up for the population to emulate was not the Party but the People's Liberation Army which Mao saw as embodying the correct virtues of selflessness and collective endeavour.

The methods to be used by the movement were not agreed by the leadership though it seems likely that all the leadership accepted the basic objectives. Despite assurances to the contrary, some leaders feared that a movement of mass participation would have an adverse effect on the revived agricultural and industrial productivity over which Liu Shaoqi, Deng Xiaoping (who at that time was the CCP General Secretary) and others had presided. In particular Liu and Deng differed with Mao over the role of the Party in the movement. They wanted the Party to remain firmly in control of the movement with the higher levels rectifying the errors of the lower levels. They ignored the idea of the peasant associations assuming a major role. The role of the peasant associations was to be taken over by work teams sent in by the higher levels which would lead and co-ordinate the whole movement. The work of investigation, according to Liu, was to be carried out secretly by these teams which were to infiltrate the peasantry and discover the corrupt cadres. Liu and Deng effectively narrowed the scope of the movement with the promulgation of two documents. In September 1963 the 'Later Ten Points' prepared by Deng were published and one year later the 'Revised Later Ten Points' drawn up by Liu were published. Their names notwithstanding, these two documents departed considerably from the radical nature of the earlier documents.

The differences of opinion between the leadership were changing from 'non-antagonistic contradictions' into 'antagonistic' ones. By January 1965 Mao had decided that Liu Shaoqi had to be removed.[26] In January 1965 a Central Work Conference issued the 'Twenty-Three Points' which mapped out how the movement should proceed. This document signalled an important change in the targets of the movement. It proceeded from the premise that the struggle between socialism and capitalism was present in the Party itself. Consequently, the principal target became 'people in positions of aurthority in the Party who take the capitalist road'. The power which the higher levels exerted over the movement through the work teams was undermined and the most important means of supervision of local cadres was adjudged to be that provided by the masses. The peasant associations were allowed to 'seize power' temporarily if it was decided that the local administration had been 'usurped' by capitalist elements. In line with this broadening of the scope of the struggle the 'Four Cleans' (si qing), which had applied to the need to clean up specific irregularities, were redefined as 'clean politics, clean economics, clean organisation and clean ideology'. As Mao became convinced that the source of the troubles lay at the heart of the Party itself, the lines were drawn for the battles of the Cultural Revolution.

3

The Cultural Revolution and its aftermath

The Great Proletarian Cultural Revolution is the most complicated and one of the most misinterpreted events in the history of the People's Republic of China. Attempts to understand it have not been helped by simplistic explanations that it was a two-line struggle between socialism and revisionism, or by the original Chinese claims that everything that happened was the result of Mao Zedong's grand strategy. As was noted at the end of the last chapter consensus had broken down in almost every policy area — although one might be able to identify two polar positions for each policy area, intervening positions were also taken up by members of the leadership. Also, it is difficult to see a consistent position taken by the same group of people on each different policy issue (this was certainly true for Mao Zedong, who, on some issues, changed his mind during the course of the Cultural Revolution). This meant that certain 'loyal Maoists' were unceremoniously dumped for continuing to follow yesterday's line. There appears to have been a number of different groups fighting on various issues, the period being characterised by a series of shifting alliances within the leadership. The following account of the events can present nothing more than a caricature of the years 1966–9.

One thing which is quite clear is that Chinese politics since 1969 have been dominated by the differences which became apparent in these years and by the resulting divisions. Certainly at the lower levels much of the struggle in the seventies has been comprised of personal revenge rather than principled

struggle, though on occasions the two have coincided. Although for purposes of analysis most writers in the West consider the Cultural Revolution as terminating with the Ninth
Party Congress of April 1969, the Chinese themselves take a
different view. The Cultural Revolution and its legacy have
remained one of the issues dividing the leadership even after
Mao's death. At the Eleventh Party Congress (August 1977)
Hua Guofeng 'brought down the curtain' on the Cultural
Revolution though he continued to make some favourable
references to it. The Cultural Revolution was seen as smashing
the 'three bourgeois headquarters' of Liu Shaoqi, Lin Biao and
the Gang of Four. Hua stated that similar political revolutions
would occur frequently in the future. Since the congress this
idea has been dropped and a negative view of the Cultural
Revolution has been adopted with one of the 'bourgeois
headquarters', Liu Shaoqi, being posthumously rehabilitated
and accorded the position of a national hero. With the
rehabilitation of its main target the view of the Cultural
Revolution that remains is of a misguided leader launching
a disastrous 'leftist' movement which led to the emergence of
the even greater excesses of the Gang of Four.

1965–9: The Great Proletarian Cultural Revolution – radicalism and disorder

Although there was serious disagreement on many major
policy issues it was in the realm of culture that the upheavals
started. Following the January 1965 meeting Mao called for a
Cultural Revolution. Later the same year a five-person Cultural Revolution Group, under the leadership of Peng Zhen,
the Mayor of Beijing, was sent to carry out investigations of
the Socialist Education Movement and to conduct the
Cultural Revolution. Controversy first became apparent when,
in November 1965, the PLA's newspaper published a criticism
by Yao Wenyuan of the historical play *Hai Rui's Dismissal
from Office.* The play, written by Wu Han, Deputy Mayor of
Beijing, told of a court official in the sixteenth century who
was unjustly dismissed from office because of his support for
the peasantry. Quite rightly this play was seen as a covert
attack on Mao Zedong for having dismissed Peng Dehuai

because of Peng's opposition to the communisation programme. The current view of these events is that academic debate was drawn out into the political sphere and that three members of the Gang of Four, Jiang Qing, Zhang Chunqiao and Yao Wenyuan, used literary criticism as an excuse to frame various people. It is claimed that Yao's article set a precedent for fabricating charges against innocent people and that the article 'far from being a prelude to the Cultural Revolution' was 'nothing but a shocking frame-up which initiated the campaign of persecution against the academic and cultural circles'.[1]

In fact the accusation laid against the initial Cultural Revolution Group was precisely that they tried to limit the debate to the academic sphere and not to broaden it into a mass political campaign. Once again Mao felt that his radical objectives were being thwarted by the Party bureaucrats who oversaw policy implementation. The February (1966) Outline Report drawn up by Peng Zhen was approved by the Politburo in Mao's absence. This tried to limit the debate to the academic sphere and criticised Yao for turning an academic question into one of politics. It also proposed that in the cultural sphere less stress should be placed on class struggle, there should be a greater toleration of ideas in the Party and that a rectification campaign should be conducted. At the same time, a countervailing tendency was also expressed. Following a forum on work in art and literature, held by the PLA and presided over by Jiang Qing and Lin Biao, the PLA's newspaper started to print articles of a far more radical nature. These articles stated that a campaign against bourgeois ideology was needed and took the view that the debate could not be restricted to the purely academic realm.

It was in this atmosphere that the Central Committee issued the 'May 16 Circular' drawn up by Mao.[2] This circular quite clearly shifted the target of the movement from the academic sphere to the political. The target was 'the representatives of the bourgeoisie who have infiltrated the Party, the government and the army', with these people described as 'counter-revolutionary revisionists' who were seen as wanting to 'overthrow the dictatorship of the proletariat and replace it with that of the bourgeoisie'. The circular stated that there were people like Krushchev in the Party who were ready to seize power. In practical terms the circular revoked Peng's February Outline, criticised him and dissolved the five-person Cultural Revolution Group.

The movement quickly took a radical turn and the reformed Cultural Revolution Group[3] took control of the media and publicised these radical viewpoints. In June it was announced that Peng Zhen, Lu Dingyi, head of the Party's propaganda department, and Zhou Yang, who was responsible for cultural affairs, had all been relieved of their posts. Having gained control of the Beijing Party apparatus Mao and his supporters sought to eradicate 'bourgeois influences' throughout the Party and state and to rebuild a more responsive Party-state system. Obviously, there was considerable opposition to this within the Party and it was very unlikely that those in positions of power would either mend their ways or hand power over to Mao's supporters. Thus thwarted, Mao had to bypass the Party machine and look elsewhere for support. The army under Lin Biao was loyal to Mao, providing him with a strong source of support. But the initial attacks were launched by a second source of support — the students.

On 25 May 1966 Nie Yuanzi put up a wall-poster at Beijing University criticising the leadership for trying to confine the current campaign to the academic sphere and calling on the students to attack them. The poster, on Mao's orders, was reprinted in the *People's Daily* and commended for its revolutionary marxist-leninist nature. This signalled an onslaught on the education system, criticising it for its elitist nature. During this onslaught the students banded together in groups which became known as Red Guards (Hong weibing). In June and July these Red Guard groups clashed with the 'work teams' which had been sent into the educational institutions at Liu Shaoqi's and Deng Xiaoping's instigation to try and prevent the movement from getting out of hand and to ensure Party control over the rising tide of criticism. The Red Guards' struggle against the 'work teams' was given Mao's support in August, when he returned to Beijing after an extended absence and on 5 August Mao pinned up his own wall-poster on the door of the meeting-room for the Central Committee — this called on the people to 'bombard the headquarters'. Early in the same month the Eleventh plenum of the Eighth CC was held but Party leaders opposed to Mao were excluded from attending. Not surprisingly the measures adopted reflected the 'radical mood'. The plenum adopted the 'Sixteen-Point Decision' concerning the Cultural Revolution.[4] This defined the aim of the movement as the 'overthrow of those persons within the Party in authority taking the capitalist road'. An important part of this struggle was the elimination of the 'four olds', the old values and customs which the 'capitalist-roaders' manipulated to enable them to dominate the masses. Clearly if the highest levels of the Party were affected they could no longer be relied on to supervise the purification of the lower levels. This meant that it was up to the masses to liberate themselves; under no circumstances was action to be taken on their behalf and the 'work teams' were criticised for dampening down the movement. Those who held 'incorrect' views were to be persuaded of their errors by reason rather than by force, but in the following months this was honoured more in the breach than the observance by the battling Red Guard groups. Finally, the decision referred to the electoral system set up by the Paris Commune which appeared to challenge the whole idea of the ruling vanguard party. The new political organisations which evolved in the struggle were to become 'permanent' mass organisations for the exercise of political power.

Following the publication of this decision debate and fighting between Red Guard groups and their opponents increased, and there was even disagreement between the Red Guards themselves as the turmoil unleashed many different grievances. After achieving the initial purpose of singling out 'those in authority taking the capitalist road', the movement fragmented and became increasingly unruly and attempts were made to bring it under control and to rebuild the Party and state structure. This was not easily done as the Red Guards could not be wished away as easily as they had been created. Also many groups opposed the restoration of a system which they felt was essentially similar to the one which they had destroyed. Even among those groups that supported the return of a modified Party–state system there was considerable disagreement about precisely what form it should take. The students proved to be good at destruction but did not prove to be very good at construction; consequently their role began to be downplayed and a more stable form of organisation than the shifting student alliances was sought to replace the old system.

At the end of 1966 and early in 1967 the movement to 'seize power' was launched to take power from the Party bureaucrats in the local Party organisations. Although power in Beijing effectively rested with Mao and his supporters the links of the national network were destroyed, and in some provinces many provincial leaders managed to resist the challenge of the Red Guards and to remain in power. As a result 'seizure of power' became the main objective of the movement and the experience of Shanghai was the first to gain nationwide prominence. In January 1967 the 'revolutionary rebels' in Shanghai had 'seized power from below' and, on 4 February, they announced the inauguration of the Shanghai Commune. This institution, which was based on the Paris Commune, did not however become the model for 'seizures of power' all over the country. Even at the time of its creation the central leadership was aware of the need to exert greater direction over the movement and as early as 15 January Zhou Enlai and Chen Boda expressed doubts about its general applicability.[5] Zhou thought that the commune was wrong to reject completely experienced Party cadres. The need to restore some kind of control was reflected by the promotion of the 'supervision formula' rather than the 'seizure and control' which gave the centre far more say about what should replace the overthrown organisations. This new approach proposed that provisional organs of power be established after the seizure of power through an exchange of views and consultations between leading members of revolutionary mass organisations, leading members of local PLA units and revolutionary leading cadres of Party and state organs. It was stressed that not all authority was 'bourgeois' and that under no circumstances were the masses to equate authority with 'bourgeois' as they had done in the past. The model to be copied was the revolutionary committee − this represented an attempt to bring together all the victorious groups in a coalition termed the 'three-in-one combination'; the first one of these being set up in Heilongjiang province.

An important feature of this new approach was the active involvement of the PLA which, with the Party machine in disgrace and the state machinery in many areas not functioning, was the only properly functioning institution. By default the job of restoring order fell to it and on 23 January 1967 the central authorities issued a directive to the PLA to 'resolutely support the left'.[6] Although, as was mentioned earlier, the PLA was loyal to Mao the PLA local commanders, when faced with the difficult task of mediating between the competing groups, often chose to side with the old, local bureaucrats rather than the more unruly 'revolutionary rebels'. The demand for order was in keeping with Mao's thought at the time, for he tried to remove the anarchistic and ultra-leftist trends which had been unleashed by the movement to 'seize power from below' and attempts were made to narrow the focus of the Cultural Revolution and bring about unity among the victors. The resistance of the ultra-left was stronger than had been anticipated and its position was strengthened by the Wuhan Incident of July 1967. On 25 July the Wuhan regional military commander, Chen Zaidao, arrested the two leftist emissaries[7] sent from Beijing to mediate the disputes which had virtually paralysed the city. Under the threat of attack Chen released the two who returned to a heroes' welcome in Beijing. This was followed by a series of direct challenges to the credentials of many military leaders by the left and, as the number of clashes increased, on 5 September a directive about how the problem should be dealt with was issued.[8] This directive commanded the PLA to restore order and to use force when necessary. This drive to restore order, although accompanied by a good deal of revolutionary rhetoric, was quite clearly intended to facilitate the reconstruction of the Party and state apparatus. Jiang Qing denounced the ultra-leftists with whom she had been closely connected, the Red Guards were ordered back to their studies, in November *Red Flag*, the Party paper which had promoted the radical line, ceased publication, and both Jiang Qing and Chen Boda appeared less in public. The blame for the disturbances of the summer was placed on a group referred to as the 'May 16 Corps' (516 Corps), who had taken their name from the radical document of that date in 1966.

The ultra-left was able to manage only one more upsurge. This followed the arrest of the PLA Acting Chief of Staff, Yang Chengwu, on 7 March 1968 when, in the months May to July, violence on a nationwide scale was again reported. This violence was the death throes of the ultra-left as policy became marked by a calculated moderation. On 28 July Mao himself, when talking to the Shanghai Red Guards, said that they had let him down and that they had 'disappointed the workers, peasants and armymen of China'.[9] The overriding priority, devoid of radicalism, was for the restoration of stability, authority and effective government. By September 1968 the last of the provincial revolutionary committees was set up with the policy of calculated moderation meaning that cadres attacked as anti-maoist served on the new committees. In April 1969 the end of the destructive phase of the Cultural Revolution was marked by the convening of the Ninth Party Congress. This set about rebuilding the Party system.

1969–78: Reconstruction and the search for successors

The Ninth Party Congress proclaimed itself to be a 'congress of unity and a congress of victory', but this fragile unity was no more than an illusion and it was difficult to see what the 'victors' had won for themselves. The years of turmoil did nothing to solve the policy differences which had led to the Cultural Revolution and actually created new problems. The two most important new problems concerned the correct role of the Party and the correct role of the PLA. The congress set in motion the process of Party rebuilding but differences existed within the leadership about the kind of Party it should be, where the new cadres should be found and about the role of the PLA in the Party system. The one group which really benefited from the years 1966–9 was the military. It had acquired a vital governing role so that at the time of the congress all but four of the provincial revolutionary committees were headed by active soldiers and almost half the Central Committee members were from the PLA. This role obviously conflicted with the maxim that the gun should always be controlled by the Party, but it is reasonable to presume that the PLA was unwilling to withdraw from the political arena unless it could be given certain assurances that the left and the mass organisations would not carry out reprisals against it. Apart from these two difficulties two other problems became more apparent as the period progressed. First, there was disagreement over how many of the innovations of the Cultural Revolution should be retained and how many should be discarded. Secondly, despite appearances to the contrary, the problem of succession which Mao had raised in 1964 had not been solved.

At the Ninth Party Congress Lin Biao stood at the pinnacle of his career for the adopted constitution designated him as Mao's chosen successor. But the congress also had the duty of reconstructing the Party apparatus which meant that Lin Biao was to supervise the removal from power of his own support base. While the PLA had been important during the phase of destruction, Zhou Enlai and the revolutionary veterans were to play a greater role during reconstruction. The first barrier against reconstruction was the remnants of the ultra-leftists for whom the main spokesman was Chen Boda[10] — he proposed that the Party be organised as it had been during the more radical phases of the Cultural Revolution, and rejected the leninist concept of the Party favouring the inauguration of institutions like the Paris Commune. At the end of 1969 the Cultural Revolution Group was disbanded and an investigation into the 'May 16 Corps' was conducted which signalled the decline of Chen and his supporters. Their fate was sealed at the Second plenum of the Ninth CC (August 1970) when the differences became apparent. It is claimed that Chen and Lin Biao launched a 'surprise attack' against the Party, with Lin making a speech without previously consulting Mao and attempting to add a provision to the constitution extolling the genius of Mao. Chen and Lin might seem a strange combination but it is possible that, despite their differences, events may have driven them together. In any event their attempts were unsuccessful and following the plenum Chen was purged and a campaign launched to criticise 'sham marxists'.

The leadership group around Mao and Zhou were now able to turn their attention to reducing the influence of Lin Biao and the milatary and so between December 1970 and August 1971 the provincial Party apparatus was rebuilt — but it did not signal the end of military influence because during this process the military actually consolidated its new-found position of power. It was quite clear that certain sections of the military were not willing to return to the barracks. This partly reflected the fears of the military commanders of reprisals against them, but also reflected a new-found power for the centrally directed units such as the air force and navy. Unlike the regional commanders of the PLA these leaders were unused to exercising political power and seemed unwilling to part with it. This problem was solved in September 1971 with the death of Lin Biao while fleeing after the failure of an alleged coup d'état.[11] Following the death of Lin the Party set about restoring its authority and five other PLA members of the Politburo were purged along with his supporters in other central and regional posts. Also a series of campaigns was launched against Lin Biao, calling on the military commanders to accept Party leadership with the Party rather than the army being once again the symbol of national unity. These campaigns against Lin culminated in the 'Criticise Lin, Criticise Confucius Campaign' (pi lin pi kong), which was launched after the Tenth Party Congress was held in August 1973. Initially Lin was denounced as an ultra-leftist and identified as the 'behind-the-scenes leader of the May 16 Corps' but during the process of criticism his label was changed from ultra-left to ultra-right. The reason for this change of label was because the identification of Lin with the left meant that there was a mounting tide of criticism directed against the left generally and the gains of the Cultural Revolution specifically. By identifying Lin with the right it made it easier to protect the 'new-born things' of the Cultural Revolution from further criticism.

The increased political strength of those criticised in the Cultural Revolution was caused by the answer given to two interrelated questions. First, with the gradual reconstruction of the Party-state system and the return of the PLA to the barracks, where were the new cadres to come from? Secondly, should the Party give greater accountability to the masses and remain mobilisational or should it revert to its pre-Cultural-Revolution role exerting leadership as an organisational decision-making body? The answer to the first of these questions provided the answer to the second. The left favoured promoting those who had been tempered during the Cultural Revolution; this included those termed 'revolutionary cadres' and those who had gained prominence as a result of the Cultural Revolution. The best example of the latter group is Wang Hongwen, who rose like a 'helicopter' to become a member of the Ninth Central Committee and a member of the Standing Committee of the Politburo at the Tenth Party Congress. In the event the bulk of 'new cadres' were not new at all but were people attacked or purged during the Cultural Revolution and subsequently rehabilitated; Deng Xiaoping is the best example of these, a man who was criticised as the 'Number Two Person in Authority Taking the Capitalist Road'.[12]

This process of rehabilitation gained momentum at the Tenth Party Congress (August—September 1973) at which a number of important figures purged during the Cultural Revolution returned to positions of power. The congress was not really one of initiatives but rather one of correctives and an assessment was made of the criticism of Lin Biao. The behind-the-scenes manoeuvres of Lin and his followers were formally brought out into the open and Lin was denounced by name, as a 'bourgeois careerist, conspirator, double-dealer, renegade and traitor'. But Zhou Enlai, in his political report, made it clear that that was not the end of the matter but just the beginning of a stepped up, concerted effort to thoroughly 'weed-out' the Lin Biao 'revisionist clique' and its 'poisonous influences in China'. Significantly, the congress reflected an attempt to put together a leadership which could command sufficient support to allow economic development not to be disrupted but at the same time could maintain some of the revolutionary momentum of the Cultural Revolution. In this context the congress abandoned the attempt to resolve the question of succession by appointing a specific individual in favour of appointing a collective leadership by electing five vice-chairmen. Some writers have pointed to the different emphasis of Zhou Enlai's and Wang Hongwen's reports as indicating that differences of opinion still pervaded the leadership and that the congress represented yet another policy stalemate. Certainly an attempt at compromise was reflected in the constitution. Teiwes has pointed out that the inclusion of traditional leninist norms and elements derived from the experience of the Cultural Revolution, if they did not exactly contradict the traditional norms, they made their implementation difficult.[13]

After the congress, although the army lowered its profile, most of the regional military leaders retained their political power through the retention of the posts of First Secretary of the provincial Party committees and chairmanship of the provincial revolutionary committees. At the end of 1973 this problem was resolved and on New Year's Day 1974 the New China News Agency announced that, with the exception of Chengdu, Xinjiang and Kunming, the commanders of the other eight military regions had been reshuffled. Some changes were also made among the Political Commissions with military leaders released from their local Party and government posts to keep them out of Party affairs and politics. In November 1973 the campaigns against Lin Biao and Confucius were linked up. The 'Anti-Confucius Campaign' sought not only to remove feudal remnants from Chinese society but also to defend Qin Shihuang (the emperor who unified China in 221 B.C.) and the legalists against the attacks of the confucianists, who were seeking to preserve their positions of power against the attacks of the legalists. In terms of the contemporary political situation Mao, who was trying to exert Party control and protect new-won gains, was represented by Qin, while the confucianists could be taken for those entrenched in positions of power and opposed to the renewed Party supremacy. When the campaigns were linked the focus was shifted much more clearly to the need to 'take a correct attitude toward the Cultural Revolution' and to protect the 'new-born things'.[14]

On 2 February 1974 the *People's Daily* called on people to 'dare to go against the tide and advance into the teeth of storms'[15] and a campaign of mass criticism unfolded. It began to appear that one of the targets was Zhou Enlai and those who had returned to positions of power under his protection. In April Deng Xiaoping presented Mao's 'three-worlds theory' in a speech at the United Nations and in May he effectively became Acting Premier when Zhou Enlai was admitted to hospital with an illness later diagnosed as cancer. Zhou's illness gave further impetus to the question of succession and during 1973—4 it became clear that serious differences existed within the leadership over the legacy of the Cultural Revolution. Deng's revived power and the large number of those purged in the Cultural Revolution who now occupied leadership posts must have served as a warning to those who sought to preserve the gains of the Cultural Revolution, but despite the differences the conflict was kept within reasonable limits and another attempt at ensuring collective succession was put forward at the Fourth National People's Congress (January 1975).

Although there was a brief revival of the Lin Biao and Confucius Campaign in the summer, it was kept under control and by the end of 1974 it had effectively ended. Certain sections of the leadership were obviously worried not only about its targets but also about the effects such a mass campaign had on production, so in July a Central Committee document was circulated stressing that the campaign had adversely affected production and that this should be prevented.[16] Attempts were made to ensure that the campaign did not escape from Party control. The memories of the years of turmoil were still fresh and by the end of the year the stress was on the stability and unity which were essential for the launching of Zhou's and Deng's programme of modernisation. At the Fourth National People's Congress Zhou Enlai outlined the policy of the four modernisations (the modernisation of agriculture, industry, national defence and science and technology), a policy which he had first presented as early as 1964. The policy envisaged a two-stage programme with the first objective being to build 'an independent and relatively comprehensive industrial and economic system' by 1980, with the second objective being to bring the national economy to the front ranks of the world by the year 2000. The balance between the competing factions was best symbolised by the balancing of posts between Deng Xiaoping, one of those who had suffered most during the Cultural Revolution, and Zhang Chunqiao, one of those who had profited most. The two were given corresponding posts in the three major institutions of Party, army and state.

This coalition was to prove too fragile to survive and began to fall apart shortly after the congress had concluded its meeting. Two things in particular aggravated the differences within the leadership. First, the ill-health of the older generation of leaders brought the question of succession much closer, for in December 1975 Kang Sheng died[17] and Zhou Enlai, Zhu De and Mao Zedong died in January, July and September 1976 respectively. Secondly, concrete economic plans had to be drawn up for implementation in 1976 and this caused the differing approaches to developmental economic strategy to come to the surface. While Deng and his supporters set about outlining programmes for their growth-oriented policies the group later denounced as the Gang of Four launched a series of theoretical campaigns directed against those who were 'whittling away' the gains of the Cultural Revolution.

Within a month of the conclusion of the Fourth National People's Congress the call was put out to 'study well the theory of the dictatorship of the proletariat'.[18] This drew inspiration from a series of comments, four in all, from Mao, warning of the need to restrict 'bourgeois rights' under the dictatorship of the proletariat in order to prevent revisionism.[19] During the spring and summer the campaign was stepped up in the theoretical journals but political practice followed the more pragmatic proposals which had emerged from the Fourth NPC, with the result that a large gap was opening up between theory and practice, reflecting the different spheres of influence of the contending factions. In autumn 1975 another campaign was launched, called the 'Water Margin [shui hu] Campaign'. The Water Margin is a classical Chinese novel concerning a band of rebels opposing the imperial court. One of the leaders, Song Jiang, was criticised in the campaign as having subverted the rebels' cause by capitulating to the emperor to advance his own interests. The relevance of this to the contemporary situation was the attack on 'class capitulation at home and national capitulation in foreign affairs';

again the veiled target was Zhou Enlai and his policies of playing down the role of class struggle at home and calling for a greater involvement in the world economic system for bringing about the four modernisations.

The differences were becoming insoluble and the First National Conference on Learning from Dazhai provided an arena within which the differences could be aired. Although the conference was concerned with the question of agricultural development it is clear that differences on this matter reflected a difference in developmental strategy as a whole and the differences which became apparent at the conference again showed that the struggle was more complicated than that of a simple 'two-line struggle'. According to Domes the three speeches delivered at the conference reflected three different approaches to the problem of rural development, but only Hua Guofeng's was published.[20] Deng Xiaoping's speech called for the confirmation and extension of the rural policies of the early sixties. These policies made use of material incentives to stimulate production but Jiang Qing's favoured the return of the commune in its original 1958 model accompanied by class struggle against the capitalist tendencies in the countryside. Hua's speech, although it tended towards the left, did not support the methods proposed by Jiang Qing; for example, he also favoured the return of the original commune model but felt that it should be brought about by the mechanisation of agriculture and the strengthening of the commune at the expense of the brigades and teams.

After the conference the campaigns stepped up further and, as was the case in 1966, the first direct attacks occurred in the universities. It was during these attacks that Deng Xiaoping's name first appeared as the target of criticism. As early as August 1975 criticism of education policy appeared at Qinghua University in Beijing and in November the Education Minister, Zhou Rongxin, was attacked in wall-posters at Beijing and Qinghua Universities; some of these posters included criticisms of Deng. In December criticisms started to appear in the national media but, as yet, they were still directed against unspecified targets who were attempting to dismantle the educational reforms of the Cultural Revolution. The New Year's editorials[21] for 1976 emphasised the position of the

Cultural Revolution, in particular the reforms in education, and linked the attempt to reverse educational policy with the 'right-deviationist wind to reverse previous verdicts' which was being pushed by 'representatives of the bourgeoisie' who stood in opposition to the proletariat. However, the editorial made it quite clear that this was not to herald the unleashing of forces as in the Cultural Revolution but that the movement was to proceed through re-education under the supervision of the Party. Significantly, a new comment of Mao's was presented which stated that 'stability and unity do not mean writing off class struggle; class struggle is the key link and everything else hinges on it'. Later Deng was charged with not appreciating this and with placing unity, development and class struggle on the same level instead of giving priority to the class struggle.

On 8 January 1976 Zhou Enlai died and contrary to general expectation on 7 February Hua Guofeng, not Deng Xiaoping, was announced as 'Acting Premier'. With Deng passed over for the post of Premier the campaign against him renewed in earnest and by mid-February 'that unrepentant capitalist-roader' was under attack. It was made clear that this attack was launched with the full support of Mao Zedong. The 10 March *People's Daily* editorial[22] continued Mao's warning that the bourgeoisie was 'right in the Communist Party' and that the 'capitalist-roaders' were 'still on the capitalist road'. For those who were still uncertain about the target it was made even clearer on 23 March when a comment of Mao's was published which stated, 'This person does not grasp class struggle; he has never referred to this key link. Still his theme of "white cat, black cat", making no distinction between imperialism and Marxism'.[23]

The movement came to a climax with the riot at Tiananmen Square in April 1976. This provided the pretext for stripping Deng of all his official posts but, significantly, he was not dismissed from the Party. On 5 April, crowds gathered to pay homage to the memory of the dead Premier, Zhou Enlai, but the removal of the wreaths and posters and the attempts to prevent new ones being placed in the square led to a spontaneous riot and demonstration. This was broken up by the PLA and militia following Wu De's[24] announcement that such actions were counter-revolutionary. The incident is now portrayed as being 'completely revolutionary' and is held up as a symbol of the masses' disapproval of the policies and political practice followed in the last years of Mao's life, but at the time a different view was taken and on 7 April the Politburo met; Deng was dismissed from his posts and Hua Guofeng was appointed First Vice-Chairman of the CCP and Premier.

Through the rest of the year the Gang of Four appeared to be in firm control and they used their control of the media to launch a campaign to discredit Deng's and his supporters' policies — particularly the three policy documents which were denounced as the 'three poisonous weeds'.[25] Deng's programme of modernisation had as its basis a policy of export-led growth; increased export of China's oil and coal was to pay for the import of advanced technology and machinery on a large scale. However, this policy also entailed the use of foreign credit and Deng was criticised for giving the authority to extract Chinese minerals to foreign countries.

The removal of Deng did not signal the end of the Gang's attacks and in August 1976 the campaign to purge other rehabilitated cadres intensified. Late in the month the *People's Daily* called for an intensification of the struggle against 'capitalist-roaders' and drew attention to those who had been 'unmasked and criticised before' but who still wanted to 'reverse verdicts'.[26] At the same time in the press, particularly the provincial press, a countervailing tendency was apparent which stressed the need for 'unity' and the 'promotion of production'. This opposition came not only from the rehabilitated cadres but also from those, such as Hua, who approved Deng's removal but feared the escalation of the movement. While Hua agreed with some aspects of the Gang's standpoint, such as the need to restrict 'bourgeois right', he appears to have differed with them over the extremes of their policies. Similarly, it seems unlikely that Hua would wish to see the campaign extended as it would soon include an attack on those cadres who had benefited from the Cultural Revolution but who now proposed a policy of compromise with the rehabilitated cadres. Since the fall of the Gang of Four evidence has been produced to show that they had differed with Hua and had attacked him for 'revisionist' and 'capitulationist' tendencies.[27] Increasingly, despite the public polemics, the Gang of Four were without the support within the Party organisation to implement their policies. This only left them with the option of launching a mass movement from without to attack the Party but the lukewarm reception that the Campaign to Criticise Deng had received from the masses showed the limits of such an approach. Also, production was severely hampered by the conflicts, and the damage wrought by the massive Tangshan earthquake in July 1976 meant that many in the Party were unwilling to see yet another mass movement unleashed.

A fatal blow to the Gang of Four was delivered on 9 September 1976 when Mao Zedong died. Mao's death removed the final legitimacy of their support. At the memorial service for Mao differences became apparent. The Gang of Four put forward the slogan 'act according to the principles laid down' (an jiding fangzhen ban) as Mao's last words, and they used this phrase to portray themselves as the chosen successors. Although the phrase was used at every provincial memorial meeting, Hua Guofeng excluded it from his memorial speech. The differences between Hua and the Gang of Four were settled swiftly and decisively on 6 October 1976 when Politburo member Wang Dongxing led the 8341 Unit of the PLA to arrest the Gang of Four. Hua Guofeng, a figure little known in the West, was a man who had gained considerably at every turn of the Cultural Revolution and was thrust to the head of the leadership when elected Chairman of the Party following the Gang's arrest.[28] Ironically, considering the claims of forgery against the Gang of Four's 'manipulation' of 'Mao's will', Hua's own indisputable right to succession was also based on a phrase written by the dying Mao: 'With you in charge, I am at ease' (ni banshi wo fangxin). To bolster this frail claim to legitimacy a limited cult of personality was launched and his credentials as Mao's successor were increased by the announcement that he was to edit volume five of Mao's selected works. This made him the most important arbiter of Mao's thought.

The initial campaign against the Gang of Four consisted almost exclusively of personal vilification and accounts of the havoc which they had brought upon the economy, but very little was said either about their theories or about their policies for the future. This was not surprising as the coalition over which Hua presided spanned a wide range of interests so policies for the future could not be presented until differences between them were settled. The source of differences now not only included one's attitude to the Cultural Revolution and the correct development strategy to be followed, but also there were the questions of Mao's legacy to the revolution and about what should be done about the 'human yo-yo' Deng Xiaoping. Deng's most virulent opponent was Wu De, the Mayor of Beijing, who, during the 'victory' rally for the smashing of the Gang of Four on 26 October, had made it clear that their arrest did not mean the end to criticism of Deng. This view was supported by other leaders such as Wang Dongxing, Ji Dengkui, Chen Xilian and even Hua himself, although Hua had used milder language when referring to Deng than had Wu. Deng's strongest supporter was Chen Yun, one of the main critics of the Great Leap strategy; he is said to have called for Deng's immediate reinstatement early in 1977.[29] This account should not be interpreted as meaning that it was a battle of personalities, for the debates also concerned how much of Mao's legacy and that of the Cultural Revolution should be retained. Too wide a criticism of the Gang of Four would inevitably lead to criticism of Mao, a development which would be disadvantageous for Hua as he claimed his right to leadership on his adherence to Mao's principles. If those principles were undermined so too would Hua's own position be undermined. Conversely, it was impossible for Deng to be returned to power without the decision adversely affecting Mao's image and without it implying approval for Deng's policies.

In March 1977 discussion articles appeared concerning the policy documents drafted under Deng's direction in 1975 (the formerly denounced 'three poisonous weeds'). These paved the way for his return and in July the Third plenum of the Tenth CC restored Deng to his posts, expelled the Gang of Four from the Party for ever and confirmed Hua as Party Chairman. In August this was followed by the Eleventh Party Congress at which Hua Guofeng announced the end of the 'eleven-year Cultural Revolution' and designated the Gang of

Four as ultra-rightists. The 'new' policy programme outlined by Hua represented an attempt to pursue 'maoism without Mao' and drew its strength from the republished 'On the Ten Major Relationships'. The stress was on unity and consolidation but a favourable attitude to the Cultural Revolution was retained. The congress signalled the broadening of the scope of the struggle against the Gang of Four to attack their policies as well as their behaviour, and cadres were exposed who had sought to 'keep the lid on the struggle'. Following the congress and throughout 1978 the Chinese press was full of accounts of 'hidden followers of the Gang' who had been removed from Party committees at all levels below the centre and of repeated references to the 'pernicious influence' of the Gang. It seems likely that this extension and continuation of the campaign was carried out against Hua's wishes because during 1976 he at least twice announced that the investigation of the Gang's supporters had, for the most part, been concluded and yet it continued.

The Fifth National People's Congress (February–March 1978) began to get to grips with the other pressing problem requiring solution – the economic plans for the future. Hua's Report on the Work of the Government declared that China was to embark on a 'New Long March', the final destination of which was to be the attainment of the four modernisations by the year 2000. The basis for this was to be the 1976–85 Ten-Year Plan which set forward a series of ambitious targets. The plan bore resemblances to Mao's Twelve-Year Plan of the mid-fifties which had preceded the Great Leap Forward and indeed the rhetoric began to mirror that which accompanied the Leap: references were made to the general line of the Great Leap of 'going all out, aiming high to achieve greater, faster, better and more economical results in building socialism'. The plan predicted the construction of 120 large-scale projects by 1985, an increase in steel output to 60 million tons (an increase of almost 150 per cent) and a rise in grain production of over 40 per cent – ambitious targets which had more in common with the enthusiastic spirit of the Great Leap than with the pragmatic policies of the economic planners such as Chen Yun. The post-Mao leadership pledged itself to restoring economic growth and providing a rise in the standard of living. This meant that power would accrue to those who could 'deliver the goods'. This gave the more pragmatic planners their chance and they began to point out the problems of the plan and argued for more 'realistic' proposals.

As China neared the end of 1978, apart from the economic problems, political problems also remained to be solved. In particular the correct attitude towards the Cultural Revolution and to Mao's legacy still had to be decided on. Although those who took the most negative view towards these two issues had made steady gains since the fall of the Gang of Four and the death of Mao, substantial opposition remained to further erosion of the legacy — but the Third plenum of the Eleventh CC (December 1978) announced a significant shift in the policy orientation.

1978–80: China since the Third plenum

The differences were not finally resolved at the Third plenum and certain compromises were worked out, but some important decisions were reached and events since the plenum have shifted the fulcrum further to the right of the political balance.

In May 1978[30] a new slogan was raised, 'practice is the sole criterion for testing truth', which provided the more pragmatic leaders with the theoretical basis for their attacks on those who sought to preserve the few remaining 'new-born things' of the Cultural Revolution. The leadership began to polarise around two main positions which became increasingly antagonistic — although there is ample evidence to suggest that some leaders, even including Deng and Hua, occupied the middle ground. Those who rejected Mao's position since 1957 became known as the 'practice faction' (shijian pai), and those who tried to protect Mao's image and policies became known as the 'whatever faction' (fanshi pai). Since the Third plenum it is quite clear that the 'practice faction' has consolidated its position at the expense of the 'whatever faction', but attempts to preserve a facade of unity have been maintained.

The plenum announced that the campaigns to criticise Lin

Biao and the Gang of Four had for the most part been completed and that the emphasis of the Party's work should be shifted to concentrate on socialist modernisation. Thus, on the surface the Chinese people were urged to forget about the past and concentrate on the future, but certain other decisions taken at the plenum ran counter to this and the past, far from being forgotten, has been almost totally re-examined. The new 'practice' slogan was used at the plenum to reverse a number of previous verdicts and the documents which had been issued by the Central Committee in 1976 concerning the movement to 'Oppose the Right-Deviationist Wind to Reverse Correct Verdicts' and the Tiananmen Incident were cancelled. The reversal of verdict on the Tiananmen Incident by the Beijing Party committee on 15 November 1978 was one of the important factors giving impetus to the 'Democracy Movement' which emerged on the streets of Beijing at the end of 1978. Among those rehabilitated at the plenum was the dead Peng Dehuai and this opened the way for the criticisms of the adventurism of the Great Leap Forward and the 'left adventurism' which led to Peng's fall and which dominated the Party from that time. The façade of unity was preserved but while there were no dismissals a number of promotions were announced. Chen Yun was made an additional Vice-Chairman of the Party and Deng Yingchao (Zhou Enlai's widow), Hu Yaobang (one of Deng's protégés purged in the Cultural Revolution) and Wang Zhen were appointed to the Politburo.

Despite these decisions no conclusive decision was made concerning the two most pressing issues. The plenum's communique[31] acknowledged that a 'satisfactory settlement' to the Cultural Revolution was 'necessary for consolidating stability and unity', and also acknowledged that there had been 'shortcomings and mistakes' during it and that it should be viewed 'historically, scientifically and in a down-to-earth way' — but it was stressed that there should be no haste in making a correct assessment. According to the communiques, the 'Great Cultural Revolution' was initiated by Mao 'primarily in the light of the fact that the Soviet Union had turned revisionist and for the purpose of opposing revisionism and preventing its occurrence'. Similarly the question of Mao was

treated cautiously. His image was preserved and the communique called him a 'great marxist' but it acknowledged
that he had made mistakes, as yet unspecified, and that his
thought should be developed in light of the new historical
conditions.

After the plenum it was apparent that there was fairly
widespread opposition to the decisions of the Third plenum
and that the implementation of its policies was blocked by
the middle and lower levels. This opposition was indicated by
the fact that the Chinese media had to devote a lot of time
and space to refuting accusations that the policies adopted by
the plenum had swung the political pendulum unacceptably
to the right. The decision to invade Vietnam in February
1979 may well have given the remnants of the left in the
leadership some breathing-space in the struggle. Despite the
assertions of victory the invasion did not prove the great
success desired and it also caused a drain on the economy at a
time when the economy could least afford it. This latter
factor in particular gave more strength to the pragmatic
planners who wanted cautious moves forward as opposed to
the ambitious targets of the Ten-Year Plan.

Chen Yun and Bo Yibo, rehabilitated at the Third plenum,
urged caution concerning economic matters and at the end of
March 1979 the *People's Daily* warned about 'economic
rashness' and the setting of too ambitious plan targets. These
warnings were reflected in the new economic policies
presented to the Second Session of the Fifth National People's
Congress (June–July 1979). The Ten-Year Plan was at best
postponed and at worst abandoned. Hua Guofeng presented
an outline which was much more closely in line with the
views of Chen and Bo, proposing that because of the problems which remained from the past, and because of the serious
imbalance within the national economy, a three-year programme of 'readjustment, restructuring, consolidating and
improving the national economy' be introduced before the
programme of modernisation could be seriously promoted.
Hua's speech also stressed the importance of material rather
than moral incentives and encouraged the promotion of rural
sideline production and rural gains – policies which owed
much more to the years of economic recovery of the early

sixties than the Cultural Revolution. In industry the emphasis was to be placed on light rather than heavy industry, a reorientation which appears to have met with some success.

Despite opposition, further progress was made on the resolution of the political issues. Following the Third plenum the play *Hai Rui's Dismissal from Office* was reassessed and in January the *Three Family Village*, which had implicitly criticised Mao in the early sixties through the use of satire, was also given a favourable assessment.[32] In February and March 1979 articles started appearing in the press which contradicted Hua's claims at the Eleventh Party Congress that no one could have pushed a line further to the right than the Gang of Four by referring to them as ultra-leftists. This view was not only more credible but also facilitated the attacks on those in the leadership who had maintained close relations with the Gang of Four. The growing number of 'reversals of verdict' built up the pressure to produce an assessment of both the Cultural Revolution and Mao, and the Fourth plenum of the Eleventh CC and Ye Jianying's speech in commemoration of the thirtieth anniversary of the founding of the People's Republic of China brought this nearer.

At the plenum the promotion of former purged officials continued: Peng Zhen and Zhao Ziyang were appointed to the Politburo and the plenum also approved Ye's speech. This speech reviewed the thirty-year history of the People's Republic and presented a negative assessment of the Cultural Revolution. While Ye said that the Party must guard against revisionism, he stated that an unrealistic assessment was made in the sixties concerning the situation within the Party, no accurate definition of revisionism was given and an 'erroneous policy and method of struggle' were adopted. Liu Shaoqi was not exonerated in the speech but when talking about the Cultural Revolution Ye only referred to the struggle against Lin Biao and the Gang of Four. When speaking about Mao, Ye continued to use epithets of praise, but he detailed some of the mistakes which had been made in the Party's work, mistakes which could only reflect badly on Mao's reputation. Ye mentioned three 'leftist' errors which had occurred in the late fifties: the broadening of the scope of struggle against the rightists in 1957; the rashness of 1958s' economic programmes; and the inept carrying out of inner-Party struggle in 1959. In all three of these incidents Mao had played a major role. A further implicit criticism of Mao was Ye's acknowledgement that the 'good name' of the Eighth Party Congress (1956) had been restored.[33] This congress is a symbolic occasion for the present leadership because it was convened when socialist transformation had been basically completed and when the Party was turning its attention to socialist construction. The congress decided that the system of class exploitation had been virtually eradicated and that the major task was to develop the productive forces, a view which finds its echo with the present leadership, so, not surprisingly, the basic contents of the documents adopted by the congress are still considered to be relevant. The major contradiction identified by the congress was that between the 'advanced socialist system' and the 'backward productive forces'. This line of thinking predates Mao's thoughts in the Great Leap, his later views on the continued existence of class struggle and the ideas developed by the left during the Cultural Revolution. To a large extent this turning back of the clocks signals a rejection of the maoist approach to development, but it should not be presumed that it will lead to the re-adoption of the Soviet model. In 1956 the leadership were united about what they did not want; the divisions occurred over how to bring about what they did want.

Those who had sought to limit the scope of the attacks had quite clearly lost in their attempts and this state of affairs was formally recognised at the Fifth plenum of the Eleventh CC (February 1980) when the attempt to maintain the façade of unity among the top leadership was abandoned. The plenum accepted the 'resignations' of Wang Dongxing, Ji Dengkui, Wu De and Chen Xilian (members of the 'whatever faction') from their top Party and state posts, elected Hu Yaobang and Zhao Ziyang to the Standing Committee of the Politburo and re-established the Secretariat with Hu Yaobang as General Secretary. The plenum also decided that the labels of 'scab, renegade and traitor' be removed from Liu Shaoqi — the accusations against him were described as the 'biggest frame-up our Party has ever known'. This rehabilitation of Liu was accompanied by the republishing of and discussion

of his writings which obviously gave more strength to those
in the leadership who favoured the reintroduction of policies
associated with Liu.

In recent years it has always been dangerous to attach too
much permanence to the contemporary state of affairs in
China, but it is tempting to see the present period as one of
the victory of a new, or rather revived, line producing a period
of relative stability. The major source of division, the events
of the Cultural Revolution, has been resolved, the policy
initiatives associated with it have been rejected and, with the
exception of the Hua Guofeng, the major figures who gained
as a result of the events of the Cultural Revolution have either
been removed from power or had their power effectively cur-
tailed. The theories which sustained the Gang of Four have
been rejected and history reinterpreted in such a way as to
discredit the left since 1956 so that the policies now being
implemented resemble those of the early sixties and mid-
fifties. Hua Guofeng announced that an assessment of Mao
would be made public at the Twelfth Party Congress and
anticipated some of the findings in an interview with a
Yugoslav newspaper.[34] Hua referred to Mao as the 'most
outstanding figure in Chinese history' but said that he was
not a God and was therefore fallible. This fallibility started
in 1957. Hua said that as Chairman of the Party Mao bore
responsibility for the grievous, serious mistakes which the
Party made during the Cultural Revolution (1966–1976).
The illness during the last years of Mao's life is used to excuse
him from the excesses of the period under the control of the
Gang of Four.

The solution of the policy debate has been accompanied
by the resolution of the problem of succession. Although
Deng Xiaoping and Chen Yun cannot pursue an active political life for very much longer they now have supporters in key
positions in the Party–state structure. As for Hua Guofeng,
although he is much younger than Deng, Chen and even some
of their successors, it is hard to see him as anything much
more than a figurehead. Events and policies with which he
was associated have been unfavourably reassessed and it is
unlikely that he would be able, should he now want to, to bring
about any significant reversal of the trends. In July 1980 it

was announced that he would give up the Premiership to Zhao Ziyang,[35] and although he will remain Party Chairman this does not guarantee him effective control of the Party apparatus. Apart from the Politburo an important source of power is the resurrected Secretariat, of which one of Deng's supporters, Hu Yaobang, is General Secretary.

The last occasion of retrenchment and consolidation (1961–3) was the prelude to the bitter struggles of the Cultural Revolution – but it is difficult to see any recurrence during this present period of retrenchment, not least because with the death of Mao there is no one, certainly not Hua, who could launch such a challenge. The tendency is to see future struggle in China settling down, as has been predicted for a long time, into one between technocratic modernisers and between different apparats competing for the allocation of scarce resources. As a possible counter to this view there is still evidence of considerable opposition to policy implementation at the middle and lower levels. Also the policies being pursued at present are similar to those which gave rise to the inequalitites and frustrations which found an outlet during the Cultural Revolution; combined with the fact that if the policies do not bring the rapid raise in people's standards of living which they have been promised, this could occasion a new wave of unrest. It is unlikely that this would result in a movement such as the Cultural Revolution but it is probable that it might find a more subtle theoretical expression than that provided by the Gang of Four.

4

Marxism–Leninism–Mao Zedong Thought

The guiding ideology of the People's Republic of China is Marxism–Leninism–Mao Zedong Thought and although one might question the extent to which the ideology serves as a guide to action, or as a *post-facto* justification for policies, an understanding of political life in China is impossible without some knowledge of its proclaimed ideology. Even after Mao's death, at a time when the leadership has stressed the collective role in the development of Mao Zedong Thought and the need to develop it in accordance with changing reality, justification for policies is still sought from the writings of Mao himself. However, particularly since the Third plenum of the Eleventh CC, the role of Mao's thought has been downplayed.

The origins of Marxism–Leninism–Mao Zedong Thought

Marxism–Leninism–Mao Zedong Thought has developed over time from a combination of intellectual, practical and cultural factors. Crucial to this development have been the following influences: those elements of traditional Chinese culture which have not only persisted but which have been actively promoted by the Chinese communists; those axioms of marxism–leninism which began to receive a greater currency after the May Fourth Movement (1919); and those theories and policies which were devised as a result of the concrete experience of the Chinese revolution.

Much academic debate has focused on the relationship between these components in the Thought of Mao Zedong, and some writers have questioned the legitimacy of his claims to be a marxist while others have seen him as little more than a faithful disciple to Stalin. Limitations of space prevent me from doing full justice to the complexities of the debate but the volume of work produced and its intensity require that the reader have some idea of the range of interpretations. Wittfogel, when attacking the work of Fairbank, Schwartz and Brandt, denied that Mao had contributed anything to the original formulations of marxism–leninism and portrayed Mao and the CCP as simply implementing the policy of the international communist movement.[1] Schwartz and Co., by contrast, were at pains to stress the other influences on the formulation of Chinese communist ideology. Schwartz's work acknowledges that new theories were developed to cope with situations which had not been dealt with in the inherited body of doctrine — a fact which is hardly surprising considering that the conditions about which Marx and Lenin wrote were vastly different from those encountered by the communists in China.[2] Fairbank in his work sees the communist movement and Mao's thought as having more in common with the Chinese tradition of rebellion, because of the movement's reliance on the peasantry, rather than the proletariat.[3]

Schram is one of the writers who acknowledges the complexity of influences on Mao's thought and who offers a carefully qualified account of it and its relationship to the marxist tradition. Schram, while feeling that 'there is little doubt that Marx would have rejected him [Mao] as a disciple',[4] does see a thread of continuity from Marx to Mao, particularly with Mao's concern about the scope and significance of human endeavour. Schram places Mao firmly in the 'leninist mainstream' but even then qualifications are added because of Mao's attitude to things such as the working class and to technology. Some writers have highlighted what is termed the 'voluntaristic' aspect in Mao's writings and have claimed that Mao Zedong Thought is a return to pre-marxist doctrines of socialism and philosophical idealism.[5] According to Harris the key factors in revolution and economic development for Mao are not the material forces of production but propaganda and education, and that this view is combined with an unmarxist usage of the term 'class' which entails a greater 'loosencess' than Marx would have allowed. The consequence of this is that 'if classes are no longer defined by their relationship to the means of production, class struggle is not what participants in the production process do'.[6] Mao has been defended against charges of 'voluntarism' by Walder,[7] who claims that this tendency to see Mao's thought as highly 'voluntaristic' — that is, entailing an emphasis on the subjective human effort over objective economic forces in promoting social change — comes from seeing the superstructure and economic base of society as separate entities rather than as an organic whole. Mao also has his interpreters, who see him as faithfully 'evolving Marxist–Leninist theory and strategy of revolutionary development aimed at realising Marx's goals in China'.[8] Pfeffer demonstrates this faithfulness to Marx's thought by asking the question what would Marx have done in China in 1949 or 1956 and by providing the answer — the same as Mao did. An interesting question maybe, but one that is fraught with methodological problems.

Given such a plethora of views, how can one interpret Marxism–Leninism–Mao Zedong Thought as it has developed in China? Certainly its marxist and leninist roots must be taken seriously but also consideration must be given to Mao's theoretical developments. This can leave it open to criticisms of revisionism but whether such 'revision' is legitimate or not is another matter. As Schram has observed,

> To argue that the structure and content of Mao's thought were essentially determined by Marxism, and bore no relation to the cultural environment in which they developed, is to ignore the evidence including Mao's own repeated calls not only for the adaptation of Marxism to Chinese conditions, but for the fusion of Chinese and Western elements in a new synthesis.

Similarly, however,

> to treat Mao's Marxism as merely one component of his thought among many others is to make light of the fact that for half a century Mao Tse-tung [Mao Zedong] strove

to guide himself by the lessons he had learned from Marx, Lenin and Stalin and to explain and justify his policies in Marxist terms.[9]

According to Schurmann[10] there are two components to the ideology, marxism–leninism – the universal doctrines which are binding on all communist parties and the Thought of Mao Zedong, which contains the principles arising from the attempt to apply the universal truths of marxism–leninism to the concrete practice of the Chinese revolution. Entailed in this second component of the ideology is the notion of the sinification of marxism. For Schurmann the former is 'pure ideology', which is identifiable with the Chinese term lilun (theory), and the latter is 'practical ideology', which is identifiable with the Chinese term sixiang (thought). As a distinction it is useful to help one examine the components that make up the ideology but it also gives rise to some problems which must be noted. Starr has pointed out that such a distinction 'provides no explanation of the origin of pure ideology or theory',[11] and treats 'pure ideology' as static and unchanging. He continues, 'Lenin's ideas are regarded as a part of present-day pure ideology, but during Lenin's lifetime they must have constituted practical ideology for the Russian revolution.'[12] Also, Schurmann's distinction makes it impossible for the Chinese to make any contribution to theory, leaving them to be content with the devising of specific policies. Despite these problems that Starr sees in Schurmann's work, he does feel that a distinction can be made between the various ideas with regard to their continued relevance. Starr argues for a three-fold categorisation of ideas: first, there are those ideas which are of permanent relevance; secondly, there are those which are relevant for a relatively long time; and thirdly, there are those which are only relevant for short periods of time. In the first category Starr only places two things, the existence of contradiction and the dialectical method of analysis. The second category includes the principles which are to guide action, but these may change over time because some may become invalid while others may be added. In the final category are ideas which are 'valid only in the instance in which they are produced'[13] and

require further testing in practice before they can be elevated
into the second category.

Having noted these methodological problems I will first
outline the elements of marxism–leninism which the Chinese
communists inherited and then outline the basic characteristics of Mao Zedong Thought. For Marx it was not sufficient
merely to record the observable events of history and link
them together in a causal sequence because he sought to
show that events moved through a succession of stages as a
matter of necessity. The analysis of this process of change
Marx referred to as the 'the materialist conception of history',
later referred to by others as 'historical materialism' and
developed by Engels into 'dialectical materialism'. The
character of each society is determined by the mode of
production by which people make their living and this mode
of production determines the social relationships and political arrangements of a given society. A change in the mode of
production brings about a consequent change in political and
social relationships. In accordance with this Marx saw history
as moving through a succession of stages from primitive communism through slave society and feudalism to bourgeois
society and then finally to communism. This interpretation
should not be taken to mean that Marx was a crude deter-
minist promoting a unilinear theory of history. Nor did
Marx intend people to believe that the economic base of a
society solely determines the superstructure. Any description
of the economic base will be bound to contain certain elements of the superstructure, and Marx was willing to include
subjective factors as well as the objective economic conditions
in his view of the dialectic.

According to Marx communist society would be brought
about by the exploited class — the proletariat — overthrowing
the property-owning class, and establishing a classless society.
The most likely place for this to occur was in those countries
in Europe where capitalism was most advanced. Marx had
little time for the 'idiocy of rural life' and, although he did
consider that the peasantry could play a role in Asiatic
countries they could only do so under the direction of and at
the initiation of the European proletariat. The important
place of the peasantry in the Chinese revolution and the

virtual neglect of the proletariat have led some writers to challenge the CCP's credentials as marxists and see the reliance on the peasants as a 'heresy' which has turned marxism on its head.

Contrary to Marx's expectation, when revolution did occur it was not in the highly industrialised European countries but in Russia, with Lenin providing the modifications to the theory to fit the new circumstances. As Schram has shown, it was in its leninist form that marxism exerted its influence in China. Following the victory of the October Revolution (1917) in Russia the study of marxism began to increase amongst Chinese intellectuals, gaining even wider credence following the May Fourth Movement (1919). Of particular interest was Lenin's theory of imperialism which appealed to patriotic intellectuals wishing to save China from the imperialist nations. In 1916 he published his treatise on imperialism which he described as the highest stage of capitalist development. Essentially capitalism was seen as operating on a worldwide scale and the exploitation of the colonies and semi-colonies by the imperialist powers meant that concessions could be made to the workers in the imperialist countries in the form of higher wages and better working conditions. Starting from this view Lenin added to the potential for revolutionary action by claiming that national revolutionary movements in the exploited countries could deal fatal blows to the imperialist countries by undermining the world capitalist economic system. This caused Lenin to take a more favourable view of the peasantry in these countries and to think that they could, in certain circumstances, constitute the main force of the revolution under the leadership of the proletariat and its Vanguard Party. The linkage of the theory of imperialism to the nationalist aspirations of certain sections of the Chinese intelligentsia proved a powerful force for revolution.

Apart from this theory Lenin also evolved certain organisational techniques which were conducive to Chinese conditions and which particularly appealed to Mao. Schram has even described Mao as a 'natural Leninist'.[14] Lenin realised that in a country such as Russia a successful revolution could be completed but not strictly in accordance with Marx's views.

Even without a large working class, revolutionary activity could be successful if led by a tightly organised and disciplined party which was drawn from the working class but which displayed a higher level of consciousness and acted as a vanguard. Democratic centralism was the operational principle of this party which meant that the free discussion of issues was allowed during the phase of policy formulation but that once a decision was reached strict adherence to it had to be observed, with the lower levels subordinate to the higher levels.

The intellectual climate of the youth of Mao and other Chinese leaders and the conditions under which the revolution took place are covered in the first chapter but it remains to highlight the major characteristics of Mao Zedong Thought.

The theory of contradictions

Most of the major interpreters of the Thought of Mao Zedong acknowledge that the theory of contradictions is the central idea around which it revolves.[15] This theory did not originate with Mao but came to him from two sources. The theory of contradictions which is more formally called the 'law of the unity of opposites' has its origins with Hegel's dialectical method, if one excludes pre-Plato-Greek thought, and was developed by Marx with his system of dialectical materialism. For Hegel the dialectical method progressed through the process of resolution of conflicting ideas, the thesis and antithesis, into the synthesis. This synthesis, in turn, then becomes the thesis of the next process of thesis–antithesis–synthesis. For Marx it was the conflict among things of the real, material world and its resolution that brought about progress and development. The second influence on Mao came from traditional Chinese thought which was more disposed to the dialectical process than its Western counterpart.[16] In classical Chinese thought there existed the notion of opposition in nature and although conflict was not ignored the main emphasis was on the complementary nature of opposites. This concern over opposition resulted in a concentration on 'the relationship of opposite forces rather than on their separate qualities'[17] and confucianism sought to maintain their harmony and restore the status quo in times of change. Schram notes the influence of Daoist dialectics on Mao's thought and points out that Mao himself has noted that many people in China regarded his interpretation of contradictions as deriving more from the 'yin and the yang' rather than from Marx's writings.[18]

These influences led to a concentration on contradictions and their resolution in Mao's writings but, unlike the traditional Chinese concern with the harmony of opposites, Mao emphasised their conflict. Unlike most people trained in Western thought, who see stability as the norm of society from which conflict deviates, Mao sees conflict and change as a continuing process and necessarily a good thing. Mao held that any view of reality which did not incorporate both aspects of a contradiction would be undialectical and any policy derived from such a view would be erroneous and doomed to failure. According to Mao, contradictions exist in any situation, at any time and even after the seizure of power, a view which runs counter to that held in the Soviet Union. This conflict in socialist society applies not only to the natural world but also to the social world where conflict may occur between individuals, groups and even classes.

In the essay 'On the Correct Handling of Contradictions Among the People' (1957)[19] two different types of social contradiction are identified — 'those between ourselves and the enemy and those among the people'[20] — which require different methods of solution. The former type is termed an 'antagonistic contradiction', to which the law of the unity of opposites does not apply as it is necessary to exert dictatorship over the incorrect part of the contradiction, once identified, and destroy it. The latter type is termed a 'non-antagonistic contradiction' and is handled in a completely different way. Where a 'non-antagonistic contradiction' exists there is only partial or misguided opposition to certain things which exist within a wider framework of unity; consequently the contradiciton can be resolved by using the method of re-education. This method of dealing with 'non-antagonistic contradictions' was developed in Yanan and is summed up in the slogans 'unity–criticism–unity' and 'learn from past mistakes to avoid future ones and cure the sickness to save the

patient'. Thus, change not only can come about by transforming the socio-economic structures but also by transforming
people's values and attitudes. Proletarian consciousness
becomes something which can be learnt and internalised irrespective of one's objective position within the economic
relations of production. It is this kind of reasoning which has
led to the aforementioned charges of 'voluntarism' against
Mao. However, there is no hard-and-fast line between those
who are considered to be 'among the people' and those who
are the 'enemies'; the dividing line can change over time
depending on the major contradiction to be resolved at any
particular moment. The major contradiction of any period is
decided on by the legitimate authority, Mao or the Party, and so
during the Cultural Revolution Liu Shaoqi was branded an
enemy of the people and 'struggled against', whereas now it is
his accusers who are the enemies and Liu is once again 'among
the people'. In 1957, when he delivered the speech, Mao felt
that antagonistic contradictions would decline and the intensity of class struggle diminish. This meant that the role of the
Party was to deal with the contradictions among the people
and prevent them from becoming antagonistic. Later Mao
rejected this position and put forward the idea that class
struggle, far from diminishing, could actually increase, and
during the Cultural Revolution the 'theory of the dying out
of class struggle' was criticised. The sources for this reversal
of views were twofold: first, there was the example of the
Soviet Union which Mao felt had abandoned the socialist
road and, secondly, Mao's fear that the same thing could
happen in China and that interest groups with a 'stake in the
system' might actually develop into a new ruling class.

'On the Correct Handling of Contradictions Among the
People' predates this train of thought, which gave credibility
to the theories of Zhang Chunqiao and Yao Wenyuan, and is
now put forward as Mao's 'final words' on domestic policy.
Similarly, 'On the Ten Major Relationships'[21] is put forward
as a major policy document which entitles the present leadership to claim its 'Maoist' legitimacy. The speech describes the
major contradictions facing Chinese society which must be
resolved during the course of the revolution. As Schram has
pointed out, although the speech evokes most of the paired

elements which are commonly regarded as symbolic of either democracy or centralism, he comes down on the side of neither.[22] Policy debates since the mid-fifties have to a large extent revolved around the contradictions outlined in this speech.

The mass-line

The previously mentioned desire to change people's attitude and the value system as a part of progress has meant that there is a strong emphasis on participation in Mao's thought. Thus it is not sufficient merely to accept passively a policy for one must be seen to support it actively. However, this participation is not just restricted to the expression of policy support but is also intended to apply to the process of policy formulation through the organisational principles of the mass-line, which Mao refers to as the 'marxist theory of knowledge'. While this idea breaks quite radically with traditional Chinese practice it does have its roots in Lenin's idea of 'democratic centralism'. This idea attempts to combine the benefits derived from consultation with those at the lower levels with those of a tight centralised control over policy formulation, but Mao added one important feature to this idea – the process was not only to apply to the Party but also to society as a whole.

Chapter 1 deals with the origins of the mass-line during the guerrilla war but its application did not stop at liberation; the idea of the mass-line was retained to engage the masses in a people's war during the struggle to transform the old society and build the new. The process of the mass-line is summed up in the following quote:

> In all practical work of our Party, all correct leadership is necessarily 'from the masses, to the masses'. This means: take the ideas of the masses (scattered and unsystematic ideas) and concentrate them (through study turn them into concentrated and systematic ideas), then go to the masses and propagate and explain these ideas until the masses embrace them as their own, hold fast to them and translate them into action, and test the correctness of these ideas in such action . . . Such is the Marxist theory of knowledge.[23]

As this quote shows, the process involves three stages. During the first stage the ideas of the masses are gathered together, an important step in a country as vast and diverse as China where actual conditions may vary greatly from place to place. But the formulation appears to go beyond this simple exercise of information gathering and suggests that the masses can also be a source of authority for policy initiation. The second stage of the process, the concentrating of ideas, makes the role of the centre seem rather like that of a processing plant, but in practice the centre's role is much more important and far-reaching than this would suggest. The final stage involves the dissemination of the formulated policies combined with education before the process is set in motion again.

The concept of the mass-line and the organisational technique of mass campaigns have been taken as evidence of Mao's 'populist' and 'voluntarist' tendencies. Mao has indeed placed a great stress on the ability of human determination to remove obstacles and to achieve the near-impossible, a view which is perhaps best summed up in Mao's rendering of the folk-tale about the foolish old man who moved the mountains.[24] In his account Mao stresses the power that determination can have in achieving a given objective; in this case it was the removal of the 'two mountains' of imperialism and feudalism which were crushing the Chinese people. It should not be construed from this that Mao saw no limit to what the masses could do, or that he was anti-organisation *per se* — as was suggested by some writers, with considerable evidence to support their views, during the early years of the Cultural Revolution. The idea that the Party might be replaced by a system ruled by Mao in 'holy communion' with the masses cherished by some was quickly crushed, and when the Shanghai People's Committee called for the abolition of 'heads' Mao denounced the idea calling it 'extreme anarchy' and 'most reactionary'.[25]

Significantly, the mass-line is intended to keep a check on bureaucratic excesses and prevent a routinisation of institutional work which would lead to corruption and the divorce of the leaders from the led. What Mao himself did not appear to realise was that the mass-line and the organisational technique of the mass campaign might themselves become routinised and counter-productive. In July 1980 the *People's Daily* criticised the past practice of the mass-line and mass campaigns and blamed the faults in implementation on the 'idealist conception of history' which promoted the view that it was the heroes who were the makers of history rather than the masses.[26] The article concluded that as a result the views of the masses had been suppressed and that 'under these conditions' the mass campaigns had become the 'materials and instruments for carrying out the "superiors' will"'.[27] The fact that the technique of the mass campaign has become devalued and the campaigns themselves highly ritualistic has made it difficult for the present leadership to use them.

Permanent revolution

Mao's view of the continued existence of contradictions under socialism, his perception that a new class could emerge even with the changed economic base, and his stress on human will as a factor for change led him to the development of the theory of permanent revolution. According to this theory continuing contradictions and newly emergent ones would be resolved by a series of qualitative changes as a part of the process of realising Mao's developmental goals. This 'permanent revolution' would prevent the institutionalisation and bureaucratisation of the revolution, things which would signify the end of the maoist vision of future society. This theory provided the basis of Mao's thinking when the Great Leap Forward was launched in 1958 and has as its basis an analogy with Lenin's ideas, as Mao understood them, on the transition from the democratic to the socialist revolution, from which is derived the conception of the transition from socialism to communism.

Mao was at pains to point out that his theory was not the same as Trotsky's theory of permanent revolution, a point wasted on Krushchev and subsequent Soviet leaders. Krushchev saw Mao's theory as a hotchpotch of anarchism, adventurism and trotskyism, but there are important differences between Mao's and Trotsky's views. For example, they had vastly different assessments of the peasantry and Trotsky was willing to give a greater degree of power to the technocrats than Mao was ever willing to concede. Also, Trotsky was concerned solely with the transition from the bourgeois-democratic to the socialist revolution without permitting society to settle down in the bourgeois stage. Mao's theory concerned a separate stage of social transformation during which all bourgeois influences would be eliminated by the maintenance of a revolutionary environment. Starr acknowledges the difference between the two theories but he does point to one similarity when he compares Trotsky's idea of maintaining upheaval in a society to prevent the attainment of equilibrium until all the tasks of the revolution have been fulfilled with Mao's statement that 'I stand for the theory of permanent revolution. Do not mistake this for Trotsky's theory of permanent revolution. In making revolution one must strike while the iron is hot — one revolution must follow another, the revolution must continually advance'.[28] It is this same speech which contains the Hunanese saying 'straw sandals have no pattern — they shape themselves in the making'[29] which characterises this approach to development.

This discussion should not be interpreted as meaning that society should always be kept at fever pitch to facilitate the advance of the revolution, but more correctly society would, as Mao said, progress in a series of waves with periods of relative calm interspaced between the periods of high activity. Many writers about the history of the People's Republic of China have been influenced by this and see the years since liberation in terms of a series of alternating periods of mobilisation and consolidation.

The dictatorship of the proletariat and bourgeois right

In the early sixties Mao began to concentrate on the idea that new classes could develop in socialist society. This meant that the continuation of conservative ideas did not derive exclusively from 'hangovers from the past', that is, that they could not be simply corrected by a series of occasional realignments as Mao's original ideas on permanent revolution suggested. As a consequence of this, a change in the Party's role was demanded. It was no longer sufficient for it to deal with the contradictions in society and to prevent them from becoming antagonistic; it was now expected to lead the population in class struggle against the new class forces generated in socialist society. The Party's role was complicated by the further notion that there were representatives of these new class forces within the Communist Party itself and thus there was a danger that the Party, far from promoting social change, might become a vehicle for restoring capitalism. Mao himself never properly formulated these ideas, which makes it difficult to assess his position, but it is important to consider because of the similar views put forward by Zhang Chunqiao and Yao Wenyuan in 1975 which played an important part in the succession struggle.

Zhang Chunqiao and Yao Wenyuan sought to explain how classes and class struggle could exist in a socialist society after the means of production had been transformed. In China the means of production are owned either by the state or by the collective which means that the economic basis of classes, according to Marx's theory, is non-existent. The theory which was developed to explain this phenomenon provided the Gang of Four's theoretical basis and established their claim to legitimacy for their attacks on veteran cadres. The phrase 'continuing the revolution' was first put forward at the Ninth Party Congress but it was a series of 'important instructions' from Mao concerning problems of theory, made public in February 1975, which gave the impetus to Zhang's and Yao's theory. Taking Mao's views as their starting-point they finished up with a theoretical standpoint which went much further than Mao's ever did in its deviation from Marx.

According to the *Peking Review* Mao had stated that 'Our country at present practices a commodity system; the wage system is unequal too, as in the eight-grade wage scale, and so forth. Under the dictatorship of the proletariat such things can only be restricted.'[30] This statement and others like it were used to justify the campaign to restrict 'bourgeois right' and to 'exercise all-round dictatorship over the bourgeoisie'. Yao Wenyuan saw 'bourgeois right' as providing the vital economic basis for the emergence of new bourgeois elements. Drawing his legitimacy from Lenin, Yao writes:

Lenin pointed out: 'In the first phase of communist society

(usually called Socialism) "bourgeois right" is *not* abolished in its entirety, but only in part, only in proportion to the economic revolution so far attained, i.e., only in respect of the means of production. . . .' However, it continues to exist as far as its other part is concerned; it continues to exist in the capacity of regulator (determining factor) in the distribution of products and the allotment of labour among the members of society. The socialist principle: "He who does not work, neither shall he eat", is *already* realized; the other socialist principle: "An equal amount of products for an equal amount of labour", is also *already* realized. But this is not yet Communism, and it does not yet abolish "bourgeois right", which gives to unequal individuals, in return for unequal (really unequal) amounts of labour, equal amounts of products.[31]

Thus, although the most blatant of inequalities have been removed, those between capitalist and worker and between landlord and peasant, other inequalities — based on relative skills, strengths or work occupation — do persist. The continued existence of these inequalities is liable to give rise to privileged groups seeking to perpetuate their vested interests in the status quo, and this would make them reluctant to see the introduction of the principle 'from each according to one's ability, to each according to one's need'. Despite Yao's reference to Lenin a crucial difference exists between their views because although Lenin thought that 'bourgeois right' would continue to exist without the bourgeoisie, his purpose is not the same as Yao's, and Zhang's, who want to show that the continued existence of 'bourgeois right' provides the basis for the development of a new bourgeoisie.

Not only is this potential seen as existing in the economic base but also in the superstructure. Zhang pointed out that in China public ownership consisted of the two types mentioned above: ownership by the whole people, which applies principally to industry and commerce; and collective ownership, which applies principally to agriculture, but in addition there were private plots and trade conducted at the rural fairs. For 'bourgeois right' to be eradicated ownership of all the means of production must be transformed into ownership by the whole people. 'Bourgeois right' also existed in the system of distribution with the eight-grade wage system and the use of material incentives to stimulate the economy and Zhang thought that these also provided a source for the development of the bourgeoisie. One final source for such a development identified by Zhang was the relationship between people, not only in terms of the relationship between economic classes but also in terms of the power relationship between different people. These superstructural elements are seen by Zhang as being as important, if not more so, for the emergence of the bourgeoisie. Zhang stressed that it was vital to attach importance to 'the relations between men and the form of distribution, and to the reaction exerted on the economic base by the superstructure; these two aspects and the superstructure may play a decisive role under given conditions'.[32]

Finally Yao and Zhang made an important distinction between form and content. Zhang stated, 'The correctness or incorrectness of the ideological and political line, and the control of leadership in the hands of one class or another, decide which class owns a factory in reality.'[33] Thus, although an enterprise might be owned by the whole people it could, in practice, be capitalist if its leadership followed the 'bourgeois line'. In order to prevent a situation occurring in which the bourgeoisie was able to take power 'bourgeois right' was to be restricted, and the 'all-round dictatorship of the proletariat' was to be exerted over the bourgeoisie. This reasoning provides the theoretical basis for the Gang of Four's policies — such as the curtailing of private plots and private rural trade and the criticism of the use of material incentives, the practical implications of which will be considered in subsequent chapters.

Ideology and the four modernisations

While the present leadership have accused the Gang of Four of breaking down the 'organic inner connection' of Mao's thought with the result that the individual sentences themselves 'cease to constitute a science as such, and are no longer the truth',[34] they could equally be charged with taking such a selective approach to the Thought of Mao Zedong by casting him in a 'positivist' light.

While a total rejection of Mao's thought is impossible because of the unique historical position which he attained, certain elements of his thought will be, and already have been, played down. The present leadership needs to establish their legitimacy by reference to Mao's thought but already the cult around Mao has been dismantled and some of his political practice has been criticised. It seems certain that sooner or later Mao will be explicitly indicted for the upheavals in the Chinese political system since 1957, with the present leadership making it quite clear that they should have the right to revise his thought in the light of new conditions arising during the march towards the attainment of the four modernisations. A mechanical approach to Mao's thought, regardless of time and place, limits the scope of policies which the present leadership can bring in, and limits their potential for developing different policies to suit the changing conditions. Mao claimed to have integrated the universal truths of marxism–leninism with the concrete practice of the Chinese revolution and the present leadership see the Party's task 'on the theoretical front' as integrating 'the universal principles of Marxism–Leninism–Mao Zedong Thought with the concrete practice of socialist modernisation', and developing it 'under new historical conditions'.[35] This process has been aided and accompanied by the attack on the cult of the individual and the stress on collective leadership. In July 1980 an article acknowledged that Mao had made the greatest contribution to the development of marxism–leninism during the Chinese revolution but also stressed that 'Mao Zedong Thought is not a product of the wisdom of Mao Zedong alone',[36] but the product of 'historical' and 'collective wisdom'. The article mentions the important theoretical contributions made by other 'early communists' to show that the revolutionary theory expounded in Mao's thought was certain to have developed in the historical course of the 'collective struggle',[37] irrespective of Mao. Such an interpretation of the origins and development of Mao Zedong Thought enables the present leadership to acknowledge the contributions made by other communists whose views may run counter to the thinking of Mao in his later years. Such views can now be put forward as a 'legitimate' part of the Thought of Mao Zedong. Similarly, 'maoist deadwood' can be cut away and the new 'collective leadership' given the right to further develop Mao's ideas.

As far as is possible the Thought of Mao Zedong has been recast in its pre-Cultural Revolution and mid-fifties mode which serves to negate both the 1975 theories of the Gang of Four and the development of Mao's ideas concerning the continued existence of classes and class struggle. Works of Mao which are now quoted to justify present policy are those which show his more conservative side. Apart from articles already mentioned such as 'On the Ten Major Relationships' and 'On the Correct Handling of Contradictions Among the People', 'On Practice' and Mao's talk at the Enlarged Work Conference in 1962 are frequently quoted. 'On Practice' can very easily lend itself to a pragmatic interpretation which fits with the slogan of 'seek truth from facts'; what is often put forward amounts to 'if it works then it must be true'. The 1962 talk finds Mao at his most conservative and while he referred to the need for discipline he spoke at great length of the importance of promoting democracy as a means to the end of centralised unification. Importantly, this article contains Mao's admission that he had made mistakes concerning the Great Leap Forward and that he should be criticised for them, an admission which contributes to the present view that Mao was after all only human and therefore liable to commit errors.

The cornerstone of this attempt to bring flexibility to the ideology is the slogan 'practice is the sole criterion for testing truth' or 'seek truth from facts' and the corresponding policy of 'correcting mistakes whenever they are discovered'. Deng Xiaoping and the present leadership, in order to claim the legitimacy of their own policies, have presented this approach as a reaffirmation of Mao's thought by trying to show that Mao always gave primacy to practice and the need to re-evaluate theory in light of it. This is a quite correct assessment but it remains to be seen whether the re-evaluation is in line with Mao's thought, whether it represents a substantial deviation from it, or whether it represents a general decline in the force of ideology as a policy outcome determinant. Zhang Chunqiao, accused of having put forward the formula of 'theory–practice–theory', is reported to have said that 'Whether one is right or wrong ideologically is determined by theory, which deals mainly with ideological problems'.[38] Such a view runs counter to the current approach for Zhang is accused of proposing that the correctness of an idea is determined by theory, and not practice, and that practice has to be tailored by theory while theory does not have to be tested in practice. In future it is claimed that struggles against erroneous tendencies will proceed from the reality, bring out the facts and reason things out so as to convince others, putting the stress on investigaiton and study. The new policy is to be 'strict in ideological criticism and lenient in taking disciplinary action'.[39] It is hoped that this approach, combined with the emphasis on distinguishing between the two different types of contradiction, will help increase democracy and debate.

At the Third plenum of the Eleventh CC it was pointed out that, at that time, class struggle was no longer the principal contradiction and that work should concentrate on the attainment of the four modernisations. *Beijing Review* stated, 'The fundamental change in the class situation in our country is the objective basis for the shift in focus of our Party's work to socialist modernisation.'[40] This view, which was presented by Hua Guofeng at the Second Session of the Fifth NPC, is to refute Zhang Chunqiao's and Yao Wenyuan's ideas about class, dismissing them as idealist, and to predate the development of Mao's thought of the sixties. It is now said that class struggle was viewed as being much graver than it was in reality, and Mao is quoted to justify the present concentration on production rather than class struggle. Again it is the 'mid-fifties Mao' who is quoted to justify this policy — 'Our basic task has changed from unfettering the productive forces to protecting and expanding them in the context of the new relations of production.'[41] The current approach to the question of class and class struggle is essentially similar to the approach for which Deng was criticised in 1976. At that time it was said that he had placed class struggle on a par with the struggle for scientific experiment and the struggle for production, rather than taking it as the 'key link'. In fact the current approach appears to go even further than this by making class struggle subservient to the struggle for production and it has been stated that 'at all times class struggle is a means; the basic goal of revolution is to liberate and develop the social productive forces. Socialist revolution is not confined to class struggle alone, for it also includes the struggle for production and scientific experiments'.[42]

Class struggle is not written off completely but the view taken is that of the mid-fifties: some bourgeois elements remain, as do remnants of bourgeois and feudal ideology, but it is denied that socialism itself can contain the seeds for the growth of a new bourgeoisie. Under the dictatorship of the proletariat it is felt that class enemies can no longer become a 'fully developed reactionary class' and openly confront the proletariat. This is conducive to the pursuit of unity and stability as it denies the necessity for 'large-scale, turbulent, mass struggles'. Class struggle is now seen in terms of people's attitude *vis-à-vis* the four modernisations, as the following quote makes clear: 'In future, class struggle will mainly centre around socialist modernisation and be made to serve socialist modernistation; its main manifestation will be the struggle between those defending the four modernisations and those trying to undermine the realisation of these modernisations.'[43]

The acknowledgement that Mao was human has enabled the leadership to put forward the view that he made mistakes and the stress on the collective nature of his thought makes a greater flexibility of interpretation possible, as does the campaign to identify practice as its core. It seems certain that before the end of 1980 an assessment will be made of Mao and his contribution to the revolution, and that this will entail branding him as the leader of a leftist tendency since liberation and guilty of left-adventurism after 1957. In the ideological sphere the legacy of Mao will remain, but it is now open to the present leadership to decide how they wish to interpret that legacy.

5

The Chinese Communist Party

The framework of rule

Before looking in detail at the three main apparats it is worth devoting a few words to some of the more general issues concerning the network of power in China. Like other communist-party states, China can be studied in terms of the classic duality of the Party and the state and their interrelationship. The general view is that the Party directs the administrative state machinery, but China's legacy from the guerrilla war has meant that the distinction between the Party and the state has been blurred and that, on occasions, the personnel of the two apparats has been identical. This has caused confusion about the division of responsibility between policy formulation and implementation. Another important inheritance is the level of military involvement in the political system — an involvement which is different from that of the military in the Soviet Union, where it acts as a pressure group pursuing 'professional' interests. In China, many people at the top levels in the decision-making process have held concurrent civilian and military posts, making it difficult to talk of a 'military interest at work'. Also, unlike in the Soviet Union, the military plays a large part in the activities of the CCP at all levels, not just at the centre.[1]

Despite structural similarities with other communist-party states, such as the parallelling of state organs by Party branches at the various levels, there have been important differences in practice. In the PRC the distinction between state and Party cadres has been less than in other communist regimes — all Party cadres are paid by the state and in the past the role of the State Council as an independent power, competing with the Party, has been over-stressed. As with the military, it is hard to identify sectoral interests because individuals have tended to express opinions over a range of issues rather than promote those of the Party, the state or the army. Certainly, the state can provide a power-base, as it did for Zhou Enlai, but in the past this base has been used to promote general rather than particular interests. On occasions the overlap of Party and state has led to the Party actually implementing policy. Normally such practice is condemned, but during the Great Leap Forward and the Cultural Revolution it was positively encouraged. At the beginning of the Cultural Revolution the organs of Party and state, at the non-central levels, were identical. Following the attacks in 1966 on the old Party and state organs they were replaced by the revolutionary committee, which was heralded as a 'brand new organ of proletarian power completely different from the exploiting classes of the old days' and, for a while, these committees combined Party and state functions in one body. This total collapse of the distinction between Party and state was rectified with the rebuilding of the provincial Party apparatus from 1969, but the revolutionary committees and Party committees continued to share functional departments, causing a persistent confusion over the division of responsibility between the two bodies. Throughout the early seventies the press stressed the need for the Party committees to strengthen their leadership over the revolutionary committees, emphasising that the Party should make the major decisions and the revolutionary committee must 'consciously accept the Party committees leadership in exercising power and carrying out its work'.[2] This problem was not helped by the fact that the leadership personnel of the two committees was often identical and Party committees in some factories were criticised for handling such trivial matters as family disputes and water temperatures in bathhouses.

The post-Mao leadership attempted to recreate a distinction between Party and state by reviving elements of the pre-Cultural-Revolution and pre-Great-Leap-Forward systems of organisation. The 1978 state constitution stressed the purely administrative function of the revolutionary committee, referring to it as the executive rather than the permanent organ of the people's congress at the corresponding level and as the local people's government at the various levels. The ubiquity of the revolutionary committee was restricted — they were to function only at the levels of government, that is, they were abolished at the prefectural level and replaced by administrative offices established by the provincial level revolutionary committee. In factories, schools, and so on the committees were replaced by a return to the 'system of a division of responsibilities with factory directors and school principals in charge under the leadership of the Party committee'. The Second Session of the Fifth National People's Congress went even further than this and abolished them altogether, with Peng Zhen making the symbolic announcement that 'local revolutionary committees are to be replaced by local people's governments' and that the posts of provincial governors, mayors and chairmen would be restored.[3]

The renewed stress on the functional separation of Party and state has been accompanied by the appointment of different people to parallel Party and state posts. Now, in 1980, at the provincial level the Party first secretaries do not hold the post of governor, etc., whereas previously it had been common practice for the Party first secretary to be the chairman of the revolutionary committee. During 1979 and 1980 all the provinces and their equivalents held people's congresses to elect their standing committees and to reestablish the people's governments. In every instance a person other than the Party first secretary was elected to the governor's post, mayor's post, and so on, and in the five autonomous regions cadres from the minorities were elected to the chairmanship. In the past the interrelationship between the Party and state personnel has been even more noticeable at the centre. Until mid-1980 all the Vice-Premiers of the State Council were high-ranking members of the Central Committee and Politburo, but in July 1980 it was announced that five of the Vice-Premiers were to resign their posts while retaining their Party positions.[4] At the same time it was announced that the highest posts in the Party and state would again be held by different people — as had been the case up until Mao's death. Hua Guofeng is to hand over his post as Premier to Zhao Ziyang, but will keep the position of Party Chairman. Previously, leaders, including Hua, have even held leading positions in all three apparats. For example, Deng Xiaoping was not only a Vice-Chairman of the Party and a Vice-Premier of the State Council but also the Chief of Staff of the PLA until replaced by Yang Dezhi.

A factor which brings a further complexity to the structure of power is the relationship between the centre and the provinces, particularly with the increasing role of the provincial leadership at the centre. Given the sheer size and diversity of China it is not surprising that there should be attempts to integrate possible conflicting ideas with those of the national decision-makers. Consequently, over time the Central Committee has enlarged to include provincial personnel, among whom can be counted Hua Guofeng, and the percentage of those whose workplace is at the provincial level has increased compared with those whose workplace is at the centre. This would suggest that the provincial leadership provides a reservoir of talent for the centre, and that it also has a degree of influence over the decision-making process,[5] but such a view is countered by the idea that the provincial leadership provides a vital cog in the transmission of the ideas of the centre to the provinces — ensuring that political power rests exclusively with the centre.[6] David S. G. Goodman, in a comprehensive study of the first Party secretary, concludes that 'there is little to suggest that the first secretary has been a local leader rather than an agent of central control'.[7]

Finally, a few words need to be said about Mao's role in the structure of power. A completely Mao-centred approach to Chinese politics leaves many gaps in one's knowledge of the workings of the political process, but nor can Mao's role in the political system be ignored. It is ironic that although Mao played a crucial role in devising the 'rules of the game' in China, it was he who was instrumental in causing a breakdown of these rules when he resorted to alternative channels of communication and more personalised form of politics. Despite constraints on his leadership, such as objective economic conditions (which in part caused his retreat from the Great Leap Forward) and organisational factors (such as the huge bureaucracy over which he presided) Mao, except for short spells, never lost his ability to initiate policy and break policy deadlock. The present stress on collective leadership implies criticism of Mao's method of leadership, particularly of those methods he used during the Cultural Revolution when legitimacy moved from the Party to the leader. One of the conventional views of Chinese politics is to see it in terms of a pendulum swinging from radical, mobilisational politics through the centre to conservative, consolidational politics. In this view Mao is seen as someone who first 'stirs things up' and then 'damps things down', keeping an undulating movement towards the final socialist objective. On occasions Mao has put forward a more conservative line which has generally reflected either the force of the opposition ranged against him or his own attempts to salvage the best possible solution. Examples can be found where the power to initiate policy was out of Mao's hands as, for example, at the Lushan plenum (1959) — when Peng's attacks caused him to beat a strategic retreat. By contrast, however, examples where Mao used his power and prestige are much more common. In 1955 he went over the heads of the Central Committee to step up the speed of collectivisation, in 1958 he launched the Great Leap Forward, in 1962 the Socialist Education Movement and in 1965 he again went over the heads of the Central Committee when he launched the Cultural Revolution.

The importance of Mao as a source of legitimacy provided him with a greater potential for action than any of the other leaders. The present leadership, with their stress on the collective, are trying to minimise this potential for any future leader. Also their reassessment of Mao makes it more difficult for any leader, or leaders, to initiate policy solely by referring to Mao for justification.

The organisational framework of the CCP

Although there are eight other political parties in the PRC[8] which accept the established system, there can be no doubt that the only party which really matters is the Communist Party. The CCP provides the tangible manifestation of the revolution and, according to the constitution, it is the political party of the proletariat composed of its most advanced elements. The role of the Party is to lead the proletariat to the ultimate goal of communism by providing the correct ideological and political line, but this line has never remained consistent and has, on average, changed every three or four years since the founding of the People's Republic. The CCP's role as the guardian of the ideology makes it the most important part of the communist system because the ideology provides the regime's legitimacy, and the Party's interpretation of the ideology enables it to justify specific social, economic and political goals.

The CCP is built on the orthodox leninist principles of organisation. Its specific formulation of these principles can be found in the Party constitution, the most recent of which was adopted at the Eleventh Party Congress (August 1977). The basic outline is quite clear but certain parts of it have been made redundant by political developments since the congress; for example, the favourable references to the Cultural Revolution in the preamble will be dropped at the next congress. As a result the Fifth plenum (February 1980) adopted the 'Guiding Principles for Inner-Party Political Life' to supplement the Party constitution. These principles are intended primarily to deal with the problems in 'Party life' which have grown up during the years 1966—76 and the principles are described as 'conforming with the unique requirement of eliminating the pernicious influence of Lin Biao and the Gang of Four'.[9]

The basic principle of the Party is that of democratic centralism. This demands that the 'individual is subordinate to the organisation, the minority is subordinate to the majority, the lower level is subordinate to the central committee'.[10] The result of this principle is a hierarchical pattern of organisation in the shape of a pyramid consisting of four and, on occasions, five levels. These levels are: the Central Organisations; the Regional Bureaux; the Provincial and Autonomous Region Organisations; the County (xian) or District Organisations; and the Basic Organisations — such as the factory or commune Party branch (see Figure 5.1). The second important principle is that of collective leadership — this is designed to avoid the tendency towards one-person rule inherent in

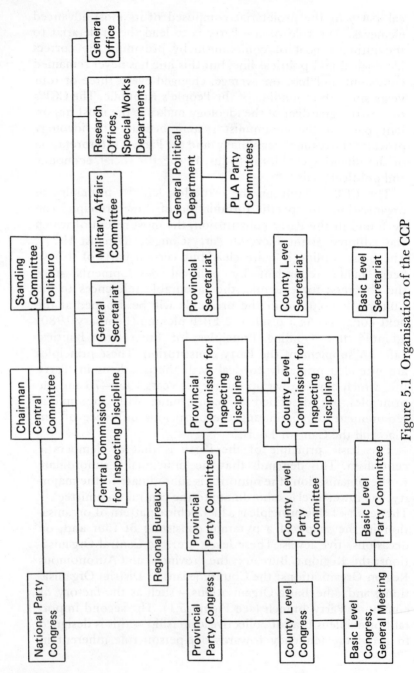

Figure 5.1 Organisation of the CCP

such a hierarchically organised structure. Party committees at all levels are called on to 'combine collective leadership with individual responsibility under a division of labour', to 'rely on the political experience and wisdom of the collective' and 'all important issues are to be decided collectively, and at the same time each individual is to be enabled to play his or her part'.[11] The third principle concerns the protection of minority rights in the Party, and seeks to enable individual members to hold different views to those of the organisation and bring them up for discussion at Party meetings. If this right is breached the individual can 'bypass the immediate leadership and report to higher levels, up to and including the Central Committee and the Chairman of the Central Committee'.[12] However, once a definite decision is made by the Party the individual must 'resolutely' carry it out.

Central organisation (see Figure 5.2)

The National Party Congress

In theory the top of the hierarchical structure is the National Party Congress (PC) which should convene once every five years. This has been the case since the Eighth PC (1956) when the 1945 stipulation that it should meet every three years was changed. The constitution acknowledges that under special circumstances the congress may be convened either sooner than or later than the arranged date. In practice this exception has proved to be more common than the rule, as the following dates of congress sessions show:

Party Congress	Year
First	1921
Second	1922
Third	1923
Fourth	1925
Fifth	1927
Sixth	1928
Seventh	1945
Eighth 1st Session	1956
Eighth 2nd Session[13]	1958
Ninth	1969
Tenth	1973
Eleventh	1977

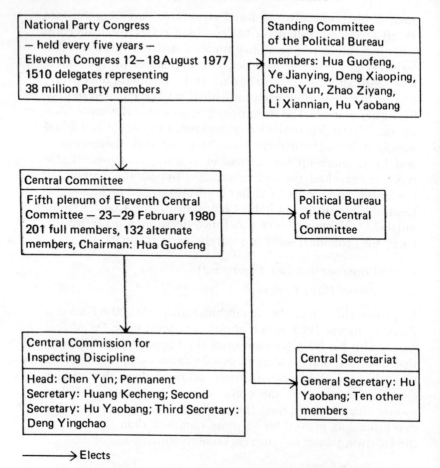

→ Elects

Figure 5.2 Central organisation of the CCP (simplified)

Also the Fifth plenum of the Eleventh CC announced that the Twelfth Party Congress will be held before its scheduled date which, most probably, will be the end of 1980 or the beginning of 1981.

The number of delegates to the Eleventh Party Congress (which only met for seven days) totalled 1510. Such a large number of delegates meeting over such a short space of time is usual, which means that it is unlikely that matters of any substance can be properly discussed at the congresses. Thus some writers suggest that the function of the congresses is a purely symbolic one. This symbolic function is obviously important, and quite clearly they are 'milestones' in the Party's history, but they do perform other important functions. The symbolic function is quite evident: the Ninth Party Congress marked the watershed between the upheavals of 1966—9 and the years of reconstruction which were to follow; the Tenth Party Congress marked an attempt to find a 'succession leadership' in the wake of the Lin Biao affair; and the Eleventh Party congress 'brought the curtain down' on the Cultural Revolution decade. The congress has the job of approving the political report which outlines recent developments and the current long- and short-term policy objectives. The political report to the Eleventh Party Congress was delivered by the Chairman, Hua Guofeng. It dealt with the 'eleventh two-line struggle' in the history of the Party and put forward the 'eight musts' which would help bring about 'great order across the land'.[14] The congress also approves the constitution and the report on the constitution. The report at the Eleventh Party Congress was delivered by Ye Jianying. Finally, the congress is responsible for the election of the Central Committee, although it is probably more correct to say that it ratifies the proposals of the top leadership.

The congress's unwieldy size, its short duration and the fact that its functions are all ones of 'approval' indicate that the centre of decision-making in the Party must lie elsewhere.

The Central Committee

When the Party Congress is not in session the Central Committee is the leading body of the Party. Although it meets more frequently than the congress its size, 201 full members and 132 alternate members at the time of election of the Eleventh CC,[15] again indicates that it cannot represent the main focus of decision-making in the Party. It is reasonable to presume that, for the most part, the Central Committee acts as a rubber-stamp to the Political Bureau (Politburo). As Schurmann has observed, 'It meets in plenary session only on

special occasions, which are marked by the announcement of
new policy decisions worked out in the Politburo or the
Standing Committee'.[16] These plenary sessions are not necessarily restricted to members and alternates, and may involve
other important personnel in the decisions which are to be
ratified. The plenums are of short duration, which again
suggests that their functions are largely symbolic. Any
decisions taken are published in the form of a communiqué.
The Eleventh CC has held five such plenary sessions: the First
plenum (August 1977) elected the central leadership positions
for the committee; the Second (February 1978) made preparations for the Fifth National People's Congress; the Third
(December 1978) marked the decisive shift in the Party's
work from criticism of the Gang of Four to socialist modernisation; the Fourth (September 1979) approved Ye Jianying's
speech for the thirtieth anniversary of the founding of the
PRC; and the Fifth (February 1980) rehabilitated Liu Shaoqi
and decided to convene the Twelfth Party Congress before its
scheduled date.

As was mentioned earlier, the Central Committee acts
largely as a rubber-stamp to Politburo decisions but this does
not mean that it is unworthy of study. The Party constitution
states that the Central Committee is responsible for the election of the Politburo and its Standing Committee, the Chairman and Vice-Chairman of the Party and the Commission for
Inspecting Discipline. Two features are worth noting about
the Central Committee. First, it can act as a transmission belt
passing down policies and passing up ideas concerning their
feasibility and implementation. Secondly, membership of the
committee can be seen as a reward for services provided, or as
an indicator of future potential. Consequently, the composition of the Central Committee is a good indicator of trends in
the political system, and a study of the composition will
indicate what the leadership considers important at any one
time, and how this changes over time. In turn, the study of
any such change over time will reveal the changing requirements of the leadership.

Table 5.1 shows the make-up of the full members of the Central Committee between 1969 and 1978 by their predominant
career background since liberation. The figures for the Ninth

Table 5.1   Central Committee composition

Classification of cadres	% of those with known backgrounds		
	Ninth Central Committee (1969)	Tenth Central Committee (1973)	Eleventh Central Committee (1977)
Party—state cadres	32%	42%	53%
PLA	50%	40%	31%
'Mass Representatives'	18%	18%	16%
Cadres purged during GPCR		12%	39%

Source: David S. G. Goodman, 'Changes in Leadership Personnel after September 1976' in J. Domes (ed.), Chinese Politics After Mao (University College Cardiff Press, 1979), p. 43.

CC quite clearly show the greater involvement of the military in the Party as a result of their political role during the Cultural Revolution. The other legacy of the years 1966—9 apparent from looking at the table is the relatively lower percentage of Party—state cadres on the committee — a consequence of the large-scale attack on the pre-Cultural-Revolution political order. In fact about 80 per cent of those who were elected to the Ninth CC were people who had not been on the previous committee — a fact which indicates the magnitude of the changes which the Cultural Revolution brought about. The Tenth CC reflects the post-Lin-Biao leadership composition with a reduced military presence and a corresponding increase in the number of Party—state cadres. This reflected the policy of rehabilitation of veteran cadres which started in earnest at the Tenth Party Congress. Approximately 12 per cent of the 'new' Central Committee members were people who had been purged during the years 1966—9. These trends continued to be reflected in the composition of the Eleventh CC, elected after the purge of the Gang of Four. The Eleventh CC's make-up, in terms of personnel, is similar to that of the pre-Cultural-Revolution Eighth CC. Nearly 40 per cent of those elected to the Eleventh CC were people who had been purged during the years 1966–9, while approximately one-third of those who were elected to the Tenth CC failed to secure election to the Eleventh (the majority of whom were purged because of their close connections with the Gang of Four).

Three other points are worth noting about the Eleventh CC. First, the number of women fell from 10 per cent to 7 per cent of full members, demonstrating the practical problems which women have in achieving the equality accorded them in theory. However, this does represent a significant increase in women's representation in comparison with the years prior to the Cultural Revolution. Secondly, the age of the Central Committee has steadily increased, which indicates that power has not yet passed into the hands of a successor generation but merely from one section of the same generation to another.[17] This fact is recognised by the present leadership and it has embarked on an extensive campaign to encourage older leaders to retire and to replace them with 'younger blood'. The problem of transition remains one of the most pressing problems facing the current leadership. Thirdly, the committee's composition reflected a reversal of the trend for an increasing number whose workplace is at the provincial level to be elected to the committee. Although the number has decreased the situation has not returned to that of the pre-Cultural Revolution when over 60 per cent had their workplace at the centre (see Table 5.2).

The Politburo, its Standing Committee and the Secretariat

The Politburo and its Standing Committee are the most important organs of the Communist Party and are the centre of the decision-making process. The constitution gives one no idea about the extent of the powers of the Politburo and its Standing Committee, and simply states that it is elected by the Central Committee, that it convenes the plenary session of the Central Committee and that when the Central Committee is not in plenary session the Politburo and its Standing Committe exercise its functions and powers.[18] We know

THE CHINESE COMMUNIST PARTY

Table 5.2   Workplace of Central Committee members

Central Committee date	Workplace % of total	
	Centre	Province
Eighth (1956)	69	31
Ninth (1969)	41	59
Tenth (1973)	36	64
Eleventh (1977)	38	62
Eleventh (Apr. 1978)	45	55

Source: Figures taken from David S. G. Goodman, 'Changes in Leadership Personnel after 1976' in J. Domes (ed.), *Chinese Politics After Mao*, p. 51.

little about the actual workings of the Politburo, except for the fact that its meetings are frequent and that discussion at these meetings is said to be unrestrained. The increasing size of the Politburo over time (11 members in 1949 and 23 in 1980) meant that the Standing Committee was set up in 1956 as a kind of 'inner cabinet'. This committee has functioned continuously since 1956 and it is the highest collective authority in the Party. It is ironical that the first major decision since Mao's death by a leadership committed to the collective principle was taken without prior consultation with either the Politburo or its Standing Committee — namely the arrest of the Gang of Four. Between the years 1966 and 1976 these two bodies had the power of decision on major policy issues and on implementation of policies, but since the arrest of the Gang of Four the pre-Cultural-Revolution system has been revived and use is made of Central Work Conferences and specialised national conferences — such as those of agriculture, science and national defence — to devise specific policies. The advantage of these conferences is that they incorporate specialists whose technical expertise is of value.

Like the Central Committee, the Politburo and its Standing Committee have experienced large-scale personnel changes during the seventies as a result of the death of top leaders, the purge of the 'leftists' and the rehabilitation of some of those purged during the Cultural Revolution (see Figure 5.3).

Ninth CC (1969)	Tenth CC (1973)	Eleventh CC (1977)	Fifth plenum Eleventh CC (1980)
Mao Zedong	Mao Zedong (d)		
Lin Biao (d+p)[a]			
Zhou Enlai	Zhou Enlai (d)		
Chen Boda (p)			
Kang Sheng	Kang Sheng (d)[b]		
	Wang Hongwen (p)		
	Ye Jianying	Ye Jianying	Ye Jianying
	Zhu De (d)		
	Li Desheng		
	Zhang Chunqiao (p)		
	Dong Biwu (d)		
		Hua Guofeng	Hua Guofeng
		Deng Xiaoping (c)	Deng Xiaoping (c)
		Li Xiannian	Li Xiannian
		Wang Dongxing (p)	
			Chen Yun (c)
			Zhao Ziyang (c)
			Hu Yaobang (c)

d — died

p — purged

c— criticised during the years 1966–9

[a] Lin Biao's death was followed by a criticism campaign against him, and had he survived he would have been purged.

[b] Criticism of Kang Sheng during 1980 indicates that had he lived he would also have fallen from grace.

Figure 5.3 Personnel of the Standing Committee of the Politburo

The present Standing Committee of the Politburo represents a leadership, with the possible exception of Hua Guofeng, committed to a programme of development similar to that proposed in the mid-fifties as an alternative to the Soviet model, but subsequently dropped in favour of the Great Leap strategy. All of them, with the exception of Hua, gained nothing during the Cultural Revolution and although some, such as Li Xiannian and Ye Jianying, did not actually lose anything either, others, such as Deng Xiaoping and Hu Yaobang, lost heavily as a result of the attacks.

The Secretariat of the Central Committee was re-established by the Fifth plenum of the Eleventh CC which elected eleven members to serve in it under the General Secretary, Hu Yaobang. The plenum announced that the Secretariat will deal with the 'day-to-day work of the Central Committee under the leadership of the Political Bureau of the Central Committee and its Standing Committee'.[19] The Secretariat provides the administrative heart of the CCP, enabling the Politburo and its Standing Committee to 'concentrate their energy on considering and taking decisions on important issues of domestic and foreign affairs'.[20] In practice this places the Secretariat in an extremely powerful position as it supervises the regional Party organisations and the functional departments of the Party which, in theory, should be responsible directly to the Central Committee and Politburo. The Secretariat existed prior to the Cultural Revolution, from 1956 to 1966, but it was abolished as a part of the attack on the Party, and its functions were taken over by the General Office.[21] The Secretariat provided a major source of opposition to Mao and his policies; only three of its eleven members survived the Cultural Revolution unscathed[22] and the General Secretary, Deng Xiaoping, was labelled the 'number two person in authority taking the capitalist road'.

The Central Commission for Inspecting Discipline

The 1977 Party constitution stated that the Central Committee and Party committees at the county level and above, regimental level and above in the PLA, should set up commissions for inspecting discipline. The commissions are to be elected by the Party committee at the same level and are given wide-ranging powers to deal with breaches of Party discipline. Although they have a new name they have similarities with the discipline inspection committees which operated from 1949 to 1955, and with the Party control committees which replaced them. These control committees were attacked and abolished during the Cultural Revolution because it was claimed that they had failed to stem the growth of bureaucracy and had, in fact, become a huge vertically integrated bureaucracy themselves. The current organisational structure is not completely clear but it may be clarified in the new Party constitution to be adopted by the Twelfth Party Congress. The discipline inspection committees which operated between 1949 and 1955 were completely subordinate to the Party committees, which meant that they were often ineffectual as a means of control while their replacement, the Party control committees, had a vertically integrated structure independent of the Party committees. Perhaps the 'new' commissions are seeking to combine aspects of these two earlier systems in their operations — it is certain that a great deal of importance is attached to them.

The Central Commission for Inspecting Discipline was set up by the Third plenum of the Eleventh CC (December 1978) and it held plenary sessions in January 1979 and January 1980. The importance attached to the new body is shown by those elected to the leadership positions of the 100-person commission. The head of the commission is Chen Yun, its Second and Third Secretaries are Deng Yingchao and Hu Yaobang, and its Permanent Secretary is Huang Kecheng, who was elected to the Central Committee by the Third plenum. During 1979 and 1980 its role has become clearer and its area of concern is much more far-reaching than a narrow definition of the term 'discipline' would suggest. As a result of the years 1966—76 discipline in the Party has become slack and the Gang of Four are accused of stifling democracy in the Party. The commission has played an important part in correcting these two problems by restoring the rules and regulations which have been flouted since the late fifties. Although it monitors minor abuses of the system its most important task is to 'ensure that the Party's ideological and political lines and organisational principles are implemented, and to ensure that the whole Party advances triumphantly in accordance with the four fundamental principles put forward by the CCP Central Committee'.[23] Since its creation the commission has investigated numerous matters concerning the history of the PRC and, most importantly, it spent a year investigating the case of Liu Shaoqi, checking the materials relating to accusations made at the Twelfth plenum of the Eighth CC. A report of the commission's findings was presented to the Fifth plenum of the Eleventh CC and provided the basis on which the plenum posthumously rehabilitated Liu Shaoqi. The commission, with the Central Organisation Department, has supervised the formation of discipline inspection organisations at the various levels in the Party, which suggests its role is more akin to that of the Party control commissions.

The Central Commission also drafted the 'Guiding Principles for Inner-Party Political Life' adopted by the Fifth plenum. The document contains twelve points, or principles, designed to restore the practice of Party life to normal and consequently it is directly critical of the practices of Lin Biao and the Gang of Four in undermining Party life. By implication it is critical of Mao's personalisation of politics. The principles attempt to revive Party life by the application of the Party norms as they functioned at the time of the Eighth Party Congress, before leadership consensus broke down. The principle of collective leadership is stressed, combined with a division of labour and a system of individual responsibility. To help enforce this principle the document introduced measures designed to curb the role of individuals. It stressed that publicity for leading members should be factual, that 'no unprincipled glorification of them is to be allowed', and that 'no museums are to be built for living persons and not too many should be built for dead leaders'.[24] The principles stress that free discussion in the Party should be safeguarded, but equally they stress that once a decision has been made it should be firmly adhered to.[25]

Also the commission has compiled an initial draft of education materials for study by cadres in the Party. The draft contains fifteen points which are to provide cadres with a code of behaviour to help cure the abuses which have existed in recent years and to prevent cadres from taking advantage of their position and power to pursue their own ends. The points outline the correct 'moral character and style' that cadres should have. They are urged to be responsible to the people, to be models of plain living and hard work, and not to seek personal gain, abuse their power, 'ride roughshod over people or to practice "what I say counts"' [26]

In addition to these activities it seems that the commission has been involved in the preparations for the trial of the Gang of Four, the preparation of charges against Kang Sheng and Xie Fuzhi and consideration of the case of Wang Dongxing.

The non-central levels of organisation

Below the Party centre there are three, sometimes four, levels of Party organisation — the region, the province, the county and the basic level. Organisation at provincial level and at the county level is basically the same as that of the centre, with Party congresses electing Party committees and so on. At the basic level congresses, or general membership meetings, are responsible for the committees at the same level, but there is no such congress or committee at the regional level.

In May 1977 Yu Qiuli, a Vice-Premier of the State Council spoke of the recreation of the regional 'economic systems'[27] but it is unclear whether this means that the Party regional bureaux have also been recreated to oversee the economic work. In the past there has been disagreement about the precise functions of these regions, and even the Chinese themselves appear to be uncertain about their function. Point ninety-four of a discussion document about the hundred major problems facing China's economic development states that China is committed to establishing economic systems in the six large regions, but then asks how is this to be done and what are they to do once established?[28] When the CCP came to power in 1949 it established the six 'great administrative regions' of north-east China, north China, east China, south-central China, south-west China and north-west China. The regions formed a part of both the Party and state systems but were abolished in 1954 only to be reintroduced in 1961 by the Ninth plenum of the Eighth CC. This time, however, they operated solely as Party organs but did not convene Party congresses. During the Cultural Revolution they and their personnel came under attack and again fell into disuse; no mention has been made of them since in any Party constitution.

On the two occasions when they were abolished the reasons given were the same, with accusations of 'independent kingdomism' being levelled against them. Basically, this meant that they were considered as providing too strong a power-base for their local leaders. This could be used to block the centre's policies and to promote regional interests. Similarly, the reasons given for their establishment on both previous occasions have been the same and have concerned the need for economic recovery. This was clearly the case in 1949 when it was necessary to revive the war-torn economy, and in 1961 when the economic disaster of the Great Leap Forward needed to be rectified. The present leadership appears to feel the need for them to aid their ambitious modernisation programmes, but this need will have to be set against the fear that they might once again provide the basis for strong centrifugal tendencies.

The provincial level is the most important non-central level of Party organisation and comprises 21 provinces, 5 autonomous regions and 3 special cities.[29] As has been noted, the provincial Party structure is similar to that of the centre, with Party congresses electing Party committees which in turn elect the standing committees, secretaries and deputy secretaries which run the provinces on a day-to-day basis. According to the constitution the provincial Party congresses are to be held every three years, but with the approval of the Central Committee their meeting may be brought forward or put back should special circumstances require it. The provincial Party committees occupy a crucial position in the party system between the centre and the local levels and they are responsible for supervising Party and economic work in the area under their jurisdiction. As a consequence of these responsibilities the provincial Party first secretary is a person who can have a great deal of power as a kind of 'political broker', balancing central and provincial interests.

The level below the province is the county in the rural areas, and the municipality for the towns; their structures and function are the same as those of the provinces. At the bottom of the hierarchy are the basic-level units which are referred to as Party branches, general Party branches or primary Party committees. According to the constitution they are set up in 'factories, mines and other enterprises, people's communes, offices, schools, shops, neighbourhoods, companies of the People's Liberation Army and other primary units in accordance with the need of the revolutionary struggle and the size of their party membership'.[30] Committees of Party branches are elected annually, but committees for the general Party branches and primary Party committees are elected every two years. The constitution adopted by the Eleventh CC calls these basic-level organisations 'fighting bastions' and gives them a sixfold task. Basically this task can be summarised as informing the people of Party policy, mobilising the people's support for the policy, while at the same time channelling back their views on the policy and recruiting new members for the Party.

Party membership

With a Party membership of 38 million (see Table 5.3) the CCP is the largest Communist Party in the world, but it is one of the most exclusive as less than 3 per cent of the population are members. The constitution gives no evidence of this exclusivity for it states that 'any Chinese worker, poor peasant, lower-middle peasant, revolutionary soldier or any other revolutionary over eighteen may become a member of the Party' on condition that they accept the constitution and 'will join and work actively in a Party organisation, carry out Party decisions, observe Party discipline and pay membership dues'.[31] However, before applicants can become members they must be recommended by two full Party members, be accepted by the next higher committee and undergo a one-year probationary period. At the end of the probationary period the applicant is admitted to the Party unless doubts remain concerning the person's suitability, in which case the probation period can be extended for one more year.[32] The

Table 5.3   *Membership figures of the CCP*

Year	Membership (approx.)	Year	Membership (approx.)
1921	57	1955	9.4 million
1939	122 500	1956	10.8 million
1941	765 000	1957	12.7 million
1949	4.5 million	1959	14.0 million
1950	5.0 million	1961	17.0 million
1951	5.8 million	1969	20.0 million[a]
1952	6.0 million	1973	28.0 million[b]
1953	6.0 million	1977	35.0 million[c]
1954	6.5 million	1980	38.0 million[d]

a Estimate on the basis of about 40 per cent increase in 1973 on 1969 given by J. Domes, 'A Rift in the New Course' in *Far Eastern Economic Review* (1 October 1973), p. 3.

b Zhou Enlai, 'Report to the Tenth National Congress of the Communist Party' in *The Tenth National Congress of the Communist Party of China (Documents)* (Beijing: Foreign Languages Press, 1973), p. 8.

c Ye Jianying, 'Report on the Revision of the Constitution of the Party' to the Eleventh National Congress of the Communist Party of China in *The Eleventh National Congress of the Communist Party of China* (Beijing: Foreign Languages Press, 1977) p. 182.

d Deng Xiaoping, 'Report on the Current Situation and its Tasks' in Summary of World Broadcasts: the Far East 6363.

Party has a series of disciplinary measures which it can take against members who fail in their duties and who ·do not respond to re-education. These range from 'a warning, a serious warning, removal from his or her post in the Party, being placed on probation' to 'expulsion from the Party'.[33] Also, if a member's performance is not deemed to be up to standard they may be persuaded to resign, and people who do not pay their membership dues for six months will be regarded as having given up their membership.[34]

For a Party which describes itself as 'the political Party of the proletariat' and 'the highest form of its class organisation', it is open to a wide spectrum of people to join. The criteria laid down at the Eighth Party Congress did not even refer to the class of prospective members at all, simply stating that 'any Chinese citizen who works, who does not exploit the labour of others' and who satisfied the general criteria was eligible to join. As this suggests, the recruitment of Party members is highly flexible, as the practice since 1921 has shown. Since the Party's inauguration recuritment policy has changed over time in accordance with the general line of the Party. Since the fall of the Gang of Four the emphasis of recruitment policy has been on cadres, intellectuals and those who possess technical skills. These groups of people are over-represented in the Party when taken as a reflection of society as a whole. Obviously, this emphasis in recruitment is linked to the policies of economic modernisation pursued in earnest since the Third plenum, which require a high level of technical skills for their implementation. One of the most frequently mentioned problems is the lack of trained cadres in the Party. An article in *Red Flag* written by the organisational department of the Anhui provincial CCP pointed out that few cadres were really proficient in professional work, and that many were 'laymen' and that 'some of the laymen' were in leading positions at the provincial level'.[35]

Another problem of recent Party recruitment is the influx of new members since the start of the Cultural Revolution. During the years 1966–76 the emphasis was on recruiting workers, peasants and soldiers rather than technicians and cadres, and the Gang of Four are accused of pursuing a reckless policy of admitting new members and promoting new cadres 'at the double-quick'. The new members joined at a time when traditional rules and regulations were under attack and this means that they are unfamiliar with traditional Party procedure. Forty-three per cent of all Party members in Shanghai were admitted during the years 1966–76 and it is claimed that a 'handful of them' do not even know what 'the Communist Party, communism or Party spirit' are.[36] To remedy this problem all Party members are to undergo a period of re-education, but although the 'unhealthy tendencies' are to be rectified it has been decided not to unfold a movement to rectify work-style.

Before the Cultural Revolution changing policies also gave

rise to changing priorities in the recruitment drive. From liberation to the mid-fifties the adoption of the Soviet model meant an emphasis was placed on recruiting the urban workers and intellectuals, as opposed to the peasantry which had provided the vast majority of Party members before 1949. The abandonment of the Soviet model resulted in a change of emphasis which again favoured the peasantry, but in the early sixties the emphasis changed yet again. At this time the emphasis was very similar to the present, encouraging the recruitment of a well-trained, urban elite at the expense of the peasantry.

The Party since Mao

By way of conclusion to this chapter it is worth considering the development of the Party since Mao's death. Essentially the period has comprised an attempt to re-establish the Party norms which were established in Yanan but which were shattered during the Cultural Revolution. The Eleventh Party Congress placed heavy emphasis on the traditional leninist principles, and the need to revive inner-Party democracy, while the Third plenum instituted a wholesale re-examination of past Party practice. This re-examination has led to the identification of two different problems as the source of the troubles. The first source is those problems which appear to be endemic to the system, and which can be subsumed under the all-embracing title of 'bureaucratism'. The evils incorporated under this range from swollen and overstaffed set-ups, which make genuine accountability difficult, to privilege-seeking and to certain cadres acting as 'masters of society' rather than as 'public servants of the people'. Three sources are identified for these problems: first, there is the previously mentioned influx of new members into the Party; secondly, there are the veteran cadres who have abandoned their 'good work-style'; and thirdly, there are 'irrational regulations which provide privileges for cadres beyond their needs and far above the average person's living standards'.[37]

The second source is those problems which come under the heading of 'feudalism' or 'feudal patriarchism' and arise from what is termed the 'slavish adherence to Mao's thought'.

The aspects criticised under this heading do not just arise because of the 'ideological hangover' from the past but, according to the present leadership, arise because the Gang of Four promoted 'feudal fascism'.[38] An article in the *Guangming Daily* concluded that not only were the years of the Cultural Revolution years of feudalism rather than socialism but so too were the years 1958–61.[39] The reason why the author describes them as feudalist was because there were no laws, no courts and there was arbitrary arrest, torture and the rule of an emperor; he concludes that, as a 'democracy', the system did not even match up to that of capitalist democracies. The main feature criticised under the term 'feudalism' is the excessive power that is given to one person, and the problems which arise from such a concentration of power. According to the *People's Daily*, 'it is impossible for mistakes not to occur if a single individual makes all the decisions' and that such a delegation of power to this 'one-man tyranny' is impermissible because 'the ability of any individual is limited'.[40] The stress on collective leadership mentioned in the chapter is designed to counter this, as is the attempt to give less publicity to individual leaders.

The revival of democracy is identified as being crucial to the solution of the problems concerning Party life. It is hoped that a revival of democracy in the Party can also bring about the revival of democracy in society as a whole. As the *People's Daily* has said:

> Political life inside the Party had been abandoned for years and democracy had been missing inside the Party. This has led to an abuse of democracy in society as a whole. So, the most fundamental lesson to be drawn today is the necessity of having full democracy inside the Party.[41]

To help resolve this problem a variety of policies have been put forward, the most important of which has been the policy of 'reversing incorrect verdicts', and pre-Cultural-Revolution organisations, such as the Commission for Inspecting Discipline and the Party schools, have been revived. It is difficult to gauge the extent of success of these policies or whether there is still reluctance to speak out, but it does seem that there has been an increase in Party life and that on occasions the 'contending ideas' have led to confusion. In May 1979 the *Jiangxi Daily* stated that China was at a turning-point, and compared the conditions in the Party to those of a car turning a corner with all the passengers shouting at each other, with some falling out of the vehicle as they argue over the direction in which it is heading.

It has been made quite clear that although democracy is to be increased it is not to be unlimited and two general groups have been identified to whom the rights of democratic expression do not extend. The first are those termed the 'whateverists', those who believe that whatever Mao said was correct. The second group are those who have misinterpreted the degree of freedom permissible. They are criticised for promoting 'so-called democracy' and have been labelled 'anarchists' or 'bourgeois liberals'. Not only is democracy to be limited but also it has been stated that democracy is not to be seen as an end in itself, but that 'giving play to inner-Party democracy is intended to increase the Party's combat strength and unite the whole Party in order to realise the Party's central task – the realisation of the four modernisations'.[42] Essentially the Party has found itself faced with the classic dilemma of democratic centralism – how much democracy, how much centralism? The present policies and organisations are attempting to find a delicate balance which will result in neither passivity nor destructure criticism. For this purpose the traditional norms of Party behaviour have been revived and past history has shown that during a time of relative leadership unity they can function. However, as history since the late fifties has shown, once this unity breaks down so, too, can the Party norms. It remains to be seen whether a new divergence of opinion over development strategy would lead to a similar erosion of Party norms. Certainly the fact that there is no figure with the capabilities for action that Mao possessed tends towards the view that conflict and conflict resolution will be more controlled.

6

The state structure

The 1954 constitution detailed the new state structure. This structure inevitably owed much to the Soviet system of government and paralleled that of the Party, with three levels of government below the centre — the province, the county or municipality, and the town or commune (see Figure 6.1). The structure has remained the same since. The role of the state is to implement Party policy although, on occasions, the implementation has been carried out by the Party itself, while at other times the state has distorted Party policy during the process of implementation. This has created problems and tensions between the two structures and to cope with them the Chinese have used the systems of 'vertical' and 'dual rule' outlined by Schurmann.[1] The exception to this was during the early period of the Cultural Revolution, when Party and state were collapsed into the one body of the revolutionary committee. Vertical rule, as the name suggests, means that a ministry at the central level has control over all the units at the lower levels which come under the scope of its jurisdiction. As a result the flow of information and command runs vertically up and down the system. This was the system adopted under the First Five-Year Plan but it caused the growth of specialised bureaux at the lower levels which were responsible to the corresponding departments at the higher levels, but which were resistant to Party supervision at the same level. As a result, in 1956 the Eighth Party Congress adopted the system of dual rule. Dual rule means that the unit at the lower level is responsible to the corresponding departments at the higher levels and to the Party committee at the same level. In practice this enables the Party to keep control over the state system, as the Party committee at each

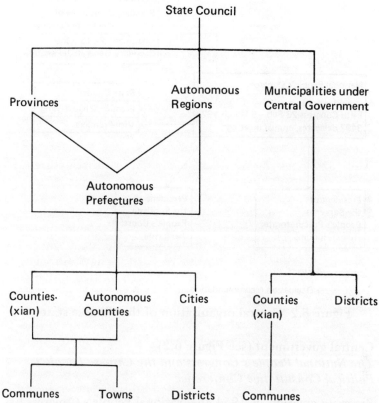

Figure 6.1 Levels of government under the State Council

Source: Beijing Review, no. 20 (1979) p. 21.

level is the only body capable of co-ordinating the activities of all the other units. During the Greap Leap Forward, following the 1957 decentralisation measures, the Party took almost total control over the state administration at the lower levels and ministries of the State Council were effectively cut off from their functional departments at the lower levels. At present, with the stress on managerial authority and technical expertise, the ministries under the State Council have been given a greater degree of authority over their functional departments at the lower levels, but the stress on joint Party supervision has remained.

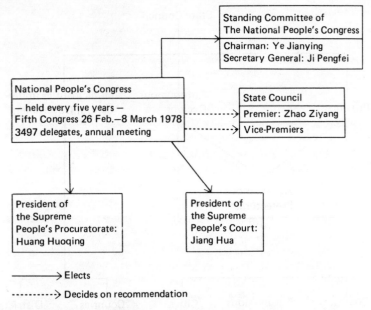

Figure 6.2 Central organisation of the Chinese state

Central government (see Figure 6.2)
The National People's Congress and the Chinese People's Political Consultative Conference

Since its creation in 1954 the National People's Congress has been the highest organ of state power but, prior to this, during the period of the Common Programme (1949—54), the highest body was the Chinese People's Political Consultative Conference (CPPCC). In September 1949 the CPPCC met in Beijing to proclaim the establishment of the People's Republic of China. The CPPCC was a manifestation of the united front policy, which meant that many of its members were non-communists, but its ultimate purpose was to bring about its own replacement as the most important administrative body. The meeting elected the Central People's Government Council and the Government Administration Council, the forerunner of the State Council, approved the Common Programme and the Organic Law which provided the principles of organisation for the new state structure. The CPPCC still functions and, since the fall of the Gang of Four, greater publicity has been given to its workings by the press. Essentially it provides liaison with the other political parties and promotes united front work, utilising expertise which is helpful for the four modernisations.

The National People's Congress is elected for a period of five years,[2] with the normal proviso concerning its extension or early termination, and to date (1981) there have been five national congresses held (see Table 6.1). The delegates to the congress are elected by the provincial congresses and by the PLA. The Fifth NPC was attended by 3497 deputies, of whom 10.9 per cent came from China's national minorities and of whom 21.2 per cent were women (Table 6.2). According to the constitution the congress has nine major functions.

Table 6.1   National People's Congresses

Congress	Time	Place	No. of delegates
First	15–28 Sept. 1954	Beijing	1226
Second	18–28 April 1959	Beijing	1226
Third	12 Dec.–4 Jan. 1964–5	Beijing	3040
Fourth	13–19 Jan. 1975	Beijing	2885
Fifth	26 Feb.–5 March 1978	Beijing	3497

Source: *Zhongguo Shouce* (Hong Kong: Ta Kung Bao, 1979), p. 99.

It can: amend the constitution and make laws; decide on the choice of Premier of the State Council, on the recommendation of the Party Central Committee; decide on the choice of the other State Council members, on the recommendation of the Premier; elect the President of the Supreme People's Procuratorate; examine and approve the national economic plan, the state budget and the final state accounts; confirm the lower levels of administration; and decide on questions of war and peace. At first glance these powers seem extensive, as indeed they are, but in practice it is not the NPC which controls them. As is the case with the Party Congress, the NPC's size is too unwieldy, and its meeting too infrequent, so that it seems more conceivable that it merely approves plans

Table 6.2   *Social composition of Fifth National People's Congress*

Category	Number	Percentage
Workers	935	26.7
Peasants	720	20.6
PLA	505	14.4
Revolutionary cadres	468	13.4
Intellectuals	523	15.0
Patriotic personages	311	8.9
Returned overseas Chinese	35	1.0

Source: *Beijing Review*, no. 20 (1979), p. 19.

and policies worked out elsewhere. With regard to the appointment of personnel the constitution acknowledges that its powers are greatly circumscribed. When the congress is not in session its Standing Committee carries out its duties, conducts the election of deputies to the NPC and convenes its sessions.[3] The Standing Committee of the Fifth NPC has 175 members and 20 Vice-Chairpersons and 1 Chairperson.

The State Council

The State Council is the executive organ of the National People's Congress which makes it the highest organ of the state administration. It is responsible and accountable to the NPC and its Standing Committee in its work, and is effectively the government of China. It is able to submit proposals on laws to the NPC or its Standing Committee as well as formulating administrative measures in accordance with the laws; to exert leadership over the non-central level organs of administration as well as the ministries and commissions; to draw up and put into effect the national economic plan and state budget; and to oversee public order and safeguard the rights of citizens. Membership of the State Council is composed of the Premier, who, from the position's inauguration to his death, was Zhou Enlai; the Vice-Premiers; and the ministers who head the bodies under its jurisdiction. Under the jurisdiction of the State Council and its General Office there is a system of ministries, commissions, committees and bureaux, the total number of which has varied over time. During the Cultural Revolution there were large-scale attacks on the administration, demanding its simplification and reduction in staff — demands which appeared to meet with some success. Although the central organisations, but not their personnel, survived the Cultural Revolution better than their non-central level counterparts, the number of central ministries and commissions was cut back. At the time of the Fourth NPC (1975) there were twenty-nine ministries and commissions whereas prior to the Cultural Revolution the total was forty-five.[4]

Since the arrest of the Gang of Four, the resultant shift in economic policies, and the stress on improving democracy and legality, have led to an increase in the number of ministries at the central level (see Table 6.3). The present economic policies have affected those ministries and commissions concerned with economic planning, the priority development of agriculture and the increase in two-way foreign trade. Thus the combined Ministry of Argiculture and Forestry has been redivided into its two component parts, a new State Finance and Economic Commission has been established under the leadership of Chen Yun, and State Commissions for Foreign Investment and Import—Export have been created. The stress on 'socialist legality' has led to the recreation of the Ministries of Civil Affairs and Justice. Apart from the ministries and commissions there are numerous specialised bureaux, agencies and committees under the State Coucil — such as the China Travel and Tourism Administrative Bureau, the People's Bank of China and the All-China Federation of Supply and Marketing Co-operatives.

The central legal organs and the legal system

In addition to its many other aspects already mentioned, the Cultural Revolution also saw an attack on the institutions of

Table 6.3   Ministries and commissions under the State Council

Ministry	Minister[a]	Ministry	Minister
Foreign Affairs	Huang Hua	Geology	Sun Daguang
National Defence	Xu Xiangqian	Coal Industry	Gao Yangwen
Public Security	Zhao Cangbi	Petroleum	Song Zhenming
Justice	Wei Wenbo	Chemical	Sun Jingwen
Civil Affairs	Cheng Zihua	Electric Power Industry	Liu Lanbo
Foreign Trade	Li Jiang	Water Conservancy	Qian Zhengying
Economic Relations with Foreign Countries	Shi Lian	Textile Industry	Qian Zhiguang
Agriculture	Huo Shilian	Light Industry	Liang Lingguang
Farm Machinery	Yang Ligong	Construction Material Industry	Song Yangchu
State Farm and Land Reclamation	Gao Yang	Railways	Guo Weizhong
Forestry	Luo Yuchuan	Communications	Zeng Sheng
Metallurgical	Tang Ke	Posts and Tele-communications	Wang Zigang
1st Machine-building	Zhou Zijian		
2nd Machine-building	Liu Wei	Finance	Wang Bingqian
3rd Machine-building	Lu Dong	Commerce	Wang Lei
4th Machine-building	Qian Min	Food	Zhao Xinchu
5th Machine-building	Zhang Zhen	Culture	Huang Zhen
6th Machine-building	Chai Shuyan	Education	Jiang Nanxiang
7th Machine-building	Zheng Tianxiang	Public Health	Qian Xinzhong
8th Machine-building	Jia Ruoyu	Grain[b]	

Commission	Head	Commission	Head
Financial and Economic	Chen Yun	State Agricultural	Wan Li
State Planning	Yao Yilin	State Energy	Yu Qiuli
State Economic	Gu Mu	State Nationalities Affairs	Yang Jingren
State Scientific and Technological	Fang Yi	State Physical Culture and Sports	Wang Meng

[a] Ministers and Heads as of June 1980. My thanks to Su Clements for providing some of the information on personnel.

[b] This is a new ministry but as yet there has been no mention of its personnel.

law and order which had existed up until 1966. The pre-
Cultural-Revolution institutions were labelled 'bourgeois' by
those who sought to abolish them. The system which replaced
that of the pre-Cultural-Revolution years has now also been
criticised, and it is said that Chinese citizens were insecure
and open to arbitrary arrest and detention. Ye Jianying's
report on the draft constitution stated that the Gang of Four
had 'raved about "smashing the public security organs,
procuratorial organs and people's courts" and put their words
into action, seriously undermining the state apparatus of the
dictatorship of the proletariat'.[5] One of the important bodies
abolished was the People's Procuratorate which operated
between the public security forces and the people's courts,
rather like the District Attorney's office does in the United
States. According to article 25 of the 1975 constitution, its
functions and powers were to be 'exercised by the organs of
public security at various levels'[6] which meant that, to an
extent, the arbitrary power of the police was enshrined in the
consititution. To correct this tendency, Ye stated that 'detention and arrests must follow legal procedures and the system
of checking and approval must be strictly observed',[7] thus
the People's Procuratorate was revived.

The new leadership has appreciated that rules and known
procedures to govern people's daily lives give a reassurance
and comfort. Consequently, 'socialist legality' should include
a system of rules and regulations applicable to all, to create
a more orderly system to replace the arbitrary practices which
occurred during the decade before Mao's death. The new
state constitution (1978) not only resurrected the procuratorate but also reaffirmed the citizens' rights to freedom of
speech, correspondence, and so on, guaranteed citizens the
'right to appeal to organs of state at any level against any
infringement of their rights', and stated that 'no-one shall
suppress any complaints and appeals or retaliate against
persons making them'.[8] After the Fifth NPC there were concrete manifestations of this drive to restore law and order,
such as the establishment of a Commission for Legal Affairs,
the resurrection of the Ministry of Justice and the introduction of a series of laws. At the Fifth NPC's Second Session
Peng Zhen introduced the drafts of seven new laws, including

China's first Criminal Code and Law of Criminal Procedure, and the Organic Laws for the People's Courts and People's Procuratorates which came into effect on 1 January 1980.

The People's Procuratorate examines and decides whether to approve a request for arrest made by a public security department, and also whether the person, if arrested, should be held criminally responsible and be brought to trial. The chief procurator, or his designate, attends the trial in the capacity of a state prosecutor to charge the accused and to see that the judicial process conforms to the law. When the procuratorate was restored it was stated that the Supreme People's Procuratorate was to supervise the work of the procuratorate at the lower levels. The procuratorate at the lower levels was also responsible to the people's congresses at the corresponding levels. Also the power of election and recall of the presidents of the people's courts and chief procurators was given to the people's congresses at the same level, from county level and above. It appears that practice created problems for the sytstem, and changes were announced at the Fifth NPC's Second Session. The relationship between the people's procuratorates at different levels was changed from one of supervision to leadership, which means that the Supreme People's Procuratorate is in charge of the local levels. The objective of this is to give the people's procuratorates a greater independence from the Party committees, but this is not equivalent to the degree of independence which they were given by the 1954 constitution. Also the role of the masses in the legal procedure has been reduced. Although it is still stated that the masses should be drawn in for discussion and suggestions on major or criminal cases[9] the phrase from the 1975 constitution that 'the mass line must be applied in procuratorial work and in trying cases' has been dropped.

There are three categories of procuratorates and courts: the Supreme Court and Procuratorate; the local courts and procuratorate (at provincial level, county and smaller city level); and the special people's courts and procuratorates which operate mainly in the military. Courts at the local level can deal with penal cases but the pronouncement of the death sentence must be reported to a court at a higher level and the sentence can be implemented only after receipt of the approval of the Supreme Court. An appeals procedure exists with a two-trial system. The appeal must be lodged with ten days of the prisoner receiving the written verdict. If, after the second trial, the accused is not convinced of his guilt the person may appeal to the court at the next level. Until the court makes its decision, a decision which is final, the original decision must be observed.

The equality of all before the law has been stressed and it has been made clear that no citizens, no matter how highly placed they are, should use their position to set themselves above the law.[10] As yet the attacks on privilege have fallen mainly on the lower-middle ranks of the bureaucracy, while those at the higher levels have remained untouched. Thus while Wang Shouxin, who was a manager of a county fuel company and vice-chairman of a county commercial revolutionary committee, was denounced as a 'good-for-nothing and an illiterate, mean woman of the old society' for misappropriating about £160 000 in cash,[11] Wang Dongxing, a former member of the Politburo's Standing Committee, appears to have avoided any legal consequences from the wall-poster accusations that he appropriated £2 million to build himself and his family luxury accommodation. In fact, as the Soviet experience has demonstrated, criticisms of privilege can be absorbed by the system over time. However, the code of criminal law and law of criminal procedure should help promote the policy of the equality of all before the law. The law forbids anyone to extract confessions by torture, to gather a crowd to beat, smash and loot, and to detain illegally and prosecute on fake charges. The law also contains the first official Chinese definition of counter-revolutionary behaviour, which is 'an act which attempts to overthrow the political power of the dictatorship of the proletariat and the socialist system'.[12] In practice, this means that it is now formally a crime to work against communism.

The non-central levels of organisation

Since the abolition of the regions in the mid-fifties the most important level, excluding the centre, is the province. The non-central government is administered through twenty-one provinces, five autonomous regions, three municipalities directly under the central government, with prefectures, counties and cities and communes under them (see Table 6.4). The prefecture does not constitute a level of political power, and therefore does not set up people's congresses and people's governments, but instead has administrative agencies set up by the province. The leading members of these agencies (administrative commissioners and their deputies) are not

*Table 6.4   Administrative division of China*a

Province	Prefectures	Counties	Cities
Hebei	10	139	9
Shanxi	7	101	7
Liaoning	3	53	11
Jilin	5	48	10
Heilongjiang	9	76	13
Shandong	9	106	9
Jiangsu	7	64	11
Zhejiang	8	65	3
Anhui	9	70	11
Jiangxi	6	82	8
Fujian	7	61	6
Henan	10	111	14
Hunan	11	90	10
Hubei	8	73	6
Guangdong	9	97	11
Shaanxi	7	92	5
Gansu	10	74	4
Qinghai	7	38	1
Sichuan	14	181	11
Guizhou	7	79	5
Yunnan	15	122	4

Table 6.4   Administrative division of China[a] (continued)

Province	Prefectures	Counties	Cities
Autonomous Regions			
Guangxi Zhuang	8	80	6
Xinjiang Uygur	13	80	7
Nei Menggu (Inner Mongolia)	4	43	5
Xizang (Tibet)	5	71	1
Ningxia Hui	2	17	2
Municipalities			
Beijing		9	
Shanghai		10	
Tianjin		5	
TOTAL	210	2137	190

[a] These divisions are as of the end of 1978 and the table has not included the number of communes in each province.

Source: adapted from *Beijing Review*, no. 20 (1979), p.23.

elected but are appointed by the higher levels. Different attempts have been made to introduce other administrative areas in the system. In some provinces, between the provincial level and county level, districts (diqu) were introduced and, in future, where they exist, they will be known as special areas (zhuan shu) and will become an agency (paichu jigou) linking county to province.[13] The three levels of government below the centre – province, county, commune and city – are organised in basically the same way as the centre. The people's congresses are the local organs of state power and are able to elect and recall members of the people's governments.[14] These people's governments at the provincial level are elected for five-year periods while those at the county level and at commune and town level are elected for three and two years respectively.[15] The people's government is the administrative (executive) organ of the people's congress and is responsible to both the people's congress at the same level and to the organs of state administration at the next higher level.[16]

One important change affecting the non-central levels was the announcement that people's congresses, at county level and above, now elect standing committees which perform the functions of the people's congresses when they are not in session. This means that the legislative and administrative organs (standing committees of people's congresses and people's governments) are now separated. Previously when the people's congress was not in session these powers were exercised by one body, the revolutionary committee.

Elections

In China there are two types of election, direct elections and indirect elections. Direct elections are those where the deputies to the representative organs of the state are elected directly by the voters themselves, and indirect elections are those where the deputies are elected by the voters' representatives rather than by the voters themselves. To help supervise cadres and prevent them from becoming 'masters of society' measures have been introduced to ensure greater accountability from those elected. A new chapter has been added to the electoral law stating that electors, or electoral units, have the power to supervise and recall their deputies. It also outlines a procedure for any such recall. Any charges against the deputy must be verified before the person can be removed and the person has the right of appeal at the 'recall' meeting. Among the new provisions on procedures is one which will ensure that elections, within limits, will become competitive affairs, as there are to be more candidates than there are places. For direct elections candidates are to exceed the total number of places by 50 to 100 per cent, and for indirect elections the number of candidates is to be 20 to 50 per cent higher.[17] Candidates for election can be nominated by 'the Communist Party, the democratic parties, the people's organisations or any other voter or deputy', as long as the application is seconded by three other people. The electoral constituencies are divided according to 'production units, undertakings, working units and residential quarters'. This role of the ballot box will diminish the importance of mass electoral meetings and although it is not intended to rule them out entirely it is now felt that the secret ballot is more 'democratic' than a mass show of hands.

Apart from being made more competitive the scope of elections has been extended. In June 1979 Hua Guofeng announced that leading members should be 'elected by the masses not only in the rural people's communes but at the grass-roots in enterprises and establishments such as factories, mines and stores'.[18] In units where it is 'inadvisable' to institute elections it is suggested that regular opinion polls be used as a method for assessing the work of cadres. Also the use of direct elections for people's congresses has been extended to include the county level,[19] but it is not considered possible to introduce direct elections throughout the whole country. During the latter half of 1979 and 1980 examples were reported in the Chinese press of county-level elections. In the second half of 1979 elections were conducted in 66 administrative units. It was intended that elections in the other 2000 county-level units would be completed by spring 1981. One of the counties which had elections in 1979 was Tongxiang county in Zhejiang province.[20] Originally, 6524 candidates were nominated, but this was reduced to between 750 and 1000 by a series of consultations with the voters' groups. Over 370 000 registered voters elected 494 deputies to the county-level people's congress (see Table 6.5). Although peasants totalled 56.5 per cent of those elected there was a positive discrimination against them in the system, with one rural deputy allocated for 1600 inhabitants while for the towns it was one deputy per 400. If this had not been the case the workers' representation would have been minimal. A complex electoral organisation was set up (see Figure 6.3) at the bottom of which there were four different categories of electoral district: first, there were those formed by a commune or town with a population of between 5000 to 20 000; secondly, those formed by several production brigades with a population between 5000 to

Table 6.5   Social composition of delegates to Tongxiang county people's congress

Category	Number	Percentage
Peasants	279	56.5
Workers	78	15.8
Government functionaries	83	16.8
Intellectuals	36	7.3
PLA	3	0.6
Others	15	3.0
TOTAL	494	100.0

Source: Beijing Review, no. 8 (1980), p. 12.

8000; thirdly, those formed by a production brigade with 1000 to 3000 people; and fourthly, those formed by an industrial or mining enterprise or a neighbourhood committee with several hundred to 3000 people.

Cadres

A cadre is any person who holds a formal leadership post in any organisation. The cadre is the key component in the Chinese system, providing the backbone of policy implemen-

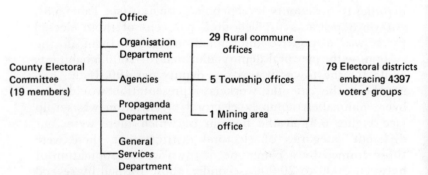

Figure 6.3 Electoral system for Tongxiang county

tation. One might refer to a military cadre, say, or Party cadre, depending upon the organisation in which they work, or to a low-level or high-level cadre depending on their respective position within that organisation. The cadre need not necessarily be a Communist Party member but will be expected to provide good leadership for the masses, listen to their views and, at the same time, remain responsive to policy directives from above. Depending on the organisation in which they work cadres have a different system of salary classification and grades. These grades used to be organised according to length of service, but the obvious disincentives to new, young cadres has meant that expertise is now included for the purposes of grading.

The Chinese press has stressed the importance of training cadres and in 1979 and 1980 has reiterated Mao's statement that 'after the political line has been fixed, cadres become the decisive factor'. However, three major problems exist concerning cadres and the cadre system. The first problem concerns the 'red–expert' dichotomy, with the ideal cadre being one who combines a specialised knowledge and ability (expert) with the consistent following of the socialist road (red). At different times one or other of these aspects has been stressed to the neglect of the other, and at the beginning of 1980 Deng offered the most recent formulation of this relationship. According to Deng, 'being expert certainly does not mean being red; however, to be red, it is also necessary to be expert'.[21] Such a definition suits the current policies which require a high level of expertise to implement them. The second problem is that there simply are not enough cadres, and what is more, the structure of the cadre system is irrational. As an absolute number there are 18 million, but this is inadequate to meet the demands of the present policies. This problem has become particularly acute following the revival of numerous institutions which were abolished during the Cultural Revolution. This break has meant that new people have not been recruited into certain spheres of work and also that those who worked in them in the mid-sixties may well not be acquainted with the most recent developments. According to Deng Xiaoping, China is between 1 and 2 million short of cadres capable of doing judicial work (judges, lawyers, special police) and about 2 or 3 million short of teachers.[22] This shortage of teachers has arisen not only because of the education policies pursued but also because of the large population growth since liberation. The third problem concerns cadres who abuse their position to press their own advantage. To counter this the Central Commission for Inspecting Discipline has drawn up education materials for Party cadres, the role of elections has been increased, the people's right of recall extended, and consequently the practice which virtually amounted to life-tenure for cadres has been abolished.

Economic management

The area of economic management has undergone a period of extensive experimentation since the Third plenum of the Eleventh CC. This, combined with two other reasons, make its consideration important. First, there are a large number of ministries and commissions in the state structure which are engaged in economic work and secondly, the 'popularity' of the present leadership is tied to its economic successes. The present leaders have gained popularity not only because they removed the Gang of Four but also because of their pledge to raise living standards. Naturally, as on other occasions when economic work has been given primacy, this has led to an increase in power for the economic planners such as Chen Yun, Bo Yibo and Xue Muqiao.

The management and planning system adopted by the Chinese after liberation was copied from the Soviets and was, therefore, highly centralised. From 1954 the major industrial enterprises were brought under the direct leadership of the various industrial ministries. The five-year plans were designed to manage the economy in a highly centralised way and, despite certain attempts at reform, this system has existed until the present policy of 'readjusting, restructuring, consolidating and improving the national economy' was introduced in the latter half of 1979. Each year the State Planning Commission works out the plans for agriculture, industry, transport and the postal and telecommunications service and the plans contain a complete set of targets.[23] Attempts have been made to break the grip of the plan which causes the power of local authorities and enterprises to be sapped by the centralised economic management. The extent of this problem was summed up in a speech by Xue Muqiao, when he said that 'the centre calls on the enterprises to tap potential, innovate and transform and yet enterprises had to ask for investment from the higher levels to even build a toilet'.[24] Until recently, all attempts at reform of the system have mainly involved readjusting the limits of managerial power between the central and non-central authorities with little consideration given to the economic relations between the state and enterprises.

The first attempts at reform came in 1957–8 during the decentralisation debate described in Chapter 2. It will be remembered that the adopted system gave the local areas policy and operational decision-making power. Under this system eighty-seven per cent of the enterprises formerly under the central authorities were place under the management of the provincial level, and the materials subject to unified distribution by the central authorities were reduced by seventy-five per cent. The localities acquired greater power to adjust targets and were able to dispose of any revenue in excess of the fixed targets. The only demand on the locality was that it had to fulfil the tasks assigned by the state. This system enabled local industry to develop, but the Second Five-Year Plan was scrapped in favour of the all-out drive of the Great Leap Forward. The Leap's over-ambitious plans, their hasty implementation and the overemphasis on the iron and steel industry meant that a serious imbalance occurred within the national economy, causing economic dislocation and scarcities. The decentralisation of powers to the provincial levels meant that each provincial unit sought self-sufficiency against the wishes of the centre, causing the collapse of national planning. Consequently the pre-1957 situation was reverted to during the years of retrenchment starting in 1961.

Two further attempts at reform were tried in 1964 and 1970. In 1964 the right of localities to handle materials, finances and investment was enlarged and in 1970 these rights were extended with about 2000 civilian industrial enterprises, undertakings and construction units directly under the central authorities being transferred to the provincial level for management. For example, power of decision concerning capital construction was divided between the central local authorities: 40 per cent of the investment was handled directly by the ministries concerned; 30 per cent was handled after consultation between the ministries and the local authorities; and 30 per cent was handled by the local authorities themselves.[25] This system has remained in operation until the experimentation which followed the adoption of the policy of 'readjustment, restructuring, consolidating and improving the national economy'. This new policy favours light industry as opposed to heavy industry (which had been favoured by the Ten-Year Plan). Between 1949 and 1978 light industrial output grew '19.8-fold whereas heavy industry grew 90.6-fold';[26] the attempts to rectify this seem to have met with some success (see Table 6.6). The related policy of narrowing the scope of capital construction has created problems, particularly because the demand for machinery has decreased with the result that many machinery works cannot find enough work to do. Factories which have found themselves in this position have been encouraged to explore other outlets, such as producing for export or manufacturing accessories and spares.

Changes have also occurred in the area of economic management. Xue Muqiao stated that 'our system of economic management is too interconnected, it is administered to

Table 6.6   Growth rates for heavy and light industry[a]

Month	Percentage growth heavy industry	Percentage growth light industry
July	9.7	12.9
August	8.2	10.7
September	10.4	13.0
October	14.8	21.2
November	9.5	20.5

[a] The figures show the percentage increase in growth in 1979 compared with the same month in 1978

death, administrative power is abused, it cannot make use of economic laws and even goes as far as overturning economic laws.'27 This reflects the view of the present leadership who see management and its improvement as one of the key problems. Methods of management are described as 'even more backward than the scientific and technological levels'28 and the change necessary to bring them up to date amounts to 'an extensive and profound revolution'.29 To help solve this problem the State Economic Commission set up a class, on 3 March 1979, for studying enterprise management and, at the same time, the Chinese Association of Enterprise Management was set up in Beijing.30 The aim of this body is to study 'the theories, systems, technology and methods and experiences in management at both home and abroad'.31

The current reforms go further than the 'administrative methods' tried before and use 'economic methods' to control the economy, primarily through utilising the role of the market. As Xue has stated, 'We should change from "using production to fix marketing" to "using the market to fix production" or, to put it even more correctly, to "using needs to fix production".'32 These ideas are not new but stem from Xue's and Chen Yun's ideas first put forward in the mid-fifties. The most important of the changes envisaged concerns the question of enterprise self-management. In 1979 2600 state-owned enterprises were given the right to run their own businesses as a prelude to tentative reforms in the whole system of business management.33 The enterprises were given extended powers to handle their own finances, materials and personnel and carry out some independent business activities. Provided that the enterprise fulfils its quotas it can decide to produce goods to sell in response to the demands of the market. Some of the profit from these sales can be used to build up the enterprise fund, which can be spent at the discretion of the enterprise itself. However, it has been stressed that an increase in enterprise profit must come from making the process of production more efficient rather than from the 'indiscriminate raising of prices'. To prevent this the State Council and Central Committee issued a circular in April 1980 dealing with price controls, to prevent the 'arbitrary raising of commodity prices stipulated in the plan'.34

There have also been changes in enterprise leadership which bring it back to a system very similar to that which existed before the Cultural Revolution. In February 1978 revolutionary committees in factories and enterprises were abolished and their 'broad based' composition of cadres, technicians and workers was replaced by a return to the system of factory directors in charge, under the leadership of the Party committee. The Party committee looks after political and ideological work which ensures the implementation of Party principles and policies, while the actual day-to-day running of the enterprise is left to the director and his staff. Also, managerial staff are no longer expected to 'participate in production'. This 'participation in production' was seen as a way of reducing the gap between mental and manual labour, but any such gap is now justified as being a necessary consequence of the socialist division of labour. Some writers have interpreted the abolition of revolutionary committees and 'participation in production' as decreasing democracy in the workplace. By contrast, however, there is now a great stress on the role of basic-level elections. In 1979 it was announced that, for the first time, Beijing Foreign Languages Printing House workers elected, by secret ballot, their own workshop cadres[35] and that the Shanghai No. 1 Printing and Dyeing Mill workers and staff dismissed a workshop director and elected his replacement 'in a democratic way'.[36]

Finally, attempts have been made to define clearly the relationship between the central and non-central levels, particularly with regard to financial arrangements. The experiment with the financial system in Jiangsu province was applied on a trial basis throughout the country from 1980. Previously when a local government increased its financial revenue through its own efforts it still had to hand back any excess over the state plan to the central government. This caused indifference to profits and losses by the provinces. The experimental system means that a fixed proportion of the province's revenue will be left at the disposal of the province, while the remainder is handed over to the central government. A further measure is the establishment of a division of revenues between the central government and the provincial-level government. The categories of tax levies which will go to the central government treasury and those which go to the local level are to be specified, and it is to be stipulated that the profit of an enterprise will go to the authorities exercising control over the enterprise. These measures will increase the power of local governments over their finances. After this division has been introduced all major construction projects will still be financed by the central government, but ancillary items and medium- and small-scale projects will be funded by the local government.

Apart from the possibility of enterprises seeking self-gain, one other major problem will have to be faced with this system. This concerns the possible unequal development of provinces. Unless more investment is given to the poorer areas they will be left behind in the race to modernise. The poorer areas will be likely to press the central government to increase centralised management and allocation of products while the richer areas would benefit from a greater decentralisation of these powers.

7

The People's Liberation Army

The People's Liberation Army, unlike armies in the West, is more than a professional standing army and has a wider field of operation than that of a bureaucratic pressure group competing for scarce resources. The role of the army in the Chinese political system owes its origins to the pre-liberation struggle described in chapter 1. Apart from causing institutional and personnel overlap, the liberation struggle has affected the functions of the military since liberation. The conditions during the Long March and in Yanan, and the need to rely on the population to wage guerrilla warfare, meant that the PLA became a multi-functional body carrying out education and production tasks. This legacy of the past, and the success of the military, led Mao Zedong to have a highly favourable view not just of the military *per se* but also as a participant in the political system. When Mao sought to purify the ranks of the Party and state during the Cultural Revolution he turned to the army for help, because he felt that under Lin Biao's leadership it embodied the 'true spirit' of the revolution. Since liberation certain sections of the leadership have tried to downgrade this 'traditional' role of the PLA, and have tried to 'professionalise' it by concentrating on its purely military functions. Until the present this tendency has been resisted, but the current policies of modernisation might well mark the change of the military from a multi-functional body to a purely military body. There are three factors which might counteract this tendency: first, the present leadership are predominantly people from the 'Yanan generation' and, in spite of their realisation of the need for change, the changes to date have been limited; secondly, the extent of the change in the PLA's functions will depend on how deeply the 'successor generation' is imbued with maoist maxims; and thirdly, a disciplined military can provide a good backbone for economic development, a function which has become a distinctive feature of the military in many countries seeking rapid development. The first reason can obviously disappear with the generation that experienced Yanan, the second reason can only be observed over time, while the third reason could persist for as long as modernisation is pursued with limited resources.

The organisation of the PLA (see Figure 7.1)

The term the People's Liberation Army includes not only the ground forces but also the navy, the air force and those divisions concerned with nuclear weaponry. Numerically the Chinese army is the largest in the world with about 4 million members, though this figure does not include the huge reserves of the people's militia which can be called on. The high membership figure conceals two major problems, the first of which is the imbalance between the various sectors, with over 80 per cent of the members belonging to the ground forces (see Table 7.1), and the second of which is the obsolescence of much of the equipment the soldiers are expected to use. The Party constitution makes it clear that the PLA is to accept the leadership of the Party[1] and the constitution of the PRC states that it is the Chairman of the Communist Party who is the commander of the armed forces.[2] This control over the military is assumed by two main bodies – the Military Affairs Commission (MAC) and the Ministry of National Defence. Of these two bodies the MAC is the most powerful and is the highest policy-making body for military affairs and the highest command organ for military operations. The MAC has existed under one name or another since 1931, when it was established on the instructions of the First All-China Soviet Congress. The Chairman of the party is the Chairman of the Commission, at present Hua Guofeng, but it seems unlikely that Hua is truly in control, given his lack of military background. Even when Mao was the Chairman it is more likely that real power rested with the first Vice-Chairman who served concurrently as the

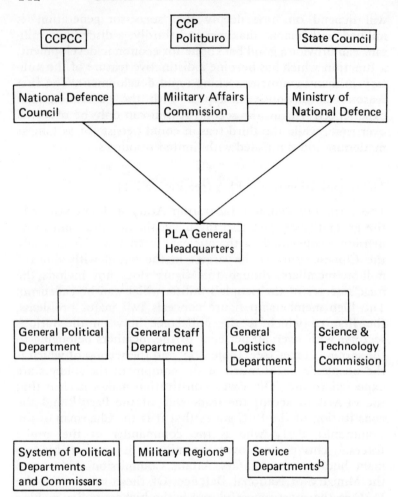

ᵃThe 11 military regions are: Beijing, Shenyang, Jinan, Nanjing, Fuzhou, Guangzhou, Wuhan, Chengdu, Kunming, Lanzhou, Xinjiang.

ᵇThe service branches are: Navy, Air Force, Artillery, 2nd Artillery, Armoured Force, Railway Corps, Capital Construction Engineering Corps, Engineering Corps.

Figure 7.1 Organisation of the PLA

Minister of National Defence. Theoretically, within the state structure the Ministry of National Defence provides a parallel administrative organisation subordinate to the State Council, but in practice the Minister of National Defence is subordinate to the MAC rather than to the State Council. The National Defence Council, which replaced the People's Revolutionary Military Council (in 1954) also, theoretically, has power with regard to military policy. The Council is elected, on recommendation, by the National People's Congress and is another example of a united front institution designed to provide co-ordination and possibly expertise. As far as effective power is concerned the Council's influence is minimal, for it has largely become an honorific body. It is unlikely that this will change in the future, despite the renewed stress on united front work.

Under these bodies is the General Headquarters of the PLA (GHQ) which consists of a number of departments, with the Chief of General Staff as its overall head.[3] The General Staff Department provides the co-ordination for the operational commands at the lower levels. The General Political Department[4] helps with Party supervision of the PLA by conducting education work in the PLA and by overseeing the system of political commissars at each level within the command structure. This network of political commissars provides a system of dual command within the PLA and helps bring substance to the dictum that, while 'political power grows out of the barrel of the gun', the Party should be in firm control of its armed forces. In theory a division of labour exists between the political commissars and military commanders, with the latter taking control of military work and the former taking care of political work — but in practice the relationship has shifted over time. Generally, when 'politics' has been 'in command' the commissars' power has been greater, and when the stress has been on 'professionalism' the power of the commanders has been greater. Under the General Logistics Department the various branches, such as the navy and the railway corps, are organised. Also under the auspices of the GHQ is the Science and Technology Commission for National Defence of the People's Liberation Army.

Below the central level there is a system of military regions

Table 7.1   Structure of the PLA's forces

Ground forces	Total: 3 million plus
	115 infantry divisions
	11 armoured divisions
	3 airborne divisions
	40 artillery divisions
	16 railway and construction divisions
	150 independent regiments
	Equipped with 8000 heavy-medium tanks
	3000 light tanks
Naval forces	Total: 250 000 plus
	68 Whiskey and Romeo class submarines
	2 Ming class submarines
	1 Golf class submarine
	1 Han class submarine
	7 Luda class destroyers with anti-ship cruise missiles
	4 Gorky class destroyers
	18 frigates
	19 patrol escorts
	150 torpedo boats
	70 hydrofoil torpedo boats
	320 gunboats
	700 fighters of naval air forces
Air forces	Total: 250 000 plus with approximately 5000 aircraft
	90 TU–16 medium bombers
	300 IL–28 light bombers
	3700 Mig–17s and Mig–19s
	80 Mig–21s
	500 Mig–15s and F–9s
	350 helicopters

Table 7.1   Structure of the PLA's forces   (continued)

Nuclear forces

2 CSS–3 (limited range ICBM 3500 miles)
30–40 IRBM
30–40 MRBM

Sources: The Military Balance 1979–80, International Institute for
Strategic Studies, London, 1979, and Cheng Tzu-ming,
'Evolution of the People's Liberation Army' in *Issues and
Studies* vol. XV, no. 12 (1979), pp. 93–4.

and military districts. The function of military regions (see
Map 2) is basically a military one and under the regions'
command there are units of the air force and the navy (with
the obvious exception of the landlocked regions — Chengdu,
Lanzhou and Xinjiang). This enables each region to operate
with a degree of independence should China be invaded or
certain key centres be 'knocked out' by a nuclear strike.
However, this does not mean that the regions have complete
independence because they are supposed to act as a trans-
mitter of policies from the centre — but their administrative
control does afford them a good deal of power. Twice during
the seventies there have been large-scale personnel changes in
the regions to prevent individuals gaining too much power
from their positions. The first occasion came in the wake of
the Lin Biao affair, when eight of the eleven commanders
of the military regions were reshuffled in the latter part of
1973. The balance of Party control was shaken as a result of
the Cultural Revolution. By reshuffling the commanders
without changing as many political commissars the process of
restoring Party control was greatly aided. The second occasion
was in late 1979 to early 1980, when a large-scale shake-up of
personnel was carried out in the military regions. Only the
Shenyang Military Region did not have its commander
changed during the reshuffle and the Kunming Military Region
had its commander changed twice.[5] In addition, the commissars of five of the regions were changed. Some of these
changes may result from reactions to the Sino-Vietnamese
conflict and may once again be designed to prevent the

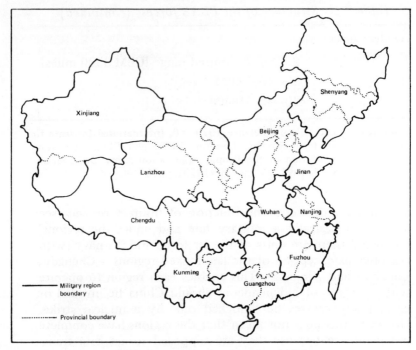

Map 2. China: military regions

entrenchment of regional commanders. Also, the changes
result from the removal of commanders who had links with
the Gang of Four, for example, Chen Xilian was replaced as
the Beijing commander by Qin Jiwei, and from the desire to
bring in younger leaders who would be more receptive to
the ideas of modernisation. It is evident that although the
function of the regions in basically military the individual
commanders, by virtue of their position, may be considered
politically important.

    The military districts,[6] which are equivalent to a province,
are more directly involved in a political role than the regions,
one of their main functions being the organisation of the
people's militia. Especially after the Cultural Revolution
many district commanders and commissars held important
posts in the revolutionary committee of the province and in
many instances were instrumental in their establishment. For

example, in August 1967 Li Desheng became commander of the Anhui Military district and chairman of the Anhui Revolutionary Committee when it was formed in April 1968, and Nan Ping became political commissar of the Zhejiang Military District in August 1967 and chairman of its revolutionary committee in March 1968. However, throughout the seventies there has been a gradual reduction in the military presence in local government, a process speeded-up by the abolition of the revolutionary committees and their replacement by people's governments containing fewer military representatives. The major cities, such as Beijing and Shanghai, have garrison commands under their jurisdiction.

The people's militia

The people's militia comes under the control of the PLA, its function being to provide a reserve for the regular armed forces. This simple outline hides a greater complexity for there has often been tension between the Party apparatus and the military over the control of the militia. The changing control over the militia has resulted in changes in its functions. At different times the militia has concentrated on political work, economic construction work, public security work at the local level, and has provided a back-up to the main forces in the event of war. On occasions it has carried out some or all of these functions simultaneously. Its military reserve and law and order functions have been predominant at times when 'professionalism' has been stressed throughout the army, while its political and economic functions have been stressed during periods of mobilisation.

During the years after liberation the militia was primarily engaged in law and order work (as the pattern of ownership in the countryside was transformed) and in providing a reserve for the Korean War. The change in policy which accompanied the Great Leap Forward fundamentally altered the militia's function. In the Great Leap Forward a 'militarisation' of society was attempted with the slogan of 'everyone a soldier', and by January 1959 the militia totalled 220 million people.[7] At the same time those who took a purely military view of the militia were criticised. It was said that they overlooked the militia's production work or that they took the view that 'the war for national defence and against aggression is the business of the army and not the whole people'.[8] The formation of the communes, combining industrial, agricultural, commercial and military functions into one unit, meant that the militia came under the effective control of the Party rather than the PLA.

The retreat from the Great Leap Forward also saw a retreat from the wide range of functions given to the militia; the emphasis was now placed on its role in economic work. On the eve of the Cultural Revolution the militia's military role was reasserted and it was stated that 'since the militia is designed for dealing with the enemy it should not take part in the people's internal affairs'.[9] Yet once again the view which sought to narrow the scope of the militia's work came under attack, this time from the Cultural Revolution. The most important change concerned the urban militia because the large-scale breakdown of order greatly increased its political and public security roles. This was compounded by two other things: first, by the extra demands put on the militia in the wake of the Lin Biao affair, and secondly by the deliberate build-up of the militia by the Gang of Four. There was an attempt to use the militia as a second armed force to counter the PLA, within which the Gang's support was limited. A month after the Tenth Party Congress (1973) an extensive campaign was launched stressing the importance of strengthened Party control over militia organisations in order to 'maintain their proletarian nature'.[10] The following year it was stated that 'the active participation in class struggles in society by the people's militia is an important experience'.[11] Of particular importance in the Gang of Four's use of the militia was the new workers' militia, promoted by Wang Hongwen. When Wang was a security cadre at the Shanghai No. 17 Textile Factory he had created a workers' militia which was not only responsible for the more traditional duties, such as civil defence, fire-fighting and law and order, but was also armed. Later this urban workers' militia was removed from the authority of the local PLA unit and placed under the direct control of the Shanghai Trade Union Federation, the head of which was Wang Hongwen. According to the *People's Daily* Wang had intended to create a national militia command headquarters with himself as the commander-in-chief.[12] After autumn 1973 the Shanghai militia was promoted as a model for the rest of the country, but the militia's activities caused resentment not only among the Gang of Four's political opponents and the military, but also among the general populace, which became critical of the immediate 'justice' handed out by well-armed vigilante groups.

The present stress on law and order and the regularisation of the legal process has resulted in the removal of the militia from its public security roles and in its control being placed back under the military. The promotion of modernisation for the armed forces, and the attendant stress on professionalism have meant that the militia's size and role have been cut back. Again the militia's role as the reserve for the regular armed forces has been stressed.[13] This downgrading of the militia's role has also been justified by claims that it absorbs scarce resources not justified in terms of the utility that it provides.

The PLA in the Chinese political system

The fundamental question is whether the military, with its involvement in politics, acts as a homogeneous group pursuing military interests against those of other apparats, or whether the most important leadership differences cut across the different apparats. Related to this question are the often-quoted dichotomies of 'red' versus 'expert', and of 'politicisation' and 'professionalisation'. Under the umbrella of these terms there has been a range of disagreements. Mao's defensive strategy is based on his experience of protracted warfare and from being in the weaker military position during battle. From Mao's experience evolved the notion of 'People's War' — the idea that 'people' are more important than 'machines' and that political mobilisation is more important than military modernisation. A consequence of this view is the idea that should China come under attack the best means of defence would be to rely on the tactics developed before liberation, rather than developing a sufficient nuclear deterrent. As has been made clear the military, especially at the non-central level, has always been involved in politics — but what is more important is the nature of that involvement. Also the use of the singular term 'military' can be misleading because different factions have existed within the military itself.

The view that policy differences have cut across apparats is not shared by all. Some writers feel that a long period without a major military involvement plus the increasing modernisation of the armed forces has driven an irreconcilable wedge between the Chinese Communist Party and the PLA.[14] This approach sees the PLA's role as similar to that of the army in the Soviet Union — purely military matters are pursued without regard to the political and ideological context. While it is true that 'professionalism' has been promoted at various times, it is extremely difficult to isolate particular leaders as having advocated a military line. One other important view which has gained currency concerns the role of the field army in Chinese communist politics. The five field armies held control over the regions after the communists first took power. During this time it is thought that a system of loyalties built up between the members of each field army; these loyalties have persisted, with the result that both the military and the civilian sector have been dominated by a series of patron–client relations. This argument contains some truth, but its importance has been over-stressed. Although many of those who fell with Lin Biao had been his contemporaries in the 4th field army, many others who fell had had no affiliation with it. Also the patron–client relationships struck in the forties and early fifties cannot fully explain the intricacies of a movement like the Cultural Revolution.[15]

The Peng Dehuai affair

The first challenge to the Yanan legacy came in the mid-fifties when a concerted attempt was made to modernise the PLA along the lines of the Soviet army. Two obvious reasons can be found for this. First, the PRC had adopted the Soviet model of development which had implications for the military because of its emphasis on heavy industry. Quite clearly the Soviet army was considered worthy of emulation

for, according to the *People's Daily*, 'the Soviet Army provided the PLA with a great example; the future PLA would
resemble the Soviet Army of today'.[16] In emulating the
Soviet army the PLA introduced a system of ranks for officers,
a new code of discipline and the use of conscription. The
second reason for modernisation derived from the Chinese
experience during the Korean War. This experience particularly affected Peng Dehuai, the commander of the People's
Volunteers. The large-scale losses and the inadequacy of the
Chinese equipment caused some to call for a greater modernisation of the armed forces.

The drive to modernise ran counter to the other functions
the PLA was to undertake after the Korean War. The decision
to abandon the Soviet model meant that greater emphasis
was placed on the PLA's non-military work. This conflict
over the PLA's roles provided the background to the military
aspects of Peng's criticisms at the Lushan plenum (1959).
The question of relations with the Soviet Union figures in
the debates – Gittings has observed that an important element in Peng's 'anti-Party' activities was a basic disagreement
over 'policy towards the Soviet Union with special military
implications'.[17] Peng was busy conducting negotiations for
a greater degree of integration with the Soviet Union at a
time when the policies of the Great Leap Forward were
stressing greater self-sufficiency. However, Peng did not limit
himself to an attack solely from a military standpoint. He
attacked the whole range of the policies pursued, even to
the extent of telling Mao how the revolution in the countryside should be carried out. One might argue that a change of
overall strategy might have benefited the military by alloca-
ting more money for investment in heavy industry, but this is
not the same as saying that Peng acted as a military man
giving an airing to his professional grievances. When Peng was
disgraced he was accused of being the leader of an 'anti-Party
group'; as Charles has stated, 'Throughout, Peng acted as a
senior member of the Politburo rather than as a dissatisfied
Minister of Defence'.[18]

The revival of the Yanan legacy under Lin Biao
Peng was replaced as Minister of Defence by Lin Biao and

under Lin's leadership the traditions of Yanan were revived
— but this does not mean that all attempts at modernisation
were abandoned. For example, the nuclear programme was
not rejected but a greater emphasis was placed on its non-
military roles. During the early sixties an extensive programme of education was carried out within the PLA, with the
result that it embodied Mao's principles to a far greater
extent than did the Party. On assuming leadership Lin sought
to intensify political education, restore the PLA's links and
image with the people, and ironically, considering the PLA's
role in the Cultural Revolution, to bring it under closer
Party control. To facilitate this process the system of political commissars was strengthened, Party branch committees
were revived in all PLA companies and Party cells were revived
in platoons. Also an intensive Party recruitment drive was
carried out among military personnel and younger PLA
members were encouraged to join the Communist Youth
League, or the Soldiers' Club. Soldiers were encouraged to
compete in the Five-Good Movement and it was from this
movement that Lei Feng emerged as a soldier worthy of
emulation.[19] The general policy was successful; by mid-
1961 Party branches were restored in all companies, 80 per
cent of the platoons had organised Party cells, about 2000
PLA personnel were expelled from the Party and another
229 000 new members recruited.[20] The success of the process
of political education is demonstrated by the fact that in
1964 a campaign was launched to 'Learn from the PLA'. As
Mao became increasingly convinced that the solution of
China's future lay in the legacy of the past he turned to the
PLA for help. In 1965 the PLA's 'revolutionary image' was
given a further boost when it abolished ranks and insignias
and introduced the 'Down to the Ranks Movement' for
officers. During the 'Learn from the PLA' campaign units
in society were called on to compare themselves to those in
the military, the training of the militia was increased and a
large number of military personnel were transferred into
civilian units. By using the PLA in this way Mao was able to
bypass an administration which was reluctant to implement
the radical policies of the Socialist Education Movement.
     Lin Biao's views and his notion of the 'People's War' were

best outlined in his 1965 article 'On the Victory of People's War'. Lin's views and the revival of the army's 'traditional' roles did not go unchallenged. The escalation of the war in Vietnam caused others to question Lin's strategy and to favour a rapprochement with the Soviet Union (at least on the military front), a decrease in the PLA's non-military roles and promotion of the idea of modernisation. The main spokesperson of this point of view was the then Chief of Staff, Lo Ruiqing, but he found his views attacked and Lo was later purged. The rejection of Lo's views did not mean that the development of things such as nuclear weapons ceased, but that their role was to fit in with the essentially defensive strategy of the People's War. Despite Lin Biao's support for the Cultural Revolution it was not initially intended that the military should intervene, but once the movement was launched the military's involvement became inevitable. The PLA was the only remaining body with national authority and the only body capable of carrying out the necessary public security role. Although Mao felt that the PLA was loyal to his commands the PLA's actions during the Cultural Revolution highlighted differences within it. While Lin encouraged the PLA to support the left and tried to prevent it from attacking the Red Guards, his regional commanders often chose to side with the 'old' regional leadership. This difference between Lin and his regional commanders was demonstrated in the Wuhan Incident of July 1967.

Party rebuilding and the fall of Lin Biao

The Cultural Revolution, although not amounting to a military takeover, did result in a massive increase in military involvement in the Chinese political system. The national Party network was destroyed and the PLA replaced the Party as the backbone of organisation throughout the country. The decision in September 1967 to allow the PLA to use force if attacked greatly aided the ability of the provinces to form revolutionary committees. It is not surprising that military representation on these committees was high; of the chairpersons and vice-chairpersons of the provincial revolutionary committees, the PLA was the largest member (42 per cent) of the three-way alliance of revolutionary cadres, PLA and mass representatives. On the committees formed during the months September 1967–March 1968 military representation was even greater — eight of the committees had chairpersons who were either military commanders or political commissars and over half of the core-group representatives were PLA personnel. Consequently, at the time of the Ninth Party Congress (1969) the military were in a powerful position and twenty of the twenty-nine provincial revolutionary committee chairpersons had a basic affiliation with the military The congress started the drive to rebuild the Party apparatus and to remove the military from positions of political power. However, this did not prove to be the case, for during the period of Party rebuilding military involvement in politics increased. While the military may have been reluctant to enter into the Cultural Revolution they were even more reluctant to vacate the positions of power gained as a result of their intervention. At the central level Lin Biao had been designated Mao's successor and had sought to expand his support base. Leaders from the centrally directed units were enjoying power which they had not experienced before. These leaders favoured continuing the status quo of 1969 with PLA members staying in their civilian positions without resigning from the army. The regional commanders also had one very strong reason for not withdrawing to the barracks. They were reluctant to hand over authority to the radical elements, with which they had clashed so violently, for fear of reprisal. PLA members in charge of study and labour at the May 7 Cadre Schools were accused of misusing their power to push their own interests. It was said that an ultra-left cadre policy was pursued and the responsibility for this was traced to Lin Biao's criteria for defining those loyal to Mao. Lin was accused of using these criteria to appoint friends and proteges to positions of authority.[21]

Despite the PLA's resistance a reduction in its political role was brought about with the removal of Lin Biao and his supporters. The purge of Lin Biao and five other PLA members of the Politburo reveals interesting information about the military's involvement in the political system, and highlights divisions within the military itself. Lin's 'fall from grace' cannot be put down solely to the pursuit of military interest and the desire to seek rapprochement with the Soviet Union, but reflects a complexity of interrelated factors. Certainly if the military had been capable of acting as a united body it is inconceivable that the alleged 'military coup' would have failed. The plotters' '571 Document' made an assessment of their support and portrayed a military which was hardly united at all. This lack of unity within the military establishment meant that Mao could rely on the acquiescence, if not actual support, of certain sections of the military when moving against Lin Biao. The two most important internal divisions were between the regional commanders and the leaders of the centrally directed units, and between those who favoured a professional, military role for the PLA and those who favoured a political role. As Lin Biao came under pressure the powerful regional commanders in the Politburo, such as Chen Xilian and Xu Shiyou, could have supported him, but they chose not to and as a result kept their high positions. This lack of support is not surprising because during the Cultural Revolution Lin Biao became increasingly identi- fied with the left, and it was with the left that the regional commanders had clashed and from whom they feared reprisals. Lin's inactivity in supporting his colleagues stood in marked contrast to the efforts of Zhou Enlai and led to Lin's isolation from his regional forces. Those who favoured a more profes- sional military sought a withdrawal from political work and may well have harboured grudges against the central military leaders for not protecting them from the Red Guards' criti- cisms. These two divisions, combined with the fact that Lin could not assure the Party leadership that the military would withdraw from politics, meant that Lin found himself in a position where he could satisfy none of the groups. Thus isolated his removal was greatly facilitated.

Since Lin's fall the military has kept a much lower profile in the political system — with the exception of their support for the arrest of the Gang of Four. Military personnel are still involved in the political process but in much the same way as during the years before the Cultural Revolution. During the succession crisis in 1975–6 the debate over the role of the military was briefly revived. In June and July 1975, at an enlarged meeting of the MAC, Ye Jianying and Deng Xiaoping made speeches on the need for the modernisation of the military and Deng, like all previous Chiefs of Staff, became a spokesperson for modernisation. This was one of the criticisms levelled against him after his second purge in 1976, when he was attacked for laying emphasis on weapons rather than men and for saying that 'the army should fight tough battles and really tough battles mean contests of steel'.[22]

Military modernisation and the four modernisations

The renewed emphasis on the four modernisations has again brought up the discussion over the correct role of the military and the need for it to be modernised. The modernisation of national defence is third in the list of the four modernisations but it has been made clear that the modernisation of defence is given the lowest priority of the four. Hua Guofeng, speaking in February 1978, made it quite clear that military modernisation would follow, and not precede, economic development. Three main areas have been identified which require modernising — military equipment, military cadres and military thinking.[23] The initial strategy pursued after the arrest of the Gang of Four emphasised the development of heavy industry. This would have given rise to a fairly fast rate of equipment modernisation and any 'time-lag' in production could have been made up for by large-scale purchases abroad. Certainly, much of the Chinese military equipment is outdated and consideration was given to how to replace it. In February 1977 conferences were convened on air defence, arms production and research into military technology and there have been numerous trips abroad to inspect the latest military technology. To help the troops gain greater expertise in using modern weapons-systems military training was stepped up, discipline tightened and the periods of military service increased. This renewed emphasis on professionalism has been accompanied by the return to high positions in the military by people such as Huang Kecheng (Chief of Staff under Peng Dehuai), Hong Xuezhi (Director of Rear Services under Peng) and Li Da (a Deputy Minister of Defence under Peng). However, the shift of emphasis away from heavy industrial output has meant that large-scale equipment renewal will have to wait. The lack of available capital has meant that the numerous trips abroad have resulted in very few purchases. Consequently, the shortage of modern equipment cannot be made up by selective imports and the backward level of scientific and technological research means that shortage cannot be made up by relying on China's own resources. The war with Vietnam (February–March 1979), like the Korean War before it, showed how inadequate Chinese military technology is when faced with modern military equipment. The casualties for the 'limited action' were high, about 20 000 killed or wounded. Also the war caused an unexpected budgetary allocation for military spending to cover the costs, at a time when the economy could least afford it. Certainly the war was disruptive for the new order of economic priorities worked out by the planners and met with some resistance internally. Sensitivity on the subject is shown by the fact that Chinese citizens were barred from discussing the war with foreigners and it was forbidden to put up critical posters about the war on Democracy Wall. Tretiak, using figures compiled by *Business China*, shows that 1979 military expenditure increased by roughly 20 per cent on that of 1978, and by approximately 35 per cent on that of 1977.[24] Despite this emergency increase it seems that Hua's policy announcement will be followed and that modernisation of the military will be gradual. Economic development will take predence over the improvement of weapons in the short term, with priority in allocation given to the economic sector. The military will have to pick up the scraps left over after agriculture, industry, science and technology have been serviced.

The main problem concerning personnel is the age of the leading cadres. Also, most of them were brought up during the years of guerrilla warfare and thus lack the technical expertise to cope with modern weapons. Attempts have been made to recruit and train younger replacements — according to the New China News Agency over 20 000 cadres were selected from the border defence troops in the provinces of Guangxi and Yunnan and sent to military installations for training under the guidance of the MAC.[25] These people are all in the eighteen to twenty-seven age group, of whom approximately three-quarters are combat heroes and all of them are said to have experience of basic-level work in the army. Also specialised training for officers is being undertaken in the military academies and an attempt to ensure a constant flow of suitably qualified personnel is being made by offering remunerative and retirement benefits. Calls to modernise military thinking and devise concepts to deal adequately with new conditions and problems have accompanied the renewed stress on modernisation and professionalism. As yet the concept of People's War has not been renounced, but as a result of a change in China's strategical and tactical outlook attempts have been made to adapt the concept to suit modern conditions. Limitations on spending will restrict too radical a change in military strategy, but unless there is another change of political line it does mean that the defensive strategy, where space can be traded for time and manpower used instead of firepower, will be replaced by the creation of a conventional deterrent force with a capability based on high-speed human resources and firepower.

It is impossible to tell whether the role of the military in the future will become similar to that of the army in the Soviet Union. However, it is possible that debate concerning military affairs may well come to focus on budgetary questions in much the same way as in the Soviet Union or in the United States. Also competition for resources within the various branches of the military is likely to increase, and decisions will have to be made about which of the particular service arms should receive priority. However, this does not necessarily mean that the PLA will cease to be a multi-functional body and neither should China's first carrier rocket test be seen as a victory for the modernisers.[26] This test, although demonstrating the commitment to modernisation, does not indicate an end to the PLA's other roles nor does it signify a decrease in the importance of political work in the PLA. Between 18–30 April 1980 an all-army political work conference was held, the main topic of which was the strengthening of Party building in the army and 'giving full play to the role of Party committees at all levels as the core of leadership'.[27] In his speech to the conference Hua Guofeng stressed that it was necessary for the PLA soldiers to be well-educated in the ideals for which they fight and that it was not enough for them to simply be good soldiers. To help with this objective a campaign was launched to foster proletarian ideology within the army and the educational role of models has been reaffirmed. New models, apart from Lei Feng, have been held up for emulation — the most important of which is Lu Shicai. Lu is reported to have said that 'moral character is the essence of a man. Without communist moral character, a man is no better than a worthless wretch who gets stuck in the quagmire of individualism and cannot smell the stink. Under no circumstances should I become a person like this'.[28] Finally, although the PLA's involvement has been substantially reduced at the provincial level it continues to play an important political role — 31 per cent of the full members of the Eleventh Central Committee came from the PLA.[29]

8

Social and political control

All societies require a high degree of loyalty from their citizens to ensure their smooth functioning. Amitai Etzioni, in his study of organisational control, shows that this control can be exercised in three ways: through the physical, the material or the symbolic.[1] This triad of force, rewards and norms can help one gain an understanding of how societies ensure obedience through a system of socialisation combined with incentives and punishments. By studying the use of force, or the threat of force, in society one can observe who employs coercion against whom, and for what particular ends. A study of rewards given for services rendered and the priority of resource allocation gives an insight into the things which a regime considers important. The study of the symbolic indicates what the values of a particular society are, how they are learnt and passed on and how they may change over time. Study of the symbolic can also reveal whether conflict exists between the values of the government and those of society. Incongruities between the two value systems will be greater when the government is trying to carry out a revolutionary transformation of society — either traditional values will be abandoned, the leadership's goals not realised, or the traditional values will be absorbed by the new values into a new synthesis.

Coercive control

The concept of law

The proclaimed aim of the Chinese legal system is reformative; prisoners are punished as a means to helping them reform. However, the system also has retributive and educative elements. Punishment is often carried out to serve as a warning to others. When a case is considered to be influential or to have an important educational significance materials concerning the case are distributed to the public for study. This information is either carried in the local press or is published in court proclamations displayed in factories, communes and other such organisations. Victor Li has shown that the Chinese legal system provides a good example of the overlapping and joint use of both normative and coercive aspects of control.[2] Two concepts of law operated in traditional China, and these two concepts have been made use of by the communist government to ensure order. The first concept is the more familiar to people in the West, comprising a system of positive law using coercion and deterrence. Since the fall of the Gang of Four it has been stressed that there is a need for this type of written law, which is known to all and which provides a set procedure for the arbitration of disputes between citizens, and between citizens and the state. Such a system requires a large number of trained administrators and institutions to operate it. The second concept, to make it function, relies on the citizen's internalisation of correct modes of behaviour through a long process of social education. Under this system people obey not because of fear but because they possess a 'proper' understanding of what is required of them as members of society. Li writes, 'Where such self-control fails, social pressure arises spontaneously to correct and to control the deviant';[3] punishment by the state is only required when this system breaks down. Such a system is relatively simple and can be readily applied by all. But problems arise when, in the absence of any codified law, arbitrary reprisals supplant the socially internalised codes. The two concepts can and have existed side by side but the general tendency is for one of them to be dominant.

The range of sanctions

The sanctions employed in the PRC exhibit this combination of normative and coercive aspects. The punishment given for a crime committed not only depends on the severity of the crime itself but also on the attitude of the criminal towards the crime. If the criminal demonstrates repentance then leniency will be used, but should he or she deny the accusations harsher punishment will be handed out. The best examples of this are the two-year suspended death sentence and the system of reform through labour with ideological re-education. As in other legal systems the penalty is reduced for those willing to provide information leading to the arrest of others.

The range of sanctions falls into three main categories: informal administrative sanctions; formal administrative sanctions; and major criminal sanctions.[4] The first category includes relatively minor offences requiring administrative sanctions and entailing a varying degree of private and public criticism. Criticism may be conducted in private by members of the local neighbourhood committee or by public security committees. The offender may be forced to write a self-criticism to be posted up in a prominent place in the area. The worst form of punishment which falls within this category is to be subjected to a 'struggle meeting'. These meetings are held in public and require the offender to suffer criticism, and sometimes physical violence, from those present. An example of the milder form of rebuke occurred in the Haidian district of Beijing, where Beijing University is situated. Both private and public criticism was carried out against former students who had been 'sent down' to the countryside but had returned illegally to try to find work.

The first of the category of formal administrative sanctions is roughly comparable to a misdemeanour. Those who are found guilty are given a formal warning followed by a small fine or a short period of detention (not exceeding fifteen days). The second sanction in the category is labour supervision. The offender is able to remain in society but does so 'under a cloud', and is liable to be regarded suspiciously by others for a fairly long, indefinite period. The offender will be required to engage, whilst under strict supervision, in physical labour and undergo a political indoctrination programme. A harder form of this is 're-education through labour' — this punishment provides compulsory measures for reeducating people whose offences are not serious enough to bear criminal responsibility. In theory the criminals' labours are to prepare them for taking up employment on release. The period of labour may last from one to three years and may be extended for one further year. During this period the offenders are paid for the work that they do; part of their pay may be deducted by the authorities to support the dependants or to be given to them when released. The category of offenders who may have to undertake re-education through labour includes people who have not responded well to criticism, those who have been found guilty of disorderly behaviour and people who have been expelled from schools or work and have no means of support. The original decision concerning re-education through labour was promulgated in 1957, with supplementary provisions added in November 1979 stating that people who had undergone the process (and their relatives) should not be discriminated against in terms of job opportunities or further education chances.

This sanction merges into the third category, that of criminal sanctions. The first of the major criminal sanctions is reform through labour. In substance this is the same as re-education through labour and is imposed by the court as punishment for a reasonably substantial crime. The sentence is rarely less than five years and the offenders are either sent to a local reform centre or, if a long-term sentence is imposed, they may be sent to the areas of 'marginal land' to work on reclamation programmes. Fixed-term prison sentences range from six months to fifteen years; also there is the punishment of life imprisonment. For sentences under six months there is detention. The sentence for all of these may be reduced if the criminal behaves well during the period of imprisonment.

People may be imprisoned for a variety of offences similar to those in Western society but also for some offences which would not necessarily carry a prison sentence in the West. One man was sentenced to ten years' imprisonment for keeping old GMD land deeds and money and for writing 'anonymous letters to foreign governments'. A male Party branch secretary of a brigade was sentenced to ten years' imprisonment because he abused his position and facilities to sleep with fifteen women, three youths, and had made obscene advances to two others. One final example is worth mentioning because the particular criminal's punishment appears to be related to his attitude towards his crime. The man, a teacher at the No. 10 middle school in Yangzhou, had slept with another man's wife. He did not accept responsibility for the initial 'crime', as it was termed, and it was said that he had tried to break up the couple's household. It appears that the man was imprisoned because of his refusal to recognise that his actions constituted a crime, and because he continued to pursue the woman. The ultimate sanction is the death penalty – but the Chinese have the unique punishment of the suspended death sentence. In February 1980 the *People's Daily*[5] reaffirmed that capital punishment was necessary in China, but claimed that the courts were very cautious in carrying out death sentences, an implicit criticism of previous practice. The death sentence is not imposed on people under eighteen years of age or on women found to be pregnant during the trial. It must be approved by the Supreme Court, a practice which fell into disuse during the Cultural Revolution. At the same time as reaffirming the need for the death penalty, the press has stressed that greater use should be made of the suspended death penalty. The offender is given a two-year reprieve during which time he or she is subjected to forced labour under strict supervision. If the offender displays a good attitude during this period the sentence can be commuted to life imprisonment or imprisonment for a fixed term.

Other sanctions in addition to those outlined above are the forfeiture of property and the removal of political rights. The new Criminal Law details under which circumstances political rights can be taken away from individuals. Those sentenced to death or life imprisonment are deprived of their political rights for the remainder of their life. Also people can be deprived of their political rights for set periods of time. Those who deprive another of personal freedom or insult or libel another may be deprived of their political rights for between one and five years. Anyone who is placed under supervision is deprived of their political rights until such time as it is considered fit for them to be released.[6]

The Public Security Bureau

The Public Security Bureau is the main agent of law enforcement although its powers have been limited by the return of
the People's Procuratorate and the general stress on law and
order. The highest body in the public security network is the
Ministry of Public Security, under which there are Public
Security Bureaux at the various levels. At the basic levels the
Public Security Bureau is helped in its data collection,
supervision and crime investigation by the neighbourhood
committees and the security defence committees. Wherever
possible civil cases are dealt with by the neighbourhood
committee instead of bringing the case before the court, a
legacy of the traditional approach to law in China. Further
back-up is provided by the people's militia, although as is
outlined in chapter 7, the militia's public security role has
diminished and the ultimate sanction of the PLA is always
available. The use of this ultimate sanction was apparent in
the Cultural Revolution during the 1975 strikes in Hangzhou
and in clearing up disturbances in Baoding in 1976 after the
Gang of Four were arrested.

Although it appears that some restrictions have been
removed concerning internal travel the public security forces
have quite considerable powers stemming from their ability
to control residence and movement. All citizens, whether in
the city or countryside, must register with the police and
possess the appropriate card designating their neighbourhood.
This registration enables then to obtain their ration allocation
tickets. To travel out of the area nationally valid ration
tickets must be acquired — overnight stays are registered and
longer visits may require approval from the local Public
Security Bureau. To facilitate this observation there are
offices of the Public Security Bureau on all major railway-
stations, at the bus termini and at airports.

Remunerative control

Material and moral incentives

The debate about whether material or moral incentives should

take precedence as the stimulant for arousing the population's enthusiasm has been one of the most important debates
in China. Neither Mao, who favoured moral incentives, nor
his opponents, promoted one to the exclusion of the other.
Mao's criticisms of the inequalities perpetuated by the
eight-grade wage system and the system of distribution
practised in the PRC did not lead him to pursue a policy of
egalitarianism. The policy adopted derived from Stalin's and
sees egalitarianism, in Zhou Enlai's words, as 'a type of petty-
bourgeois outlook which encourages backwardness and
hinders progress. It has nothing in common with Marxism
and a socialist system'.[7] Certainly, in the countryside significant differences have persisted, whatever the policy pursued
by the centre. However, there is disagreement about whether
these differences have decreased over time as a result of the
CCP's policies. Whyte concludes that income inequality
within production teams is relatively low, but that this may
be the result of a relatively equal pre-liberation distribution
rather than because of the post-liberation transformation of
agriculture.[8] In his rejoinder Blecher uses a more sophisticated
statistical analysis to claim that land reform and collectivisation did bring about a significant redistribution of income
within small rural communities.[9] Particularly during the
Cultural Revolution the stress was placed on the need to
scale down such income differentials rather than to allow
them to remain static or even to increase.

The fall of the Gang of Four and the 'new' modernisation
programme have meant that the emphasis has been placed
on material incentives. In October 1977 wage rises of about
10 per cent were given to 64 per cent of the urban workers.
Forty-six per cent of workers were given wage rises by being
moved up one grade on the wage-scale, while the other 18
per cent was granted 'an upward adjustment in pay'.[10] Following the Third plenum of the Eleventh CC the procurement
prices of agricultural products were raised, giving the peasants
a higher income in an attempt to stimulate production.
Other measures, such as the greater use of private plots, the
encouragement of rural markets and the reduction of or
exemption from agricultural tax in some areas, have also
helped to raise peasant incomes and productivity. In his

report to the Second Session of the Fifth NPC Hua Guofeng stated that the total income for the communes, production teams and peasants would increase by 13 000 million yuan as a result of these measures. In 1978 the average income for peasants, excluding that from sideline and private plot production, was 13 per cent up on that of 1977. This was the largest increase in any one year since 1966.[11] Although the collective is still considered to be the most important sector, officials in Chongqing have acknowledged that farmers are twice as productive when they work for themselves. [12] Hua Guofeng laid down the bare outlines of this policy in his report to the First Session of the Fifth NPC when he stated, 'Throughout the historical period of socialism, we must uphold the principles of he who does not work, neither shall he eat' and 'from each according to his ability, to each according to his work'.[13] The two extremes of egalitarianism and a wide wage spread were to be avoided. Remuneration for work done was to be 'primarily on a time-scale basis with piecework playing a secondary role and with additional bonuses'.[14] Greater reward was to be given for jobs which required a higher labour intensity or which had bad work conditions. However, Hua made it clear that material incentives were to be combined with moral incentives and that the latter would take precedence. In practice this does not appear to have been the case and the use of material incentives gained a greater currency. As a result in April and May 1980 there was a renewed stress on the need to make use of both kinds of incentive.

After Hua's report a series of articles was devoted to the defence of the slogan 'to each according to his work', and to refuting the Gang of Four's criticisms of it.[15] It is said that the Gang of Four negated socialist material interest altogether and concentrated on subjective factors. Wang Hongwen is claimed to have said that 'piece-rate, payment by the hour, or bonuses, have nothing whatsoever to do with the welfare of the workers. It is a positive insult to workers'.[16] The criticisms against the Gang of Four are exaggerated but they do contain some truth. Certainly their policies were designed to contain and reduce differential and the stress on political and educational work meant that production time was lost.

Shoudu brewery has calculated that in 1974 it lost 13 500 hours of production time through the organisation of 36 courses.

An important part of the use of material incentives to stimulate production is the bonus system. Since the Third plenum of the Eleventh CC there have been extensive experiments with the bonus system in the industrial enterprises. Initially, these systems were much simpler than those in operation before the Cultural Revolution, but during the period of experimentation the systems became more complex. One of the first models held up for emulation was the Kailan coal-mine in Tangshan. As early as 1973 this mine, to stimulate production, had reintroduced material incentives and greater wage differentials for key sectors. The mine operates a daily wage system on the time-rate basis, with those working underground receiving more than those who work above ground, and with auxiliary workers receiving less than those engaged on the main jobs. This basic wage is supplemented by a simple bonus system. Before the Cultural Revolution as many as seventy different kinds of bonuses existed and, for some, earnings derived from bonuses exceeded the basic wage. Under the post-Cultural-Revolution system a monthly bonus is issued to a group of workers who fulfil the quantitative and qualitative quota. The largest bonus for mine workers is 22.6 per cent of their standard wage, the smallest 12.1 per cent. For cadres the amount of their bonus is in inverse proportion to their wages. This bonus system is not intended to apply to those whose monthly wages exceed 100 yuan.

However, in Sichuan province a more complex experimental system has been introduced in 100 enterprises.[17] In general four types of bonus schemes are in operation. First, there is the fixed package bonus scheme (one for fulfilment and overfulfilment of quotas) which is promoted by provincial departments. Under this system the factory authority hands out the average bonus to each individual according to the extent of target fulfilment of each economic management committee. Secondly, there are individual bonuses. Rewards are given for overfulfilment, quality and safety with priority given to overfulfilment. Thirdly, there are composite bonuses which are commonly instituted among ancillary production workers and office cadres. Fourthly, there are bonuses for reducing production costs and bonuses in the form of shares in the profits for overfulfilling plans. During the period of experimentation two particular shortcomings were high-lighted: the method of drawing bonuses and the level of bonus are not in line with the demand for close integration of reward and production. Bonuses are directly linked with the fulfilment of production quotas but the bonuses are still drawn from a fixed percentage of the workers' standard wages and such a static figure gives 'a contradiction between the total amount of bonuses and demand'.[18] Secondly, it is said that a problem arises from instituting a bonus scheme 'which derives its bonus by deducting a percentage from the profit of overfulfilment' or a bonus scheme 'for the reduction of production cost alongside the existing scheme of drawing bonuses from the wage fund'.[19]

More general criticisms of the bonus system have been raised. The criticism of the Gang of Four's views has led to an excessive emphasis on material incentives and the practice of indiscriminately giving out bonuses has been attacked. During 1980 this tendency has been criticised on ideological and pragmatic grounds. Those who object on ideological grounds fear that the individual might supplant the collective as the most important economic unit. These people want to promote the policy as first outlined by Hua at the Fifth NPC. This view has gained a greater currency among the leadership because of more practical considerations. As has been found in the West, the payment of bonuses does not automatically lead to increased production; workers may see the bonus as a 'natural' part of their wage regardless of their productivity. Also, there is the problem that wage rises often lead to the demand for more rises, particularly if prices increase. In October 1979 it was announced that prices for some food-stuffs and service charges would go up as of 1 November 1979.[20] This 'blow' was softened by giving office employees, workers and the army monthly subsidies, and by giving 40 per cent of office employees and workers promotions and wage increases. Finally, there is little surplus cash available for the giving out of bonuses. Deng Xiaoping stated that over

5000 million yuan had been given out in bonuses and that in some areas workers were able to double their incomes as a result. Of the total he estimated that 2000 million yuan too much was paid out, causing work to be stopped on a number of capital construction projects.[21]

The Shoudu brewery has been cited as an example where 'bonuses in command' produced production difficulties.[22] The brewery decided that the best way to speed up the overhaul of the tanks was to give larger bonuses to the workforce. The leadership were willing to offer the workers 94 yuan on top of their monthly wages, roughly doubling them but the workers put in requests ranging from 500 to 1000 yuan. Eventually the leadership made an agreement with the older workers to give them an extra two months pay, but this was rejected by the younger workers who received a lower monthly rate. Although the project was only delayed for four days it was enough to persuade the leadership that such large-scale bonuses were to be avoided. Eventually more workers were added to make up two shifts of ten workers so as to cut down labour intensity and eliminate overtime work. When bonuses were decided, four workers received 56 yuan, fourteen received 51 yuan and two received 30 yuan. This example demonstrates some of the problems encountered with the bonus system and indicates how ideological and pragmatic reasons can fuse together to prevent too large a growth in material incentives at the expense of moral incentives.

Income inequality: urban workers

Even before bonuses are taken into account considerable differences exist between people's incomes. In 1979 the average *per capita* income for peasants from the collective was 83.4 yuan (a 11.3 per cent increase on 1978) while for workers in state-owned enterprises it was 705 yuan (a 9.5 per cent increase in 1978 but only a 7.6 per cent increase in real terms). While living costs are much lower in the countryside, no rent or water fees are payable and most basic foodstuffs are obtained without cost, wage-earners in the city are better off. Also, these average figures conceal differences between different regions and between wage-earners on different salary grades. Present policy will serve to widen such gaps as already exist and it has been acknowledged that more pay should be given for more work done. It is now considered that some people and some areas should become prosperous first.[23]

The wage structure in China was established during the fifties and appears to have altered very little since. This consists of a system of overlapping grade systems depending on one's occupation. The complexity of the system makes it difficult to gauge the overall spread of incomes. Most wage-earners come under the eight-grade wage system for workers and staff in the public sector economic enterprises. In this system, workers and staff are graded according to their skill and experience. The salary range of the grades is approximately three to one from grade eight to grade one, but these grades are not fixed and vary between different industries and between different regions. At the lower end wages start from about 30 yuan and rise to about 120 yuan. Generally, workers are placed in three industrial categories according to the requirements of work. The first category covers heavy industrial work, such as the iron and steel industries and coal-mining; the second category includes manufacturing industries and those such as machinery and electrical power, and the third category includes light industries such as textiles and foodstuffs. A worker on the first grade in category one would receive more than a worker on the same grade in category two who, in turn, would receive more than a worker in category three. China is divided into eleven different regions on the basis of living standards and commodity prices — although Shanghai is given an artificially beneficial position, presumably because of its industrial importance.[24] The span is such that a worker on the same grade in the highest-ranked region (number 1) may earn 30 per cent more than a worker on the same grade in the lowest-ranked region (number 11). Outside the grade system are the apprentices who receive a monthly income below that of a grade one worker.

The eight-grade system is not the only one in operation; technicians and engineers are graded on a scale with between eighteen and twenty-four grades, while workers and staff in state administration, welfare and educational organisations are covered by a thirty-grade wage system. For the former Meisner reported a wage range in Shenyang from 230 yuan to 34 yuan or 6.8:1.[25] The latter pay-scale has the widest wage range and includes the top state administrators. The top rate of this scale in 1975, according to Deng Xiaoping, was 400 yuan, which was paid to about 100 people in the PRC. Older professors in the universities may receive between 300 and 360 yuan while their most junior colleagues receive between 50 and 60 yuan. A study by Doak Barnett showed that the wage range in one national ministry was almost 10:1, with the minister receiving close on 400 yuan, the bureaux chiefs between 200 and 250 yuan, divisional chiefs 150 to 200 yuan and section chiefs receiving 45 yuan.[26] In addition to these basic wages there are other incomes, such as the bonus system and the 'hidden benefits' for higher-grade cadres. The 'hidden benefits' are difficult to quantify but, for example, such cadres will have access to the use of cars, rail and air travel and are able to claim expenses. People such as Ba Jin and the trade-union leader Ni Zhifu receive sizeable additional incomes from royalties – Ni from the drilling-bit that he invented, and Ba Jin royalties from his literary works, one of which is claimed to have made him 200 000 yuan.[27]

Finally, outside of this wage system there are those who work in the collective enterprises, which appear to be reasonably remunerative and those, such as unemployed women, engaged in factory piecework either at home or in small workshops. This latter kind of work is not very remunerative, with wage levels equivalent to, or slightly lower than, those of an apprentice.

Income inequality: the peasantry

The peasants do not receive wages but are allocated a certain number of work-points for each day's work. At the end of the year the profits of the collective are calculated and after certain deductions, such as welfare funds, accumulation funds and taxes, have been made the money is divided out in accordance with the total number of work-points. Those who have accumulated more points get more money. Consequently,

in any particular commune the wealth of a family will
depend on the number of active workers it has as compared
to those that are non-productive. However, those that are
non-productive in the collective sector are not necessarily a
drain on the family income because they can supplement this
income by working on the private plots or by engaging in
sideline production. Not only are there differences between
families within the communes but also there are great differences in income according to the area in which the commune
is situated. Since the Third plenum of the Eleventh CC these
differences are seen as a stimulus to production and it has
been argued that 'getting rich first' is actually egalitarian in
nature. It is claimed that the poorer areas or individuals will
strive hard to catch up with the richer ones, thus turning
inequality into equality.[28] A high correlation exists between
the natural resources of a particular area and the *per capita*
income of the peasant. Thus, while Jikou commune in a hilly
area of Fujian province had a *per capita* income of over 130
yuan in 1976, in the same year the suburban Yihui commune
in Yunnan had a *per capita* income of 242 yuan.[29] The
proximity to market is a crucial factor and, although the
peasantry in general are less well off than urban workers, the
suburban peasants as a social group are one of the richest in
China. Where they are able to grow fruit and market garden
produce their incomes can be very high[30] and become even
higher once extra earnings are taken into account. Income
derived from the collective went up by 13 per cent in China
in 1978, but on the outskirts of Beijing, Tianjin and Shanghai
it went up 27.1, 24.4, and 39 per cent respectively.[31]

The peasants' incomes are supplemented by other sources
such as the money derived from produce grown on the private
plots, sideline occupations (such as pig-rearing) and handi-
crafts. Especially in the present political climate these earnings can be considerable; for example, a married couple with
seven children received 1700 yuan from the collective (after
deductions for grain, edible oil and vegetables) and a further
1000 yuan from their other occupations.[32] Another family
with three children received 1320 yuan after deductions
from the collective, while they were able to raise another 300
yuan from pig-rearing.[33]

This brief survey of incomes gives some idea of the differentials in Chinese society. These differentials correlate with other inequalities, such as social status and one's chances for advancement. Not surprisingly, it is better to be an urban worker rather than a peasant, skilled rather than unskilled, experienced rather than inexperienced, highly placed in the hierarchy rather than lowly placed and male rather than female.[34]

Normative control

Normative control is important in any society to ensure acceptance and support for the regime by its citizens, but equally it can be used to facilitate the transformation of society by replacing traditional values with ones more acceptable to the regime. On assuming power the CCP was confronted with powerful traditional values, values which it was necessary to upset in order to change society's goals. This change of values involved a twofold process — first, those already alive had to be convinced of the benefits of the new system and, secondly, a suitable programme of education had to be devised for those born into the new society. This redirection of goals and an inculcation of new ones is an important stage in the consolidation of power and helps to legitimise the regime. This process is given added importance in China because of Mao's belief in the need for participation as a means of bringing about attitudinal change. This view has been opposed within the leadership, especially at times when mass participation has led to criticism of the Party (as in the Hundred Flowers Movement, 1956–7), or when it has led to chaos (as in the Great Leap Forward, 1957–8). Those who oppose Mao stress that economic development should be pursued first and criticise the 'excessive concentration' on attempts to change values.

Intellectuals

The most problematic group to exercise control over is the intellectuals, and Party policy towards them has fluctuated over time.[35] When economic development has been emphasised greater freedom has been accorded to them, but when mass mobilisation has been pursued they have come under attack and have had their field of enquiry limited.

The present policy of modernisation means that it is necessary to draw on the expertise of the intellectuals, who in return must be given certain freedoms and sureties to ensure their support. Consequently, the intellectuals are enjoying an unparalleled freedom for any time since 1949, and have been positively encouraged to write about and investigate the hitherto 'forbidden zones'. It has been stated that 'without democracy, there can be no science' and that 'science and culture cannot develop without free discussion'.[36] The present approach is summed up by the slogan 'letting a hundred flowers bloom and a hundred schools of thought contend'.[37] This slogan has been put forward during times of liberalisation to signify the encouragement of debate. However, as the Hundred Flowers Movement showed, criticism, even when officially encouraged, may suddenly be suppressed if it goes beyond the acceptable limits. Previous experience explains why the initial reaction of the older intellectuals to the new policies of liberalisation was tentative. The most problematic field of intellectual enquiry is that of art and literature. The calls for free academic exchange have been balanced by the stress on the need for Party leadership over artistic and literary work. It does appear that persuasion rather than coercion is the means used to dissuade erring writers.[38] The ideological conformity of works written during the years of the Cultural Revolution has been relaxed; writers are now allowed to write 'unsuccessful or even defective works' and critics to publish 'immature, defective or erroneous comments'.[39] Criticism of such works is to be conducted in a 'truly comradely, convincing, reasonable and appropriate way'.[40]

The present policies have reopened some of the basic policy formulations laid down by Mao in Yanan at the Forum on Art and Literature in 1942. At this time Yanan experienced an influx of intellectuals who saw the CCP as providing the best vehicle for national salvation but who were not necessarily willing to commit themselves to the Party's ideological rigour. The intellectuals wanted less interference by the Party in cultural and intellectual activities, more opportunities for debate and greater tolerance of differing viewpoints. Criticisms of the Yanan regime came from people such as Wang Shiwei and Ai Qing. Ai Qing felt that he could not describe 'ringworms as flowers' while Wang wrote that 'statesmen were the leaders of society, the directors of the revolution and the formalisers of policies; artists reformed man's spirit, mind and ideas . . . and stimulated the moral strength of the revolution'.[41] At the forum Mao gave his reply. Art was not independent of politics and was to be surbordinated to the revolutionary tasks prescribed by the Party at any given time.

Since Mao's death and the arrest of the Gang of Four the relationship between politics and art has again been discussed. Although the view has been put forward that art is separate from politics, the dominant view is that Party leadership is still important and that art and literature must contribute to the current major task of the Party — the four modernisations.[42] However, the strict approach towards intellectuals, art and literature which was adopted by the Gang of Four has been rejected in favour of the more liberal approach outlined above. Mao, in his Yanan talk, rejected Wang's concept of human nature. For Mao, there was no abstract human nature or universal emotion which could be revealed, but only specific forms belonging to specific classes at specific times. The role of literature was to reflect these differences and not to cloud them by writing about universal qualities. Finally, Mao stated that the function of literature was not to reveal the dark side of (communist) society as impartially as the bright side. Defects in society were not to be pointed out by intellectuals but were to be handled by the Party alone. During the years 1966–76 this function of literature was exploited to the full, with euphoric portrayals of the masses and the Communist Party. Present policy is that writers should praise the bright aspects of society but also that they should expose to criticism the dark aspects. Literature can be critical but not entirely so for, while it is recognised that realism is the lifeblood of art, this is not taken to mean that one should write about everything in life.[43] Liu Binyan put forward the writer's view of this question when he said, 'When literature mirrors what is undesirable in life, the mirror itself is not to

blame; instead, disagreeable things in real life should be
spotted and wiped out. An ugly person cannot be turned into
a beauty simply by smashing the mirror'.[44]

The current policy has resulted in a variety of measures to
improve the conditions of intellectuals and ensure their
support. There has been a large-scale reversal of verdicts on
cases concerning intellectuals, particularly for those who
were designated 'bourgeois rightists' in 1957 following the
Hundred Flowers Movement. Intellectuals' status is to be
raised, working and living conditions are to be improved and,
where possible, their incomes increased. Certain intellectuals
have been held up for emulation and 160 of the 340 model
workers at the December 1979 National Model Workers'
Conference were intellectuals.[45] Their prestige has been
further enhanced by the restoration of academic titles for
those in universities, colleges and research institutes.[46] This
new policy has been accompanied by a Party recruitment
drive among intellectuals. In 1979 Guizhou province recruited 1916 intellectuals to be Party members. This was
15.4 per cent of the total number recruited[47] with 2600
(15 per cent) admitted to the Beijing Party.[48] Also, there is a
drive to promote both Party and non-Party intellectuals into
leading positions; in Shenyang almost 1000 scientists and
engineers have been promoted to leadership positions in
factories and colleges. Finally, and perhaps most importantly,
intellectuals are now a designated part of the working class.
This means that on future occasions, when re-education is
considered necessary, it will be dealt with in the same manner
as other contradictions among the people. It will no longer
be a case of remoulding the intellectuals' world outlook but
will be a case of mild reform. The Gang of Four are reported
to have said that 'remoulding teachers is like pressing a rubber
ball under water. Press hard and it goes under, but as soon as
you let go, up it pops again, thus requiring that pressure
should always be put on them to keep them in deep water'.[49]
Three categories of intellectuals are identified: those from
pre-liberation society; those who supported the revolution
before 1949; and those who have been trained since 1949. It
is calculated that the third category contains 90 per cent of
those labelled intellectuals. As a result the present leadership

considers intellectuals to be a legitimate part of the working class and not the 'stinking ninth category',[50] as they were labelled during the Cultural Revolution. Differences between mental and manual labour are seen as a necessary division of labour, and the Gang of Four are criticised for having promoted the view that 'mental workers govern the people while the physical labourers are governed by others'.[51]

Education

There are two main reasons for looking at education in China. The first is that it provides the main agent of socialisation, inculcating the values the leadership deems important. Secondly, education, particularly higher education, gives access to positions of power and prestige within the hierarchy. The aim of the CCP is to create a modernised, socialist state but there has been a continual tension between the demands of modernisation and those of socialism. Particularly since the mid-sixties education has provided a major focus for this tension. The desire for modernisation has led to a priority being placed on education and, more particularly, on the cultivation of specialist skills. A major problem has been how to find the right balance between elitism and popularisation and between the need to concentrate resources and the need to cultivate a mass, literate and technically competent population. This problem has been increased by attempts to use education as a redistributive tool, which has resulted in changing education policies over time. The current meritocratic policies pursued since the arrest of the Gang of Four contrast markedly with the downgrading of academic requirements during the years 1968–76. During these eight years greater importance was attached to the individual's class stance and the recommendations of fellow workers. In general the education strategy resembles that of the Soviet Union, Eastern Europe and most of the developing world. A rapid expansion of the formal education facilities has been combined with curriculum emphasis on practical and scientific subjects. The state plays an increasing role not only in the funding of education but also in deciding which materials should or should not be used for teaching.

In primary and secondary schools there are 210 million children — a high number, but one which does not include the whole school-age population. The Education Minister, Jiang Nanxiang, has designated the attainment of universal education as one of the major tasks for education work.[52] Apart from the problem of providing education for all there are also problems with standards. Hunan province announced that over 95 per cent of school-age children attended but that of these only 70 per cent finish the five-year elementary course and less than half reach the required standard. The schooling system is highly standardised and centralised.[53] According to the outline programme for national education the length of primary and secondary schooling is to be ten years for those in urban areas, with five years spent in primary school and five in secondary school, while in rural areas it is hoped to provide eight years' education with a five—three-year split.[54] (See Table 8.1.) This puts those in the rural areas at an immediate disadvantage in terms of their chances of going to university because a ten-year schooling period is normally expected from those taking the entrance exams.

In schools children are divided according to their ability into three streams of 'quick' classes, 'medium' classes and 'slow' classes.[55] Those children placed in the 'medium' or 'slow' classes receive extra tuition in an attempt to improve their performance. In addition to this streaming there are annual competitive examinations in selected courses for junior and senior secondary school students. Those who achieve the best results are sent to better schools.[56] This re-emphasis on the meritocratic aspects of education has led secondary schools to concentrate on those students who will go on to college. However, as only about 4 per cent of students go on to higher education such a concentration of time and resources is wasteful. As a result this tendency has been criticised by the Chinese media and the dual function of education has been stressed. Not only are secondary schools expected to provide students for university but also they are expected to pay attention to providing a skilled workforce.[57] This factor, the stress on modernisation and the need to aid technical training, has meant that technical schools have reopened.

Table 8.1   Primary and secondary school education

Primary school

Entrance age	Duration	Courses[a]	Study/Labour time allocation
Seven[b]	Five years	Chinese, arithmetic, elementary knowledge of nature, foreign languages, politics, physical culture, music, drawing	Nine and a half months' study per annum. Fourth- and fifth-year students do nine months study and one-half month labour.

[a] Nature, foreign languages and politics are only for third years and above. Foreign languages are only taught in some urban primary schools.

[b] Children aged six or six-and-a-half may be admitted.

Secondary (Middle) school

Entrance age	Duration	Courses	Study/Labour time allocation
Twelve	Five years total[a]	Politics, Chinese language, mathematics physics, chemistry, biology, foreign languages, history, geography, basic farm knowledge, hygiene, physical education, music and drawing	Nine months' study and one month physical labour per annum.

[a] There have been discussions in the press about extending this to six years.

Source: Adapted from *Beijing Review*, no. 1 (1980), pp. 20–2.

In 1965 approximately 30 per cent of secondary school students were studying in agricultural or vocational secondary schools but these schools were closed down during the Cultural Revolution. Apart from reviving these vocational schools there have been attempts to introduce technical courses in ordinary secondary schools.

China has 598 colleges and universities with around

850 000 students. Entrance to university from secondary school is by way of the national entrance examinations. These unified entrance exams were reinstituted on the decision of the October 1977 Education Ministry Conference on College Enrolment. This conference decided that 20 to 30 per cent of the places would be reserved for students straight from secondary school, meaning that they would not have to complete the normal two-year work period before going to university.[58] This number of students allowed to proceed directly from school to higher education is to be gradually increased. Exam success is the most important criterion for university entry; only after satisfactory marks have been gained are political assessment and a physical examination carried out. This same process of selection came under strong attack during the Cultural Revolution because of its 'meritocratic excesses'. During these years the stress on politics and the preference for 'correct class stance', as opposed to purely academic ability, led to a change in university enrolment policy. Favoured treatment was given to children from the families of workers, soldiers and peasants, or to the educated youth 'sent down' to the countryside. Also, greater emphasis was placed on the opinions of one's comrades in the workplace. The actual effect that this change of emphasis had on university recruitment is difficult to gauge. It is likely that the representation of groups such as peasants may have been exaggerated as some of those admitted were educated youths who had been 'sent down' to the countryside and who were subsequently reclassified as peasants. However, it is certain that the replacement of the examination system by the 'recommendation system' removed the major advantage possessed by the children of urban intellectuals. White has observed that these reforms did have a limited redistributive impact but that the impact was less than was hoped for. He sees the failure for this as being primarily attributable to the failure of the Cultural Revolution to alter radically the power structure of society. There was a significant impact in altering differences between different urban strata but not in altering differences between city and countryside.[59]

Whether this redistributive impact was great or not, educationalists in China felt that standards had fallen and that politics had been set in opposition to professional competence. Zhou Rongxin, the Education Minister in 1975, put forward criticisms along these lines, stating that academic standards at university were only on a par with those of the pre-Cultural-Revolution technical secondary schools.[60] In an attempt to discover the standards a test was given to 1977 science graduates working in the Shanghai area. The questions covered the basic secondary school syllabus and those tested were informed of the questions beforehand. The results were staggering: 68 per cent failed mathematics, 70 per cent failed physics and 76 per cent failed chemistry.[61] New regulations on entry have been designed to improve this standard by improving the quality of those selected for university. Future rewards for those selected are obviously high, and warnings have been issued to parents not to push their children too hard. It is stressed that worthwile contributions can be made to society by those who do not go on to university.[62] Postgraduate education is again encouraged and about 200 institutions of higher education, and a similar number of research institutes, have started enrolling postgraduates. In May 1980 exams were held for graduates (or equivalents) and graduands to provide the basis for selection for postgraduate work. If the propspective students are full-time workers they will continue to draw their salaries, while if they are just graduating the enrolling institution will provide them with a grant to the value of 90 per cent of the wage of the average college graduate in that locality.

The 'Key Point' system is an important feature of the present education strategy — a system which came under attack during the Cultural Revolution for its 'elitist' nature. The system represents in microcosm the whole question of resource allocation. The key points are to serve as an impetus to promote the gradual development of the whole system by relying on the concentration of resource allocation in a few areas to maximise returns on minimum costs. Certain schools, from primary level upwards, and certain universities, are designated as key points. As a result they receive greater funds from the state to provide the best facilities and to pay the best and most experienced teachers. The key points enrol the best students and are expected to produce the best results.

There are both national key points[63] and local ones. Unlike ordinary schools and colleges they can recruit from a wider area, thus increasing their ability to recruit the best students. The problems of this system are self-evident and already warnings have been published about the dangers of concentrating exclusively on the key points. In Rushan county, Shandong province, the education bureau has allocated what it terms 'competent leading comrades' to work in schools of an average standard to help raise standards.[64]

Mass participation

Chapter 4 considers the theory of the mass-line and some of the problems related to it and to its practical implementation. Here some of the organisations for mass participation and the different types of mass campaign are considered. The lowest participating unit is the small group.[65] These groups are organised by the higher levels in a person's workplace and consist of up to about fifteen people. Although it carries out other activities its most important function is to conduct political study. These small groups are of increasing importance during mass campaigns when the leadership is seeking to mobilise the population towards some particular goal. However, at all times they have the important function of spotting and correcting deviant behaviour. Whyte has pointed out the importance that these groups have in the process of communication.[66] They act as a channel for information from the leadership to the individual and as a forum for discussion of policy initiatives. Any misgivings that the small group or individual members may have about the policy or its implementation are reported to the higher level. When not engaged in any particular campaign the small groups discuss matters relating to work and the neighbourhood, or engage in discussion of theoretical writings. It is difficult to estimate the success of these groups; for example, sometimes the political study periods of the small groups simply consist of reading aloud the main article of the *People's Daily* for the benefit of those who are illiterate or only semi-literate. This obviously fulfils the function of communicating the leadership's policies but would appear to do very little else. During the movement to criticise Deng Xiaoping one study group opposed to the movement spent their time discussing family matters, thus avoiding discussion of the issue at stake. Although this example may be atypical it does show that the level of group involvement depends on the particular subject matter.

Membership of a mass organisation provides another avenue for participation in the political process, but there is disagreement about whether they can faithfully promote the interests of their members or whether they are simply a channel for implementing Party policy. Since the fall of the Gang of Four the most important mass organisations have been revived and encouraged to play an active part in the political system.[67] These organisations, like the small groups, are responsible for transmitting policies to the lower levels and for providing the leadership with feedback. It is difficult to use these organisations to promote interests counter to those of the leadership because Party members are placed in leading positions in the organisations, and the organisations operate under the leadership of the Party. Townsend concludes that 'the mass organisations are the CCP's primary assistants in transmitting Party policies to the mass level'.[68] However, he also feels that despite Party control these organisations have been successful in giving meaning to the concept of the mass-line by providing opportunities for mass political participation.

Mass campaigns are organised movements, instigated by the leadership, requiring participation and commitment from the people. People's attention is attracted to the object of the campaign by the use of slogans, newspaper articles and meetings. Once people's attention has been focused and all have identified with the struggle, the level of involvement is stepped up by the dissemination of study materials to help the people evaluate themselves and others. This phase leads on to active participation, when particular individuals are held up for praise or are singled out for criticism. Punishments and rewards are handed out as the campaign moves into the phase of summing up its relative successes and failures.

The campaigns vary in subject matter and in the number of people affected. Generally speaking the campaigns fall into three main types. First, there are emulation campaigns. The objects held up for emulation can be people, such as the soldier Lei Feng, or places, such as the agricultural brigade at Dazhai, and will embody an ideal or ideals for the people to copy. Secondly, there are struggle campaigns. In these campaigns a definite object has to be struggled against, such as a class or social group; thus, during land reform the landlords were attacked, and during the Cultural Revolution the targets were 'capitalist-roaders'. The targets of these campaigns may also be certain social customs or malpractices. During the movement to criticise Lin Biao and Confucius, the position of women in society was identified as one of the social, as opposed to political, targets of the movement. Thirdly, there are campaigns aimed at attitudinal and ideological reform. These campaigns entail certain individuals, for example, Party cadres during rectification movements, undergoing a process of thought reform. The present leadership has not abandoned the organisational technique of the mass campaign, but its use will become less frequent because of 'mass disillusionment' and because of the stress on achieving development using an orderly set process.

9

Urban China

The People's Republic of China is, quite rightly, thought of as a rural country, but it has a numerically large urban population and is governed by a Party which, according to its constitution, represents the interests of the working class. However, the practical experience of revolution led Mao in particular to see the city as a corrupting influence while the countryside was seen as embodying the 'revolutionary virtues' of thrift and hard work. This anti-urban bias was evident during the Cultural Revolution and, as Bergère has written, 'although the birth of a "new class" was not an exclusively urban phenomenon, it was closely associated with an élitist urban culture'.[1] In the countryside the communists have been able to realise their policy of combining work and living places but in the cities this has not been possible. Accommodation for workers and their families has been built on or near the workplace to try to solve this problem. The most extensive experiment to combine work and living space was the introduction of the urban commune in 1958 as an extension of the rural communisation launched in the Great Leap Forward.[2] The urban commune tried to create integrated units of production, administration and living as was the case in the rural communes. These either focused on existing factories, schools and so on, or small-scale industry was brought to residential areas. Because of the insurmountable problems encountered the movement was abandoned in December 1958, only four months after it had been started. However, one thing which was not abandoned was the small street industries set up during the movement. The retreat from communisation has left Chinese city-dwellers with a dual system of organisation – through the workplace and through the place of residence.

Although China's urban population is high in total it is quite specifically concentrated. The most urbanised areas of China are the north-east and the lower Changjiang (Yangtse) River basin. China's cities and towns number over 3400. Of these, 192 are municipalities with a total population of more than 70 million,[3] and there are 13 cities in China with populations of over 1 million.[4] If one includes the cities' immediate agricultural population the number of cities with populations over 1 million rises to 29. The policies of modernisation will mean that in the future there will be a greater population to be absorbed by the urban areas. There is general agreement that the major cities should not soak up any more population because of the problems already apparent. For example, the size of Beijing's population has led to a lowering of the water table; both Beijing and Shanghai are heavily polluted and all the major cities are overcrowded. At a forum held early in 1980 two major approaches were put forward as a solution to the problem.[5] The first view favoured a continuation of present policy, involving the development of small cities and towns throughout the countryside combined with the expansion of commune- and brigade-run enterprises. Under this scheme small towns would be set up in commune seats with a sphere of economic activity of between ten and fifteen kilometres. Five such towns would be set up in each of the country's 2000 counties, making a total increase of 10 000 towns. The population estimates for these towns are between 20 000 and 50 000 residents; as a result a displaced rural population of between 200 million and 500 million could be taken up. The second view does not discount such developments but places the emphasis on the construction of big and medium-sized cities. The proponents of this viewpoint think that the policy of building up small cities and towns in the past resulted in more failures than successes. The output value, profits and products from the small interior industrial towns are far below those of the big coastal cities which have greater labour productivity. Supporters of this view argue that the development of small cities will mean that they cannot properly fulfil their functions; they suggest that big cities should be developed first, facilitating the construction of smaller ones.

Territorial organisation

Residents in urban China are subject to two sets of organisational arrangements, one of which is territorial, the other functional. At the basic level the workplace is the most important of these two organisations. Much of a person's life, including social and leisure pursuits, will revolve around one's work-unit. For those who do not work there are organisations based on one's place of residence. In the early months of 1980 a more active role was outlined for these organisations.[6]

The largest of the urban organisations is the municipality. The three most important of these are Beijing, Shanghai and Tianjin, each being the equivalent of a province. There are other municipalities at the level of the prefecture and county. These municipalities not only include the city proper but also the cities' suburbs and any rural communes with which the city has an important exchange. It is at this level that work-based organisations and territorial organisations are joined. Municipalities have their own Party committees and people's governments elected by the people's congresses. Below the municipality is the district, which also has a people's congress. Districts vary in size but have populations of over 100 000 and are the lowest level of local government in the urban areas and equivalent to the commune in the countryside. If the municipality is sufficiently large sub-districts are set up below the level of the district. These sub-districts are branch offices set up by the municipal or district people's government in an urban area with between 50 000 and 100 000 people.[7] Municipalities where the population exceeds 100 000 must set up sub-districts, but their establishment is optional for municipalities with a population of between 50 000 and 100 000. In municipalities where the population is under 50 000 no sub-districts are set up. Because sub-districts are branch offices their officials are not elected but are appointed by the municipal or district people's government.[8] Their task is to act as a transmission belt between the people's congresses and the neighbourhood (residents') committees, directing the work of the latter while passing up residents' views to the higher levels.

The neighbourhood committees are self-governing, their officials elected directly by the residents living in the area. These committees were first set up in 1951 in an attempt to establish order from the general confusion arising from the *ad hoc* organisations in existence. By December 1954 the leadership felt that their value had been demonstrated and on 31 December 1954 the Organic Regulations of the Urban Neighbourhood Committee were issued. Over time the importance of these committees has varied. During the anti-rightist campaign of 1957—8 and in the initial phase of the Great Leap Forward these committees played a major role. Although they were never abolished the short-lived urban communes meant that the committees' role was downgraded and nearly all their time was spent organising production and the communal mess-halls. From 1966 their importance relative to the workplace declined, although in January 1980 the 1954 regulations were republished, signalling a revival of their role.[9]

The committees are established under the leadership of the basic-level government or the sub-district office and have between 100 and 600 households under their jurisdiction. The households are organised into residents' groups of between fifteen and forty households with a maximum of seventeen small groups to each committee. The regulations list five main tasks for the committees: (1) to handle things concerning the public welfare of the people; (2) to pass on the opinions and suggestions of the residents to the local people's government[10] or its branch agency; (3) to mobilise the residents to respond to the government's calls and to comply with the law; (4) to direct public order and security works of a mass nature; and (5) to mediate disputes between the residents. Each of the small groups elects one member to serve on the neighbourhood committee. The committee has a membership of between seven and seventeen and serves for a one-year term. The committee members select a chairperson and one to three vice-chairpersons, one of whom is responsible for women's affairs. Neighbourhood committees which have a relatively large number of people under their jurisdiction can, if necessary, set up work committees on the approval of the local people's government. These work committees can be either permanent or temporary bodies. A maximum of five permanent committees can be set up to deal with matters such as public welfare, public security, work relating to culture, education and health, dispute mediation and women's work. While these committees should 'draw from the most enthusiastic members', as far as is possible it is ensured that each person only has one job.

As a rule organisations, schools and relatively large enterprises in the area do not participate in the neighbourhood committees, though they do send representatives to any meeting that concerns them and are expected to comply with decisions taken by the committees concerning the residents' welfare. Similarly the residents must comply with any regulation designed to promote their public welfare. The committees in carrying out their work are to avoid 'commandism' and are to promote democracy through the use of democratic centralism and 'mass voluntarism'. With the permission of the people's government, work departments of the municipality may give tasks to the neighbourhood committee and its work committees, and the work departments may also give them vocational guidance. Miscellaneous expenses of the committees and supplementary living allowances for their members are borne by the local government. With the residents' agreement and the approval of the local government, funds for welfare services can be collected from the residents and any accounts must be made public. No other collections from the residents can be made.

The small groups provide the basic level for political participation for those who are not employed or who work at home or in a collective enterprise. For others the group serves as the forum for discussing social and welfare problems. The small groups elect a leader who usually is concurrently their representative on the neighbourhood committee. In addition the group can elect one or two deputy group leaders. If a group's member of the neighbourhood committee is elected chairperson or vice-chairperson of the committee the small group can elect another leader. Anyone is eligible to become a member of these groups but those who are under surveillance or who are deprived of their political rights cannot stand for office and can be barred from attending certain meetings.

Certainly these neighbourhood committees and small groups provide local inhabitants with the opportunity of participating in matters concerning their immediate environment, but control over the most important matters lies with the higher authorities. Also, the committees and groups must always operate within the parameters of Party policy.

In January 1980 the *People's Daily* also republished the Regulations of the People's Mediation Committee and the Social Order and Security Committee.[11] The people's mediation committees are 'self-governing bodies of a mass nature' whose officials are directly elected by the residents.[12] They carry out work under the guidance of the basic-level government and people's courts. The committees have between three and eleven members, their tasks being to: mediate in civil disputes; to handle minor criminal cases; to publicise the government's decrees and edicts; and to promote unity among the people. The social order and public security committees are also self-governing organisations, described as having a 'mass character '. The work of these committees keeps them in close contact with the neighbourhood committees and they form a part of the public security system. The size of the committee varies from three to eleven people, including one chairperson and one or two vice-chairpersons. Where the conditions require it, and if the municipal or county public security bureau approves, small groups can be set up with between three to five 'activists'. These small groups work under the direction of the social order and security committee and are elected by the people. The most important tasks of the committees are to help the public security organs apprehend and exercise supervision over criminals and counter-revolutionaries. In addition the committees help with the re-education work for criminals and counter-revolutionaries and help educate the population in matters such as crime and fire prevention.

Organisation at the workplace

This section considers the organisation of the factories and offices which are in the state-controlled sector. The literature covering the field of organisation and management emphasises the dichotomy between what may be termed the 'red' and the 'expert' approach to the problem. Schurmann sees the former approach as asserting that 'organisational unity can only be produced by perfecting the network of human organisation', while the 'expert' approach asserts that 'organisational unity can only be produced by a rational division of labour supported by modern technology'.[13] Richman identifies this dichotomy as being one shifting between 'ideological emphasis' and 'managerial, technical and economic rationality',[14] while Gray sees it as a difference between the Soviet-Stalinist model and the model developed in Yanan.[15] In practice organisation and management in industry have consisted of a mixture of the two. What has been in question is the relative weight to give to each aspect and which, if either, should dominate.

During the Great Leap Forward and the Cultural Revolution managerial authority came under attack and there was an attempt to scrap 'unreasonable rules and regulations'. The proposed system was not to rely on complex rules to express the division of labour. Efforts were made to blur the distinction between management and workers by increasing worker participation in management and by making technical and managerial staff engage in productive labour. The most far-reaching changes of the Cultural Revolution were very short-lived as industry ran into production difficulties. From 1968 there were pressures to reintroduce many of the abolished rules and regulations concerning labour discipline and a greater reliance was placed on technicians. By the early seventies the practice of industrial organisation greatly resembled that of the pre-Cultural Revolution and debate centred on which of the new practices should be kept and which of the old practices should be discarded. Thus, while limited material incentives were being reintroduced the 'reactionary theory of material incentives' was being criticised and continued participation in management by the workers was combined with the revival of precise regulations outlining work requirements. The People's Daily, when criticising those who advocated that 'systems are useless', was at pains to stress that the question of their revival was not important for the Cultural

Revolution had shown that production could be stimulated without recourse to a system of rules and regulations.[16]

The present system has moved even further towards the 'management' end of the spectrum, with the stress on the need for rules and regulations to revive production after the 'years of anarchy' under the Gang of Four. The debate about workers' participation in management has not been about whether workers should participate, but about the amount of participation and about the level at which they should participate. However, any future participation will be quite formally organised to prevent it from affecting production. In the workplace there is a functional separation between policy initiative and policy implementation. The duplication of work which arose from the revolutionary committee, containing personnel in many instances identical to the Party committee, is obviously not in line with the main thrust of the new policy. A return to the pre-Cultural-Revolution system is seen as the solution to this problem and as the way to facilitate speedier decisions in the production process. Now policy decisions of the Party are implemented by the director and his assistants or working committee. However, the director does have a reasonable freedom of action and more likely than not will be a Party member himself. A typical example of the present set-up is the Shoudu Iron and Steel Company. All decisions must be made by the Party committee before being put into practice by the factory director, but in cases of emergency the director has the power to take prompt action before reporting to the Party committee. In charge of the day-to-day affairs there is a working committee comprising the director, four deputy directors and 'responsible technical and administrative cadres'.[17] It is thought that this makes the revolutionary committee redundant and in fact many of its members serve on the working committee, but now there is said to be a clear-cut division of responsibility which did not exist before.[18]

Party committees comprise a secretary, deputy secretaries and committee members.[19] The main administrative body under the Party committee is the political department. This department supervises the work of the sections such as the organisational, propaganda and militia sections. In addition the political department supervises the work of other bodies in the factory, such as the trade union, the Youth League and, if it has one, the school. The director is the responsible administrative member of the factory who carries out his work with the aid of his deputies[20] and other technical and administrative cadres. Under the factory director's leadership there are the general office and a number of sections dealing with matters such as production, planning, technology, safety, quality examination and wages. Also under the director's leadership are the workshops; these are divided into sections, shifts and groups.[21]

The main forum for workers' participation is the workers' congress. These congresses are convened at regular intervals by the factory, under the trade union's guidance, rather than by the workers, and are attended by delegates elected by the workers.[22] Before the congress delegates canvass for opinions and suggestions from fellow workers and these are then presented to the factory leadership for consideration. The congress discusses major issues concerning the enterprises, and works out and puts into practice resolutions relating to production plans, management regulations, labour organisations, financial expenditures, welfare and labour protection. Any proposals which the leadership considers 'feasible and rational' are taken up. Although the workers have been removed from administrative bodies concerned with the day-to-day running of enterprises, these congresses continue to give them some say in enterprise management. However, their power is limited by the fact that the leadership decide when a congress should be convened and which suggestions should be taken up. Should there be any particular problem which is difficult to solve then three-in-one combination groups of leading cadres, technicians and workers can be formed to deal with it.

Elections are seen as an important force ensuring that there is democracy in the workplace. In fact, it is now stated that the right of workers to elect and remove leading cadres at the grass-roots level is an important guarantee of their participation in enterprise management.[23] At the Ninth National Trade Union Congress in October 1978 Deng Xiaoping put forward the call that heads of workshops and shifts in factories should be elected directly by the workers. For the higher levels, approval and removal of personnel by the workers are not governed by direct elections for two reasons. First, each of the administrative sections only has four or five personnel, which is considered an insufficient number to be worthwhile or to make the election representative. Secondly, the electorate is not extended to include the workers under these sections because it is said that they have little daily contact with the section chiefs. As a consequence of this lack of contact it is felt that they would not know who to vote for. The compromise is to use an opinion poll conducted among the personnel of the administrative sections and representatives of the workers, such as the workshop heads.[24] At the Shoudu Cement Works opinion polls were conducted prior to the reappointment of chiefs to the sections of planning, production, design and finance. In total four of the twenty-one cadres under consideration were removed from office because of their failure to secure majority approval.

Trade unions

The trade-union system was yet another casualty of the early years of the Cultural Revolution. The establishment of the revolutionary committee with members drawn from the workers enabled people to put forward the argument that the trade unions were redundant. The revolutionary committee took over the economic and welfare duties of the trade unions while their representative functions were taken over by the workers' congresses.[25] These workers' congresses were renamed 'trade unions' in 1973, the unions functioning with a reduced role compared to the previous one, under the supervision of the revolutionary committee.

The abolition of the revolutionary committee has led to a revived role for the trade unions under the Party committee. This revival has been especially marked since the Ninth National Congress of the All-China Federation of Trade Unions was convened in 1978. The trade union is described as a mass organisation and essentially this means that it acts as a conveyor of information and directives between the

union's members and the Party. Membership is voluntary and
open to any person working in a factory, shop, school,
hospital or scientific research institute. Applications for
membership are discussed by other members and must be
approved by the union at the basic level. Members pay
monthly dues to the union amounting to 0.5 per cent of their
wage and these dues are kept by the basic-level union to help
cover basic costs. Additional revenue for the union comes
from three other sources: monthly allocations from the
management of the unit (amounting to 2 per cent of the
total wage bill); subsidies from the enterprises and governments at various levels; and income from cultural and sports
activities sponsored by the trade unions. These funds are used
to cover things such as expenses for workers' and staff
members' spare-time education courses, their recreational
activities, trade-union offices, cadre training and subsidies for
members in financial difficulties. The unions are organised
both by trade and by geographical location. Each factory or
shop will have a union, and at regional and national levels
there are unions according to the profession. The All-China
Federation of Trade Unions is the leading body of this network and under its supervision local federations are set up in
provinces and municipalities. At the various levels there are
trade-union congresses or conferences and these elect the
administrative body, the trade-union committees.

When one considers the work of the trade unions it is quite
clear that they are concerned with the avoidance of conflict
or with conflict management rather than with conflict promotion. While it is stressed that the unions should uphold the
interests of their members it is made clear that the best way
to achieve this is by gaining their members' support for Party
policies. The central task for trade unions revolves around
promoting production, and to this end its most important
political task is 'to organise the workers and staff to take an
active part in the four modernisations and strive to fulfil
and overfulfil the state economic plan'.[26] Consequently,
the solution of problems concerning workers' conditions is
seen as being conducive to efficient production rather than as
improving the workers' conditions *per se*. To help with this
task the union organises the workers' congresses, conducting

its work under the leadership of the enterprise's Party committee. The trade union is also to 'represent the interests of
the majority of the workers and support their correct views
and reasonable demands'.[27] What this actually means is that
the union has an educative role designed to screen out or
correct any views considered unreasonable. It is to 'guide the
workers in correctly exercising their democratic rights,
maintaining order in production and observing labour discipline'.[28] This role is best seen in the unions' position on
strikes. In general, strikes are considered unnecessary because
it is thought that adequate channels for expression of grievances exist. Also, the theoretical standpoint that the working
class is the ruling class in the country makes the possibility of
any substantial difference between leaders and led inconceivable. However, should a strike occur the trade unions
co-operate with the local industrial and labour departments
to discover its causes and to devise a solution. Even if the
demands of the workers are considered reasonable it may still
be necessary for the trade unions to oppose them if there is
a lack of financial and material resources to meet the demands.[29] If the strike arises because of the bureaucratic
faults of the enterprise leadership, then the unions are to
offer full support to the workers and to prevail on the
management to solve the problem.

Apart from general, political and ideological education the
unions organise full-time and part-time training courses in
technological subjects for the workers. It is hoped that these
courses will mean that by 1985 most workers will have
reached the level of senior-secondary-school students.[30]
Trade unions also organise labour emulation drives with the
aim of increasing efficiency and production. These emulation
drives may seek to encourage people to learn from a particular individual, to achieve a certain target or to compete with
others. In a Harbin linen mill workers were encouraged to
emulate Ma Lina, who produced 80 000 metres of cloth
without a defect. For her achievement she was promoted
from the position of a second-grade worker to a fifth-grade
worker.[31] Also there are '100 day contests' between individuals to produce one hundred days of work without
faults.[32] These drives and competitions are not necessarily

restricted to a single enterprise but may include a number of enterprises in the same city or province. In Harbin a competition was set up between the turners' groups in the city after workers at the city's rolling-stock factory challenged their counterparts in other factories in the city. Under the direction of the city trade-union headquarters, the 944 turners' groups were divided into 54 competition zones with results compared and appraised twice a year.[33]

Finally, trade unions are concerned with the well-being of their members. The extent to which the members' welfare can be promoted is limited. It is stressed that the economic backwardness of China means that the living standards of the workers can only be improved gradually on the basis of increases in production and labour productivity. Within these confines the unions lobby the enterprise leadership to build and improve the workers' housing, improve service at the canteens and to allocate funds for sanatoriums, nurseries, kindergartens and so on. In the social sphere the unions organise sports contests and other recreational activities, including cultural entertainment.

Collective enterprises

Apart from the state-run enterprises there are collectively owned enterprises in both the city and the countryside. At present such enterprises are actively encouraged. Unlike the large state-run enterprises they are small or medium-sized ventures, the means of production and the products of which belong to the collective's workers. The Gang of Four described these enterprises as the 'capitalist-tail' of industry and tried to limit the scope of their activities. Between 1966 and 1978 the wage scales for those in the collectively owned enterprises were lower than that of those in the state-owned enterprises, their supply of materials and fuel was not guaranteed, and many of the enterprises were taken over by the larger state-owned enterprises. Now they are considered an important part of China's economy. Table 9.1 shows the relative importance of these enterprises in the national economy, particularly in terms of employment. Future plans envisage an even greater role for these enterprises and the previous idea of

Table 9.1   *State and collective industrial output and*
                employment

Form of ownership	Total industrial output value (%)	Fixed assets of industrial enterprises(%)	No. and % of workers and staff
Owned by the whole people	80.7	91.8	30.4 million 71.5
Owned by the collectives	19.3	8.2	12.1 million 28.5

Source: Beijing Review, no. 6 (1980).

curtailing them has been criticised for running counter to
the objective economic laws. The low level of the productive forces in agriculture and in industry is now stressed, and
the collective enterprises are seen as providing an important
supplement to what the state can provide.[34] The state-
owned and the collectively owned economy are described
as the two legs on which China must move forward.[35] Positive
help is given to establish collective enterprises; for example,
in Beijing the municipal people's government helps them
market their products and helps with the supply of raw
materials. During the first two or three years of their existence no industry or commerce tax or income tax is collected.
Also aid is given by lower levels; for example, a Beijing neighbourhood committee lent a snack-bar enterprise 4000 yuan
to help get it off the ground.[36]

There are three main reasons for the current stress on the
importance of collective enterprises. First, they help with the
problem of unemployment, which will become more acute as
the process of agricultural modernisation progresses. During
1979 jobs were found for over 7 million who were unemployed
in the urban areas, most of these new jobs being in the collectively owned sector. Between 1980 and 1985 employment
will have to be found for an estimated 18.65 million school-
leavers.[37] Such a high number cannot be coped with by the
state sector. Although the state sector will expand, modernisation and increased efficiency will lead to the employment
of fewer people. Consequently, the burden of providing
employment will have to be carried by rapidly expanding

the collective enterprises. In Jiangsu province 82.7 per cent of the existing enterprises are collectively owned and, despite difficulties, between 1965 and 1977 collective enterprises provided 46 per cent of those looking for employment with jobs. In more recent years they have provided 70 to 80 per cent of the new employment.[38]

One major advantage of the collective enterprises is that they can provide these new jobs cheaply and will yield quick returns on any outlay. In the state sector it can cost more than 100 000 yuan to create a new job. Also, the variety of trades which are included in the collective enterprises means that they can take on a large, diverse workforce. Secondly, their size, the ease with which they can be set up and flexibility means that they can fill the gaps left in the economy by providing a diversity of goods not otherwise catered for. Unlike state enterprises they can have a more flexible approach to production, according to the demands of the market. In Beijing alone 1335 collectively owned enterprises exist covering a wide range of activities (see Table 9.2). Their importance in terms of output is demonstrated by the fact that in 1978 they provided 79 per cent of the total output (33 500 million yuan) of the second light industrial department.[39] The efficiency of these enterprises is ensured by

Table 9.2   Collective enterprises in Beijing

Number	Type of enterprise
636	Factories
352	Repair shops
134	Retail shops and snack-bars
95	Architectural repair teams
47	Cultural troupes and units
36	Transportation service teams
35	Others

Source: Beijing Review, no. 6 (1980).

their internal structure. Purely economic interests provide the motivation for the workers as they are rewarded directly in proportion to their efforts and expertise. The enterprises are responsible for their own profits and losses and thus the workers' welfare is directly related to the success or failure of the enterprise. The wages are roughly comparable to those in the state sector. For one enterprise the highest monthly income was 60 yuan while the lowest was 40 yuan, roughly equivalent to the wages of workers on the fourth and second grades in the state sector.[40] The efficiency of the enterprises has had an effect on the state-owned sector. In Beijing the early start and energetic work of the photographers' collective, taking pictures of the tourists in Tiananmen Square, forced the photographers employed by the state also to make an earlier start. Another example was reported where a collectively owned restaurant took away the trade from the nearby neighbouring, inefficient, state-owned restaurant, causing it to reduce its prices, improve the quality of food and adjust its business hours in accordance with the customers' needs.[41]

Thirdly, the development of these enterprises is seen as being crucial to the development of the small towns needed to soak up the displaced rural population. The obviously excessive cost rules out a dispersal of large-scale state-owned industries, which means that the build-up of smaller towns will occur primarily through the development of the collectively owned enterprises, by providing industry closer to the raw materials and its potential markets. An example of this proposed form of development is Weihai in the province of Shandong.[42] The city has a large potential workforce in the countryside for developing industry, but limited state investment is available. Thus the city has built a number of collectively owned industrial enterprises integrating industry with agriculture. At city level there are 83 industrial enterprises, of which 32 are state-owned and 51 collectively owned with a workforce of 6000 and 11 000 respectively. Expansion is achieved mainly by developing existing enterprises through a method known as 'hens laying eggs'. With this method new products are produced on a trial basis in specially designed workshops in an existing factory. If they prove successful the workshop is gradually expanded into a new factory.

Urban problems

One of the major urban problems has already been mentioned
– unemployment, particularly unemployment among the
young. In the seventies any visitor to China will have been
aware of the groups of young people 'hanging around' with
nothing to do, and this unemployment has been reflected in
the high instance of petty crime in the urban areas. This
problem will increase as the baby-boom of the early sixties
works its way through the system. There are three main
categories of young people seeking employment: first, there
are those who have just finished secondary school and who
have not been given a job assignment. Secondly, there are
those who initially were unable to work because of illness or
because they had to take care of sick relatives but who now
require work. Thirdly, and most problematically, there are
the educated youths who have returned from the countryside either legally or illegally. These are secondary school
graduates who were sent down, either permanently or temporarily, from the cities to settle in the countryside and to
engage in physical labour. This group has provided one of the
major focuses for social unrest in the urban areas. The role
of collective enterprises in providing employment has already
been mentioned, and of the 7 million people employed in
1979 nearly 50 per cent were employed in these collectively
owned enterprises. However, other proposals have also been
put forward to deal with the problem. In the textile industry
it is suggested that a four-shift, eight-hour work-system should
replace the present three-shift, eight-hour work-day, thus
providing more jobs. In the chemical industries, where
workers are in contact with poisonous or harmful substances,
a system is being experimented with under which workers
are given one to three months a year off to recuperate, study
or work in rotation in places without such substances.[43]

A second major problem is that of housing. Although 1979
saw an increase of 50 per cent in housing construction over
1978, the biggest annual increase since 1949,[44] the problem
of housing shortage remains. In the 192 big and medium-
sized cities and towns in 1978 *per capita* living floor space
only totalled 3.6 square metres (excluding kitchen, lavatory

and corridor floor space) and it is calculated that one-third of the inhabitants live in overcrowded conditions.[45] One of the major causes of this problem is that housing has just not kept up with population growth. While population in the 192 main cities has risen by 83 per cent since 1949 to 76.82 million, the total increase in housing floor space by 1978 was only 46.7 per cent (a total of 277.18 million square metres). This meant that floor space per person actually decreased by 0.9 square metre per person.[46] This problem has been exacerbated by the declining ratio of housing projects compared to factory buildings. During the First Five-Year Plan (1953–7) the ratio was set at 1.13:1, but as the construction of production premises increased the building of residential quarters and facilities did not expand at the same rate, and the ratio fell to 0.7:1.[47] The amount of state investment in urban housing construction constituted 9.1 per cent of the total investment for capital construction, but by the time of the Third Five-Year Plan (1966–70) it had dropped to 3.98 per cent,[48] further increasing the pressure on housing. To help solve this problem the building materials industry and new housing projects have been designated key sectors in the national economy. It was hoped in 1979 to raise 6000 million yuan from a variety of sources for housing construction. This would amount to 10 per cent of the total state investment in capital construction.[49] Also the amount of private housing is being expanded. Those with their own money are able to get supplies from the state to build their own houses. If the house is built on privately owned land it belongs to the individual but if it is built on public land the owner has to pay rent for the land.

The third major problem for the urban areas is environmental pollution. This problem is particularly acute in the large municipalities such as Beijing, Shanghai and Tianjin. A recent survey conducted in the south-eastern suburbs of Beijing revealed the extent of industrial pollution. Each year factories discharge a total of 180 000 tons of more than 40 kinds of gaseous waste; waste water was found to contain more than 50 000 tons of silt and more than 100 kinds of other waste. In winter the level of dust, carbon monoxide, sulphur dioxide and other toxic matters in the air was well above the state limits.[50] To help solve this type of problem stricter controls concerning the production process have been introduced. Any new industrial plants must meet designated pollution standards and existing factories which do not meet the requirements are instructed to solve the problem or move out of the city. As a result forty-two factories have moved or changed their production process while another thirty-five are to follow suit.[51] In September 1979 China adopted its first law on environmental protection, including provisions for the protection of wildlife and natural vegetation.[52] The major hindrance to the implementation of these measures, apart from technical knowledge, is financial constraint, because money for reducing pollution will have to be taken from funds which could otherwise be used for production.

10

Rural China

In spite of thirty years of rule by the Communist Party China has remained a predominantly agricultural country. Consequently the success of its agricultural policy will be the key to the success of the whole programme of the four modernisations. Approximately 800 million peasants live in 50 000 people's communes, but population concentration is very high, with about 90 per cent of the total population living in 40 per cent of the land area. The scale of the problems facing agriculture means that the state must make an enormous investment in agriculture to introduce modern machinery and to carry out large-scale agricultural capital construction. This is the objective but it is not economically feasible nor is it possible to rectify quickly the unequal exchange in value between industrial and agricultural products. This means that policies to achieve growth and raise living standards will still have to be based largely on making use of the large population and on development through incentive.

The Socialist Transformation of Agriculture

During the first decade of communist rule the Chinese countryside witnessed a massive transformation from individual farming to communisation. By the early sixties the basic organisation of the rural areas settled down. The communes functioned as a co-ordinating agency and administrative unit, the production brigades as the level of management and the production teams as the basic accounting unit. This has not meant that debate over rural policy has ended. Since the early sixties there has been a fluctuation in policy emphasis.

As with other areas of debate the problem has not been one of a battle between competing exclusive programmes but a question of how to balance the component parts of agricultural policy. The now criticised policies of the Gang of Four placed a greater emphasis on what may be termed the more 'radical' measures. The present leadership proposed a more cautious and 'conservative' approach to the problem of agricultural development. This section considers the transformation of agriculture and the next section the parameters of policy debate and the current agricultural practice.

The first step in the transformation of the relations of production in the Chinese countryside was land reform. As Chapter 1 shows, the CCP came to power with the support of the peasantry; an important reason for this support was the CCP's commitment to the land-reform programme. Experiments with land reform had been carried out in areas liberated before 1949.[1] Land reform was crucial in breaking up the traditional social order and power relationships in the countryside. The redistribution of land greatly increased support for the communists but the policy was not one developed in isolation by the CCP. The movement had considerable spontaneous support from peasants seeking to throw off landlords and exact revenge from those whom they saw as their exploiters. In February 1948 it was necessary for the Party to launch a rectification campaign for its over-zealous cadres. 'Leftist excesses', such as allowing landlords no land at all, were heavily criticised during the movement. The implementation of the land reform process was carried out by the peasants' associations set up to hold meetings, decide on redistribution and hand out punishments. Land reform had the advantage not only of breaking up the power of the landlords but also it forced an identity of interests between the peasantry and the Communist Party. This formed a bond very hard for others such as the GMD to break.

The fact that land reform was seen to be an integral part of the Party's policy helps explain why a cautious approach was taken to the question of collectivisation after 1949. The Party felt that it would not be possible to 'skip' this stage for fear of losing support. Also, during the years of reconstruction the Party sought to unify as much of the population as possible. This meant that they did not want to alienate the middle and rich peasants by introducing 'premature' collectivisation. Other factors also contributed to the cautious approach. The Soviet experience of forced collectivisation without the support of the peasantry showed what a disastrous effect it could have not only on regime popularity but also on agricultural output. Collectivisation of the small peasant economy needed a large number of technically and administratively competent cadres. These cadres could not be produced overnight, but had to be trained over a long period. As a result the policy approach adopted was one of caution and persuasion; any excesses came from the basic levels rather than because of directions from above.

The Agrarian Reform Law of 1950[2] brought the process of land reform closely under Party control in an attempt to restrain the spontaneous activities of the peasants. A fivefold categorisation based on property relations was drawn up to enable cadres to unravel the complexities of the rural Chinese life.[3] The law enabled land reform to remain based on the interests of the labourers and poor peasants while at the same time not alienating the middle and rich peasants. This was done to minimise the disruption of production. The category of middle peasant was the vaguest, but essentially a middle peasant was one who worked the land himself without engaging in exploitation. The land worked did not necessarily belong to the peasant. Landlords were to have their land confiscated or requisitioned for redistribution. However, the land of the rich and middle peasants, including those designated as prosperous middle peasants, was to be protected. The blow of being designated a landlord could be softened if the person had supported the revolution or if the person had a dual status. Further complication was introduced by the fact that it was possible for different members of the same family to be classified in different categories. The bulk of land reform was completed in the eighteen months after the 1950 autumn harvest. Seven hundred million mu of land was redistributed among approximately 300 million peasants, giving them between 2 and 3 mu each on average.[4] However, there was considerable variation from region to region, and minority areas and Xizang (Tibet) did not undergo land reform at all. Production on such a small scale brought obvious problems. The landholdings were too small to be really profitable and there were too few farm implements to go round. Such small units made it impossible to make rational use of the land, to popularise new farming techniques effectively and to carry out large-scale capital construction projects.

These problems prompted the need to reorganise Chinese agriculture into larger units. For agriculture to feed the industrialisation programme satisfactorily a huge financial investment would have been necessary, but obviously this was impossible. The emphasis on the development of heavy industry meant that little capital was available for investment in agriculture. So it became imperative for agriculture to be more efficient — but this had to be done without increasing spending. The solution was to co-operativise agriculture. This process began slowly at first in 1952 with the formation of mutual-aid teams, but gradually gathered pace until the communisation programme was embarked upon. The first stage in this transformation consolidated and promoted the traditional forms of co-operation. This took the form of creating mutual-aid teams; about five to eight households combined for work in particular seasons and up to twenty households co-operated on a year round basis. Through 1953—4 the process was intensified and in 1954 it was basically completed. Animals, tools and the redistributed land remained in private hands but labour was pooled. After the mutual-aid teams were set up Party policy moved on to encourage the formation of lower-stage agricultural producers' co-operatives (APCs). These grew out of experiments with the co-operatives created in certain areas, normally those areas which had been liberated early. They were voluntary associations of roughly thirty households and introduced the idea of pooling not only labour, but also property, land, farm implements and draft animals. The co-operative was run as a unit. The peasants received their income in relation to their stake in the enterprise, that is, in proportion to the size of the shares of property they had originally invested. In January 1954 a directive was issued concerning their development. By the end of that year, as Schurmann has calculated, there were 114 165 such APCs.[5]

The following year was a crucial one for the transformation of the countryside because the question of whether mechanisation should precede social transformation or vice versa came to the fore. Mao Zedong argued that given the country's conditions it was imperative to first of all co-operativise and than mechanise. The small size of peasant holdings meant that it would be impossible to mechanise without increasing the size of the working unit. His opponents argued that mechanisation had to precede co-operativisation if it was to work, because the peasants would lack both the organisational and technical skills to run the collectivised agriculture. Mao argued that when agriculture was collectivised the peasants would be able to accumulate the capital required to purchase agricultural machinery. His opponents put an alternative view that the amount of machinery necessary could only be supplied at low cost by industry over a long period of time. Initially Mao was held in check and in March 1955 the process of transformation was slowed. The First Five-Year Plan (27 July 1955) set a target of one-third of all households to be organised into co-operatives by the end of 1957. At this juncture Mao decided to intervene personally in the political process and in his speech 'On the Question of Co-operativisation of Agriculture' (31 July 1955) he called for a rapid increase in the speed of co-operativisation.[6] His speech fixed a target of one-half of all households to be co-operativised by the end of 1957. In practice the speed of transition was even quicker, with the formation of lower-stage APCs completed by the end of 1955. By the end of 1956 higher-stage APCs had been set up across the country. This basic policy of collectivisation preceding mechanisation is still supported but the speed of transformation is criticised, a criticism which is even stronger for the following programme of communisation. Xue Muqiao said that after co-operativisation was completed, 'everybody got overexcited'.[7] Despite the fact that co-operativisation was only completed in 1957, by 1958 several provinces had already started setting up communes. Indeed, the programme of communisation was completed in half a year and Xue criticises this transformation as not resembling the 'typical model of co-operativisation that is spreading step-by-step'.[8] The speed of its introduction meant that it was carried out by relying on 'commandist' methods rather than persuasion.

The higher-stage APCs were much larger in size than the lower-level APCs and contained between 100 and 300 households depending on the terrain of the particular area. The method of income distribution was also altered and one's income was no longer decided on the basis of one's original share but on the basis of work-points.

The next stage in the process of transformation was the creation of the people's commune during the Great Leap Forward. In early August, following his visit to the newly formed commune in Hunan, Mao promoted the creation of communes throughout the country. This was endorsed by the enlarged meeting of the Politburo which met in the latter half of August at the summer resort of Beidaihe. Once the decision had been made the process of communisation moved swiftly, and by 1959 the 750 000 higher-stage APCs had been amalgamated into just 24 000 people's communes. The small number of communes meant that some of them were an impractical size. Below the level of the commune was the production brigade, equivalent to the higher-stage APCs, and below this was the production team, equivalent ot the lower-stage APCs. The communes not only carried out agricultural work but were also responsible for industrial work, trade, education, military affairs, health, village administration and social welfare. Many areas used the commune to unify their accounting and allocation units. Some counties (xian) went even further and organised the 'xian federation of communes' (xian lianshe) and the whole county unified allocation. Communal living was organised and dormitories and mess-halls set up to increase the available productive labour. Work was to become more like work in the cities, with payment of wages replacing the accumulation of work-points. Also, the individual peasant's relationship to his place of work was broken up.

The speed of transition quickly led to serious problems. The size of the communes made them unwieldy units. The speed of the changes meant that there was a shortage of skilled administrators because no one had had any experience of organising units of such a size. Peasant resentment increased as they were moved away from their homes and into the dormitories. The relatively smooth transition prior to communisation had led to an atmosphere of optimism, causing a great miscalculation in the potential of the national economy. This miscalculation led to the setting of over-ambitious targets. The disastrous effect on production might not have been so severe had it not been accompanied by three years of extremely bad weather.

At the end of 1958 the Sixth plenum of the Eighth CC was held in Wuchang and it made an attempt to moderate the 'leftist' excesses by slackening the pace of communisation. In February 1959 the meeting in Zhengzhou criticised the 'communist wind' and advocated that communes should practise the 'three-level system of ownership, the three-level system of management, the three-level system of accounting with the team as the basic accounting unit'. Prior to this the unit in the countryside responsible for decision-making had been consistently raised (from mutual-aid team to commune). Now it was to be moved back down again. This was completed in two stages. First, from spring 1959 the brigade was made the basic unit of account with it owning and controlling most of the means of production. Practice showed that the brigade was still too large a unit and from 1961 the team was made the basic accounting unit and was given ownership and control of most of the means of production. The commune remained as the basic administrative level. In 1962 the number of communes was increased from 24 000 to 74 000, making them into more manageable units. The communal experiments in living were terminated, the use of material incentives allowed and private plots restored.

In September 1962 the 'Regulations on the Work in the Rural People's Communes' (the 60 Articles) were published. These laid down the basic organisation for the countryside and this has remained virtually unchanged since. The regulations stipulated that the system of 'three levels of ownership with the production team as the basic accounting unit' was to be adopted. Also, it was stated that this should not change for thirty years. The production teams were made smaller so as to include only thirty or forty households. The regulations clearly stressed the principles of 'from each according to his ability, to each according to his work', 'more pay for more work' and 'one who does not work, neither shall he eat'. The commune operates as the basic level of local government, procuring grain, collecting taxes, providing public security and channelling information to the higher levels. In addition it draws up the precise production plans for the commune in accordance with the state plan, supervises large-scale capital construction projects and manages the small-scale industry on the commune.[9] Below the commune is the production brigade and this oversees the work of the production teams and provides the link from the team to the communes. The production teams are the most important unit in the commune because they can make the final decisions concerning both the production of goods and the distribution of income according to the work-points accumulated.

Current agricultural policy

Before looking at current agricultural policy in detail it is worth highlighting the major areas of debate in the sphere of agriculture. The first major area of debate is dealt with in the preceding section and concerns the general question of the relationship between technical transformation and social transformation. The second area of debate concerns the amount of sideline production the peasant may engage in outside of the collective. The focus of this debate has been on what constitutes legitimate sideline production and what constitutes 'spontaneous capitalist tendencies'. The policies of the Gang of Four were not designed to eliminate sideline production altogether but to contain it. This was to ensure that the peasants did not attach greater importance to individual rather than collective production. While present policy still stresses the prime importance of the collective, a much greater role is given to the initiative of the individual peasant. Thirdly, there has been discussion over the correct level for the accounting unit in the countryside. For the vast majority of communes the basic accounting unit is the production team, but the eventual objective is to raise the level. The Gang of Four are accused of having prematurely attempted to raise the level of accounting from the team to the brigade before the objective economic conditions would permit. It is said that these attempts caused both production and the income at team level to suffer. Finally, there has been debate about the permissible level of inequality in the countryside. Chapter 8 shows that there is a considerable variation between incomes. There have been differences of opinion about whether such variation should be held in check, narrowed or allowed to increase.

In addition to the other important decisions, the Third plenum of the Eleventh CC (December 1978) decided that when shifting the main emphasis of the Party's work to socialist modernisation it should concentrate its main efforts on promoting agricultural development. The main priority of the four modernisations is agriculture and this was reaffirmed in June 1980 by Yu Qiuli. He stated that 'Only if and when its [China's] farming problems are resolved can obstacles in the modernisation of industry, science and technology and national defence be reduced'. To facilitate this, the low level of investment in agriculture is to be raised and an 'expert' leadership trained. However, despite this pledge only 14 per cent of the total state funds for investment went to agriculture in 1979, while investment in heavy industry exceeded 46 per cent.[10]

The Third plenum distributed two important documents for discussion — 'The Decision on Some Questions Concerning the Acceleration of Agricultural Development' and 'The Regulations on the Work in Rural People's Communes' (draft for trial use).[11] The former summed up previous experiences and put forward twenty-five measures designed to improve the rural situation. This document refers to the 'twists and turns' of previous policy and acknowledges that development has barely kept up with population growth. The years up until 1957 were the years of best growth, with an average annual increase of 7 per cent in the output of grain. According to the document, between 1957 and 1978, while population increased by 300 million, the area of land for cultivation diminished. In 1978 the average *per capita* grain ration was the same as that in 1957. The collective property of an average production brigade was valued at an average of less than

10 000 yuan. It was acknowledged that in some places this amount was not even enough for simple reproduction.[12] The Regulations on Work stipulated that the state's laws should protect the right of ownership of the people's communes, brigades and teams and their power of decision. Also the use of private plots, sideline production and rural gains was assured. This document was not endorsed by the Fourth plenum of the Eleventh CC (September 1979), indicating that some differences still exist concerning its stipulations. One possible point of contention is the statement in Article 1 that 'a rural people's commune is an organisation merging government administration with commune management'.[13] The success of this merger has been questioned in the Chinese press. In December 1979 an article in the *Guangming Daily* concluded that experience had shown that the combination of government administration with commune management had more drawbacks than it had advantages.[14] The article commented that this practice overlooks the actual condition of the development of China's productive forces and leads people to 'rattle on in an abstract way about the advantages of ownership by the whole people and exaggerates the restrictive nature of collective ownership'. The article criticises the fact that commune cadres are on the state payroll and consequently are not immediately concerned about or affected by the economic interests arising from the proper management of the communes. Instead it is said that the cadres are more concerned about the implementation of the administrative orders of their superiors. It does not, however, seem likely that government administration and commune management will be divided. Such a division would only mean that at some future time the two would have to be merged again.

The gist of the proposed policy measures was outlined in the *People's Daily*. Five major rules were to be observed when implementing policies: (1) the right to self-determination by the people's communes and their subdivisions must be respected; (2) systems of responsibility in production must be established and the principle of each according his work must be abided by; (3) initiative in family sideline production, farming and private plots must be encouraged; (4) rural fairs must be allowed; and (5) the state purchasing

prices of agricultural and subsidiary products must be raised.[15]
The package of policies offered resembles that put forward
in 1962 under the slogan 'three freedoms and one guarantee'.
Consequently, they represent a substantial shift away from
the 'radical' end of the spectrum. Present policy relies on the
use of material incentives to regenerate the rural economy.
The use of incentives and their resultant inequalities are seen
as the way to improve the peasants' productivity. It is proposed that some peasants and areas should be allowed to
become better off first. The possibility that such a policy
may lead to resentment and polarisation is dismissed. It is
envisaged that poor areas, brigades, and so on will catch up
with the more advanced by a mixture of aid and their own
efforts. The more advanced areas once caught will be 'encouraged' to move further ahead — 'thus through emulation, all
will advance along the socialist road towards common pros-
perity and the difference between them will be reduced step
by step'.[16]

There is an emphasis on agricultural specialisation and
diversification. Key bases have been set up using the most
advanced machinery and equipment for grain production,
cash crop production, livestock rearing, and so forth. The
objective is to turn these bases into 'giant, modern agricultural
enterprises with high labour productivity and marketability'.[17]
Initially experiments were carried out designed to bring
about a marked increase in production and a rapid rise in
the peasants' income in areas comprising one-fifth of the
population. This policy is very similar to that of the 'green
revolution' tried in many developing countries. Basically,
heaviest investment is put into those areas capable of producing the speediest returns. The previous over-emphasis on
grain production is used as justification for the emphasis on
specialisation and diversification (see Table 10.1). The
emphasis on grain production is seen as a legacy of China's
traditional grain-oriented, small-peasant economy. The use of
the slogan 'take grain as the key link' has been criticised. It is
claimed that the emphasis on grain production has had a
disastrous effect on areas forced to grow grain in unsuitable
conditions. For example, soya bean production was forced to
give way to maize and pastures were 'ruthlessly ploughed up

Table 10.1   *China's agricultural components*

Total agricultural output value in 1978: 145 900 million yuan.

Component	Percentage of total
Crops	67.8
Forestry	3.0
Animal husbandry	13.2
Sideline occupation[a]	14.6
Fishery	1.4

[a] Includes 11.7 per cent from the output value of brigade-run small industries, but excludes the output value of commune-run industries.

Source: *Beijing Review*, no. 4 (1980), p. 20.

to grow grain so that the number of livestock was reduced'.[18] However, the abandonment of this policy might increase rural inequality because areas with good arable land can now concentrate on producing high-return cash-crops rather than engaging in grain production for self-sufficiency. This problem has been recognised by the leadership and explains the large increases announced for grain procurement prices. The increases were intended to prevent a wholesale rush away from grain production to more lucrative products. In accordance with the Decision on Agricultural Development, the purchase price for grain was put up by 20 per cent when the summer harvest was put on the market. An extra 50 per cent was paid for any surplus grain marketed. These prices were not passed on to the consumer. This decision is in accordance with calls for using economic methods to manage the economy rather than administrative ones.

To help promote diversification the ownership rights and decision-making powers of the agricultural units have been re-emphasised. The ownership rights of the people's communes, production brigades and teams are to be protected by state laws. As long as they operate within the guidance of the state plan all basic accounting units can cultivate whatever they like, decide on their own methods of management and

distribute their own products and income. According to Xue
Muqiao, in the past many production teams were deprived of
their initiative by the enforcement of regulations about what
to plant where, the method of planting and the frequency
of multiple cropping. In his view many counties had only
'one head' of the production team (the county Party committee secretary)'.[19] The use of the workforce and materials of
the production team by the higher levels is criticised. On
occasions brigades, communes and government departments
have used the workforce, materials and land of teams, without
providing compensation, to build roads, water conservancy
projects, factories, and so on. Between 1966 and 1976 total
agricultural income in the county of Wuxian, a high-yield
area, increased by 12 million yuan but expenses rose by 24
million yuan. Average individual income in 14 of the county's
37 communes was lower than in 1966.[20] The main cause of
this state of affairs is said to be the unpaid use of the production team's workforce. An account of the situation in Jinshan
commune stated that the commune owed its teams 73 000
yuan for work on a canal project, 110 000 yuan for money
borrowed for industrial enterprises and compensation for
requisitioned land, and 10 000 yuan compensation for peasants' houses occupied by the commune's afforestation farm.
This total debt of 193 000 yuan meant a 950-yuan burden
for each team in the commune.[21] The position of the production team as the basic accounting unit has been reaffirmed.
The Gang of Four are criticised for promoting a 'premature'
raising of the level of account, a form of transition dubbed
by the present leadership as 'transition in poverty' (qiong
guodu). The present stress should not lead one to think that
this means an end to raising the level of account. For some
areas the advantages to be gained from greater mechanisation
will prompt the raising of the level of account. However, the
desire to raise the level is now rarely referred to publicly and
any transition which does take place is to be one predicated
on wealth.

Apart from the greater power of initiatives and freedoms
given to the collective they have also been given to the individual. The relationship between individual production
and that of the collective has provided one of the most

acute debates in rural policy. The redistributed 'Regulations on the Work in Rural People's Communes' make it
clear that domestic sideline occupations are a necessary
supplement to the socialist economy. As long as it does not
detract from the collective, communes are to encourage their
members to 'avail themselves of their leisure time and holidays
to develop domestic sideline-occupations, increase the output
of society, augment the members' income and enliven the
rural markets'.[22] The term 'domestic sideline occupation'
includes a variety of activities within it: the cultivation of
private plots[23] allocated by the collective; the use of a fodder
plot[24] for pig-rearing; the raising of sheep, rabbits, chickens,
ducks, geese, cattle and horses; domestic handicraft production such as knitwear, sewing, embroidery; side occupations
such as gathering, fishing, hunting, sericulture, apiculture;
and the management of private trees and bamboo. Despite
assurances of protection of these rights, policy with regard
to private plots, sideline production and rural markets has
varied over time. The official attitude towards them has often
been ambiguous and at times hostile. Their existence as a
necessary extra to the collective was recognised, but at the
same time so was the potential disruption of the collective
by them. From the start of the Cultural Revolution they were
regarded suspiciously as the 'tails of capitalism'. There is
ample evidence to show that particularly at times when
'leftist' ideas held sway cadres in some areas eliminated them
altogether. In other areas strict limits were put on the
amount of time the peasant could spend working on the
private plot and how much income could be derived from it.
For example, a quarter of the production teams in Baoan
commune in Wuxian county stopped their members raising
chickens and the Lingyan production brigade in the same
county limited each household to growing only fifteen
cabbages on its private plot.[25] The notion that these activities
represent capitalist tendencies and are harmful to the collective is now refuted. Past practice is criticised because the
inability to consolidate socialist relations of production was
put down to the continued existence of classes and the two-
line struggle. This analysis meant that the methods of class
struggle, large-scale criticism of capitalism and 'cutting off

the capitalist tail' were necessary. These large-scale movements are now seen as unnecessary and as actually sabotaging the productive process.

Current practice is to adopt measures favourable to the private sector. This is combined with criticism of measures curtailing private initiative. The agricultural model of Dazhai has been criticised for this practice because of its adoption of policies to 'block the capitalist road'. While the collective is to remain the main source of income for the peasantry, earnings from sideline occupations can make up a sizeable supplement. For example, in 1979 one family in south China got 1700 yuan from the collective and another 1000 yuan from their sideline occupations.[26] It is apparent that this relaxation of policy has led to calls for greater independence for the peasants from the collective. In some areas peasants sought to reduce the size of teams and called for the fixing of production quotas based on individual households. This tendency has been criticised as a breach of Party policy because it 'turns the collective economy into an individual economy' and does not accord with the production responsibility system practised in the collective economy.[27] In some areas, although quotas have not been based on the household, they have been based on small work groups within the production team. Such a system of work allocation and reward distribution is bad for popularising new technology, developing brigade and commune enterprises, organising welfare undertakings and carrying out agricultural capital construction.

To facilitate the sale and exchange of the privately produced goods rural fairs are encouraged. Apart from providing a medium of exchange they give the consumers a greater variety of goods to buy and foodstuffs to supplement their diet. Products marketed at the fairs are subjected to restrictions by the state. Generally any goods normally procured by the state are banned from being sold in the markets. This revival of the rural markets has helped ease the problems of speculation and black-market dealings. Such problems tend to increase during periods of tighter controls. By the end of 1978 it was estimated that there were 33 000 rural fairs throughout the country. In early 1979 a national conference of directors of industrial and commercial administrations in Beijing reaffirmed their 'positive role' in stimulating the rural economy, improving the peasants' life and promoting farm production and sideline occupations in the country-side.[28] Their revived role was borne out by the findings of a survey of 206 markets. The survey showed that total sales in the last quarter of 1978 went up 30 per cent compared with the corresponding period of 1977.[29] Prices in the markets are higher than those in the state retail outlets but there is evidence of the prices coming down. The survey showed that the price of grain, edible oil, pork, eggs, vegetables, etc., fell by 7.3 per cent. Another survey showed a 6.5 per cent drop in prices (in the same period of comparison) and that some goods were actually cheaper than the state fixed prices.[30] In the cities peasant markets are permitted. In Beijing by November 1979 there were about 1500 stalls selling over 80 kinds of farm produce. Total transactions between March and August 1979 came to over 2 million yuan. This represented 0.133 per cent of the city's total retail trade during this period.[31] These markets help ensure the inter-flow of goods between city and countryside and enable more of the non-staple goods to be supplied to the city. As with private plots and sideline occupations there is recognition of continuing problems. The revival of rural markets could lead to over-concentration on the private sector. *Beijing Review* acknowledges that the markets, if allowed to get out of control, are 'liable to become hotbeds for capitalist tendencies and may even upset the planned socialist market'.[32] Local rural cadres are given the difficult task of striking a balance that will stimulate production but, at the same time, will not let private production get out of hand. Past practice has shown that it is usual to lean more to one side than to remain in the middle.

Collectively owned enterprises

The programme of local industry was launched in 1958 as a part of the Great Leap Forward and although its fortunes have fluctuated since, it has continued to play an important part in commune life. At the end of 1979 there were more than 1.5 million enterprises in the Chinese countryside run by communes or brigades with a workforce of 28 million.[33] Their importance to the rural economy is show by the fact that this means there is an average of 30 such enterprises per commune. Their total annual output value amounts to nearly one-third of the commune income.[34] The Qianzhou commune of Wuxi county in Jiangsu province has 80 small commune- and brigade-run enterprises with an output value in 1978 of 25 million yuan and a net profit of 6 million yuan (see Table 10.2).

The range of these kinds of enterprises is wide. They range from small-scale coal or ore mining to chemical fertiliser production to production of goods for export (for instance, embroidery, lacquer ware). The enterprises are owned collectively and are financed predominantly by the commune or the brigade. The state will, if required, provide low-interest loans through the agricultural bank. The labour force in the enterprises is drawn from the commune or brigade running the enterprise. During the busy season for agriculture these workers return to work on the land. Depending on the requirements of the industry a number of technicians may also be employed. The lack of these skilled workers is one of the major problems facing the collective enterprises. Articles at the end of 1979 and early 1980 considered the problem of how the commune- and brigade-run enterprises could best be made to serve the interests of the production teams.[35] It was suggested that in the end-of-year allocation these enterprises should assign part of their profit to be distributed to the teams in proportion to the teams' inputs of investment, labour, land and materials. This would strengthen the team's collective economy and boost the peasants' incomes. Also, it was suggested that shares be bought with collective investment. Profits from this would then be divided up to create enterprises run jointly by a number of production teams.

During the Great Leap Forward when this programme was launched both economic arguments and ideological arguments were put forward to justify it. Currently the economic advantages to the countryside are stressed and seen as the more important. The benefit to income is mentioned above but also they provide advantages for the process of mechanisation.

Table 10.2   Output value for Qianzhou commune

Year	Grain (per mu) output	Total agricult. output value	Total output value of sideline prod.	Total indust. output value	Per capita income from the collective
	kg.	yuan	yuan	yuan	yuan
1952	145	1 805 000	356 000		
1957	155	2 180 000	430 000		42
1970	450	3 760 000	925 000	1 530 000	75
1979	835	5 500 000	5 450 000	36 000 000	165

Source: Beijing Review, no. 15 (1980), p. 19.

Not only can the enterprises help provide the majority of the required medium- and small-sized machinery but also they will be able to soak up the population displaced by the increase in mechanisation. Another advantage of these small-scale industries is that they can make use of scattered raw materials. Finally, they can help ensure the availability of consumer goods for the countryside. The main ideological argument advanced is that the development of these industries will help to overcome the 'three differences' — those between industry and agriculture, mental and manual labour, city and countryside. The expansion of these industries would involve more peasants with higher technological knowledge working in industry rather than on the land. Gradually the amenities and facilities available in the city could be extended to the countryside.

State farms

In the PRC, apart from the collectively owned communes, there are 2048 state farms owned by the whole people with 4.8 million workers working 4.33 million hectares of land.[36] Unlike peasants in the communes, the workers on the state farms receive wages complete with a bonus system. The farms operate under the provincial level reclamation bureaux. The farms are situated in the border and hilly regions, beside the sea or on marshland and wasteland. They are larger and more mechanised than the communes. In 1979 402 of the state farms were commended as advanced units most of which were grain-producing. On average each worker turned out over 10 tons of grain a year, of which over 50 per cent was marketable.[37] Also cotton, oil, rubber and a variety of cash-crops are produced for the market. Since 1978 these farms have again become profitable following the reintroduction of economic accounting and a system of business management similar to that in state-owned factories. Between 1966 and 1976 these farms made a loss of 3500 million yuan and it was not until 1979 that they again recorded a profit — 300 million yuan.

11

Epilogue

As China entered 1981 it was clear that the trends outlined at the end of chapter 3 had continued. There had been a further erosion of the policies, and power, of those associated with the Cultural Revolution. In particular, it became clear that Hua Guofeng's period as one of China's top leaders was coming to an end. The Third Session of the Fifth National People's Congress (August–September 1980) confirmed that Hua Guofeng would give up his post of Premier to Zhao Ziyang.[1] In part this represented the culmination of the general trend to ensure that leading Party and state posts were not held by the same person. This reason was acknowledged by Hua himself. When announcing his resignation he stated that the division of posts was to prevent 'over concentration of power and the holding of too many posts concurrently by one person' and is aimed at 'effectively and clearly separating Party work from government work'.[2] However, in Hua's case, it also represented a part of his removal from top positions of power. Hua's attempts to promote 'maoism without Mao' which had seemed to be an acceptable compromise in the first couple years after Mao's death were now seen to be increasingly anachronistic. As criticism of Mao moved further back in time, the portrayal of Hua as Mao's faithful follower since collectivisation in the mid–fifties became damaging. Also, in the present climate the manner in which Hua assumed the post of Chairman is unacceptable. His claim to legitimacy rests on the words allegedly written by Mao – 'With you in charge, I am at ease'. This can too readily be portrayed as the Emperor passing on the 'Mandate of Heaven' to his chosen successor – a portrayal not helped by Hua's deliberate attempts to cultivate a personality cult on assuming power. It is possible that Hua could have weathered these storms had it not been for his role in the supression of the Tiananmen Incident in April 1976. At this time Hua was Minister of Public Security and as such was responsible for the Incident's suppression. The 'reversal of verdicts' concerning the Incident did not augur well for Hua and it would appear that during the trial of the Gang of Four his position with respect to this, and the movement to criticise Deng Xiaoping was irretrievably compromised. On 27 Norverber 1980 Hua made his last public appearance and at the CCP's New Year Party it was the General Secretary Hu Yaobang, not Hua who made the important speech. Hua's name did not even appear on the guest list.

Under the jurisdiction of a special court of the Supreme People's Court the trial and sentencing of the 'Lin Biao and Jiang Qing cliques' was carried out between 20 November 1980 and 25 January 1981.[3] In total ten people were put on trial in two groups: those military leaders associated with Lin Biao, and the Gang of Four and Mao's former secretary Chen Boda. The delay between the final hearing on 29 December and the pronouncement of sentence indicates that the final document was the subject of some debate. Its historical im portance as a chronicle of what 'crimes' were committed during the years 1966—76 and the leadership's fear that Jiang Qing may become a martyr, if sentenced to death, were presumably the foci of discussion. In the end the question of what to do with Jaing Qing was avoided when she was given the death sentence with a two-year reprieve. Four major charges were brought against the defendent containing a total of forty-eight specific offences.[4] The trial revealed a great deal of new information, including details of a plot to assassinate Mao in September 1971, and formally charged that there was a concious link between the activities of Lin Biao and Jiang Qing. The prosecution claimed that after Lin's demise Jiang had 'gathered the remnants of this [Lin's] clique and continued to carry on counter-revolutionary activities'.[5] The prosecution continued 'if it is said that there were subsequent contradictions within the Lin Biao and Jiang Qing counter-revolutionary cliques, this only shows that they were jackals of the same lair in stealing, but contradictions arose when they divided the spoils'.[6] Earlier in the proceedings Jiang had denied collaborating with Lin Biao, claiming that she had fought against him.

Despite the fact that some of the defendents were found innocent of some of the charges the trial was unsatisfactory when viewed solely in terms of an advertisement for China's new legal system. However, the trial had a number of other important implications. It had educative value and provided those persecuted during the Cultural Revolution with a form of retribution. Also, it seems probable that it was intended to mark the end of an era, hence the importance of the judgement as an historical document. Important repercussions were felt in the political sphere. Apart from the implication of Hua, inevitably the name of Mao Zedong was drawn into the proceedings. It appears that the substance of Jiang Qing's defence was based on the claim that she had acted on Mao's behalf. This claim was rejected by the Chinese press and leaders. While it was acknowledged that Mao had made mistakes it was stated that these mistakes were 'entirely different in nature from the crimes of the gang'.[7] This distinction between 'crimes' and 'mistakes' helps distance Mao, and other leaders, from some of the events of the Cultural Revolution but is not entirely satisfactory. For example, the 'slander' of Liu Shaoqi by those on trial was considered a crime while the fact that the Party Central Committee had passed a resolution denouncing Liu as a 'renegade and traitor' was considered a mistake.

Explosions in Shanghai and some other cities between the end of the trial and the pronouncement of sentence has shown that there are still some supporters of the Gang of Four willing to actively support them. Early in 1981 the Chinese press contained numerous articles stating that the main task was to promote stability and unity in order to ensure that the programme of economic readjustment is carried out successfully.[8] However, a number of factors, apart from the existence of elements supporting the Gang of Four, suggest the possibility of potential future conflict. One important group which could provide a problem are those who, while not necessarily supporting the Gang of Four or their policies, owe their official positions to their advancement during the Cultural Revolution decade. These people would be opposed to a continued criticism of the past. For example, the 18 million Party members who joined during the years 1966—76 would be unwilling to see a reduction of their chances for advancement which a large scale purge or rectification movement in the Party would bring about. Despite the appeal for unity, past experience has shown that once a movement gains momentum it is very hard to stop it. Deng Xiaoping has made several calls for consolidation and unity but there may be others in the leadership whose 'thirst for revenge' is not yet satisfied and may eventually pressure Deng. Indeed the view of the present conflict as a two-way fight between Hua and Deng is too simplistic. Deng's own record is not blemish free: in the mid—fifties he supported Mao against Chen Yun and Xue Muqiao during the debates over decentralisation; in 1957 he supported the now criticised 'anti-rightist campaign'; the now derided post-Mao economic policies owe as much to Deng as they do to Hua,[9] and his reputation was damaged as a result of the miscalculations concerning the Sino-Vietnamese conflict.

Towards the end of 1980 an article in *Red Flag* dealing with work-style criticised not only the years 1966—76 but also the years from Liberation until the Cultural Revolution. The article criticised 'nostalgic people' who 'show their bias by their special feelings for the seventeen years preceeding the "great cultural revolution" '. The article continues:

the 'great cultural revolution' was not a sudden occurrence. If we look at the great catastrophe in those ten years, we will notice that many errors already germinated before the 'great cultural revolution'. A qualitative leap forward only happens after a gradual quantitative accumulation. The 'great cultural revolution', a grave overall error which brought great disaster to the people, was only the continuation and development of seventeen years of errors. . .. If we are contented with merely liberating our minds from the ten years of catastrophe, yet dare not liberate ourselves from the errors of the preceeding seventeen years, our minds will still be ossified.[10]

Finally, the attempts to loosen the grip of the Party over state and society could also lead to problems. As the experience of Poland has shown once concessions have been granted it is very difficult to call a halt. According to Reuters, a Chinese provincial newspaper has written that workers and students in central China have been trying to set up independent trade unions.[11] The paper, acknowledging that the Party had made serious mistakes in the past thirty years, stated that these people had not acted out of ulterior motives but because they represented the ultimate in ignorance. It remains to be seen whether the Party can find the maintain the right balance to ensure continued central control while at the same time allowing the necessary flexibility to promote initiative.

January 1981   A. J. S.

References

Chapter 1

1. See E. Balazs, *Chinese Civilisation and Bureaucracy* (Yale University Press, 1977), and M. Elvin, *The Pattern of the Chinese Past* (Eyre Methuen, 1973).
2. Ho Ping-ti, *Studies on the Population of China* (Harvard University Press, 1959), p. 270.
3. Hsiao Kung-chuan, *Rural China* (University of Washington Press, 1960), p. 380.
4. J. Levenson, *Confucian China and its Modern Fate* (University of California Press, 1965).
5. B. Schwartz, *In Search of Wealth and Power, Yen Fu and the West* (Harvard University Press, 1964), p. 42.
6. See B. Schwartz, *In Search of Wealth and Power*.
7. Contrary to the practice employed elsewhere in the book I have not adopted the Pinyin romanisation of Sun Yat-sen's name, Sun Zhongshan, because of the widespread usage of the other form. The Alliance Society was the precursor of the Guomindang. The Guomindang deliberately traced its history to the revolutionaries who had fought to overthrow the dynasty. In so doing it attributed a far greater role to Sun and the Alliance Society in overthrowing the emperor than had actually been the case.
8. Following China's defeat in the Sino-Japanese War (1894–5) Yuan Shikai was given the task of organising an army along Western lines. Yuan created the Beiyang Army and it became China's most modern and efficient fighting force. After the October 1911 uprising Yuan was summoned to lead the Beiyang Army to put down the rebels. However, Yuan delayed and demanded almost full powers to handle the situation while, at the same time, negotiating with the revolutionaries. The revolutionaries offered Yuan the Presidency of the Republic if he would renounce his allegiance to the dynasty. In February 1912 the Qing dynasty published a decree of abdication, and a month later Yuan assumed the Presidency.
9. See M. Meisner, *Li Ta-chao and the Origins of Chinese Marxism* (Harvard University Press, 1967).

10. J. Chesneaux, F. Le Barbier and M.-C. Bergère, *China from the 1911 Revolution to Liberation* (Harvester Press, 1977), p. 86.

11. Maring, alias H. Sneevliet, was a Dutchman who was a minor Comintern functionary. Maring was the Comintern delegate to the CCP's first Party Congress. Before this he had worked with the communists in the Dutch Indies and had taught them how to operate the united front policy. It was Maring who ordered the actual entry of the Communists into the Guomindang.

12. L. Eastman, *The Abortive Revolution* (Harvard University Press, 1974), pp. 7–8.

13. Ibid., p. 8

14. Ibid., p. 40

15. G. Alitto, 'Rural Reconstruction During the Nanking Decade: Confucian Collectivism in Shantung' in *China Quarterly (CQ)*, no. 66 (June 1976), p. 213.

16. Peng Pai had already established a base area in Guangdong province at Haifeng and Lufeng. The base area was crushed by the GMD early in 1928.

17. Li Lisan gained effective control of the Party at the Sixth Congress. Prior to this power had been in the hands of Qu Qiubai, who was blamed for the failure of the policy of 'continuous uprisings' at the end of 1927. Qu had replaced Chen Duxiu, who was blamed for the failure of the united front policy because of his programme of capitulation.

18. See Mao Zedong, 'Report on an Investigation of the Peasant Movement in Hunan' in *Selected Works* (Beijing: Foreign Languages Press, 1966), vol. 1, pp. 23–58.

19. See G. Benton, 'The Second Wang Ming Line' in *CQ*, no. 61 (March 1975), pp. 61–94.

20. Zhang Xueliang was the commander of the North-eastern Army that was sent to crush the communists at the end of 1935. Yang Hucheng was a former warlord in the north-west who, at this time, was the pacification commissioner for Shaanxi.

21. These were the principles of Sun Yat-sen put forward in his book *The Three Principles of the People*. They were the principle of Nationalism, the principle of People's Democrary and the principle of the People's Livelihood.

22. Yanan is situated in the province of Shaanxi in the north-west of China.

23. See Mao's lecture, 'Reform in Learning, the Party, and Literature' in Boyd Compton, *Mao's China Party Reform Documents 1942–44* (University of Washington Press, 1966), pp. 9–32. A cadre is any person who holds a formal leadership position.

24. Mao Zedong, 'Some Questions Concerning Methods of Leadership' in *Selected Works*, vol. 3, p. 119. The concept of the mass-line is considered in greater detail in chapter 4.
25. For example, 'Better Troops and Simpler Administration', 1941–3, 'Campaign for Reduction of Rent and Interest', 1942–4 and 'Campaign for Mutual-Aid-Teams and Cooperativisation', 1942–4.
26. C. Johnson, *Peasant Nationalism and Communist Power: The Emergence of Revolutionary China 1937–1945* (Stanford University Press, 1961).
27. L. Bianco, *Origins of the Chinese Revolution, 1915–1949* (Stanford University Press, 1971).
28. Deng Xiaoping, 'Report on the Current Situation and Tasks' in Summary of World Broadcasts: the Far East 6363.

Chapter 2

1. Mao Zedong, 'The Chinese People Have Stood Up' in *Selected Works* (Beijing: Foreign Languages Press, 1977), vol. 5, pp. 15–18.
2. The transformation of Chinese agriculture is covered in greater detail in chapter 10.
3. The campaigns are often referred to in the literature by their Chinese names San Fan (Three-Antis) and Wu Fan (Five-Antis). The targets of the Five-Antis Campaign were bribery, tax evasion, theft of state property, cheating on government contracts and stealing state economic information. See J. Gardner, 'The Wu-Fan Campaign in Shanghai: a Study in the Consolidation of Urban Control' in A. Doak Barnett (ed.), *Chinese Communist Politics in Action* (University of Washington Press, 1969), pp. 477–539.
4. See Mao Zedong, 'On the People's Democratic Dictatorship' in *Selected Works*, vol. 4, pp. 411–23.
5. Figures from Xue Muqiao, 'Economic Work Must Grasp the Laws of Economic Development', translated by the author in *Documents on Communist Affairs* (Macmillan, 1980).
6. Gao Gang was the head of the Party and state apparatus in the north-east, the most industrialised area in China, and in November 1952 he was made head of the newly created State Planning Commission which oversaw the Five-Year Plans. Rao Shushi was the Director of the Central Committee's Organisation Department and was Party and state leader of the East China Region.
7. Mao Zedong, 'On the Ten Major Relationships' in *Selected Works*, vol. 5, pp. 284–306.
8. Mao Zedong, 'On the Correct Handling of Contradictions Among the People' in *Selected Works*, vol. 5, pp. 384–421.
9. See Ye Jianying's speech at the Meeting in Commemoration of

the Thirtieth Anniversary of the Founding of the People's Republic of China in *Beijing Review (BR)*, no. 40 (5 October 1979), p. 14.

10. These two solutions have been termed 'Decentralisation 1' and 'Decentralisation 2' by Schurmann. See F. Schurmann, *Ideology and Organisation in Communist China* (University of California Press, 1968), pp. 175–8.

11. See S. Andors, 'Revolution and Modernisation: Man and Machine in Industrializing Society, the Chinese Case' in E. Friedman and M. Selden (eds.), *America's Asia: Dissenting Essays on Asian–American Relations* (Vintage Books, 1971), pp. 393–444.

12. See, for example, Xue Muqiao, 'Economic Work Must Grasp the Laws of Economic Development' in *Documents on Communist Affairs*.

13. In total output, not output *per capita*.

14. For a more detailed discussion of the theory of 'permanent revolution' see chapter 4.

15. Extracts of the former are in S. Schram (ed.), *Mao Unrehearsed* (Penguin Books, 1974), pp. 91–5. The latter can be found in J. Chen, *Mao Papers* (Oxford University Press, 1970), pp. 57–76.

16. In particular see V. Lippit, 'The Great Leap Forward Reconsidered' in *Modern China*, vol. 1, no. 1 (January 1975), pp. 92–115.

17. From a report of Li Xiannian's interview with the American journalist Harrison E. Salisbury in *The Times* (28 July 1980).

18. See *The Case of Peng Teh-huai (Peng Dehuai) 1956–68* (Hong Kong: Union Research Institute, 1968), pp. 7–13.

19. See Mao Zedong, 'Speech at the Lushan Conference' in S. Schram (ed.), *Mao Unrehearsed*, pp. 142–6.

20. Ibid., p. 139.

21. This information was supplied by David S. G. Goodman, who, at the time, was a student at Beijing University.

22. *People's Daily (Renmin Ribao)* (8 March 1979). Before the Cultural Revolution Lu Dingyi was the CCP Director of Propaganda and Minister of Culture.

23. The rural sector of Chinese society is organised into three levels. The lowest level is the production team, above this is the production brigade which consists of a number of teams. The third level is the commune which is the basic level of government in the countryside. For a fuller explanation see chapter 10.

24. See Mao Zedong, 'Speech at an Enlarged Central Work Conference' in S. Schram (ed.), *Mao Unrehearsed*, pp. 158–87. This speech is also referred to as the '7,000 Cadres Speech'.

25. Mao Zedong, 'Speech at the Tenth Plenum of the Eighth Central Committee' in S. Schram (ed.) *Mao Unrehearsed*, p. 189.

26. See E. Snow, *China's Long Revolution* (Pelican Books, 1974), p. 26.

Chapter 3

1. *Beijing Review (BR)*, no. 10 (1979).
2. See *Peking Review (PR)*, no. 21 (1967), pp. 6–9.
3. The group functioned under the jurisdiction of the Standing Committee of the Politburo and was led by Chen Boda, Jiang Qing and Kang Sheng.
4. See, 'Decision of the Central Committee of the Chinese Communist Party Concerning the Great Proletarian Cultural Revolution' (Beijing: Foreign Languages Press, 1966), pp. 1–13.
5. P. Bridgham, 'Mao's Cultural Revolution in 1967: The Struggle to Seize Power' in *China Quarterly (CQ)*, no. 34 (April–June 1968) pp. 9–10.
6. 'Decision of the Central Committee of the Chinese Communist Party, the State Council and the Military Affairs Committee of the Central Committee and the Cultural Revolution Group of the Central Committee, Concerning the Resolute Support of the PLA for the Revolutionary Masses of the Left' in *Chinese Communist Party Documents of the Great Proletarian Cultural Revolution, 1966–67* (Hong Kong: Union Research Institute, 1968) p. 195.
7. The two were Xie Fuzhi and Wang Li. Xie became chairman of the Beijing Municipal Revolutionary Committee in 1967 and a member of the Politburo in 1969 and died in 1972. Wang was a leading member of the Central Cultural Revolution Group but was dismissed from all his posts because of his alleged connections with the 'May 16 Corps'.
8. 'Order of the Central Committee of the Chinese Communist Party, the State Council and the Military Affairs Committee of the Central Committee and the Cultural Revolution Group of the Central Committee Concerning the Prohibition of the Seizure of Arms, Equipment and Other Military Supplies from the PLA' in *Chinese Communist Party Documents*, p. 507.
9. J. Gittings, 'Stifling the Students' in *Far Eastern Economic Review* (29 August 1968), pp. 377–8.
10. Chen had been elected to the five-person Standing Committee of the Politburo.
11. For a more detailed discussion of Lin's fall see chapter 7.
12. In April 1973 Deng was introduced by Zhou Enlai at a reception for Cambodian military officials as a Vice-Premier of the State Council.
13. F. Teiwes, *Politics and Purges in China: Rectification and the Decline of Party Norms* (M. E. Sharpe, 1979), p. 624.
14. New Year's Day editorial in *People's Daily (Renmin Ribao RMRB)*, *Red Flag* and the *Liberation Army Daily* (1 January 1974).

15. 'Carry the Struggle to Criticise Lin Biao and Confucius through to the End', *RMRB* (2 February 1974).
16. Zhongfa no. 21, 1974, in *Issues and Studies*, vol. XI, no. 1 (January 1975), pp. 101–5.
17. Kang Sheng has been posthumously denounced as the originator of many of the theories developed by the Gang of Four.
18. See, for example, 'Study Well the Theory of the Dictatorship of the Proletariat', *RMRB* (9 February 1975) translated in *PR*, no. 7, p. 4.
19. For a fuller discussion of this campaign see Chapter 4.
20. See J. Domes, 'The "Gang of Four" — and Hua Kuo-feng: Analysis of Political Events in 1975–76' in *CQ*, no. 34 (September 1977), pp. 481–3. The following points concerning the agricultural debate are based on this analysis.
21. New Year's Day editorial in *RMRB*, *Red Flag* and *Liberation Army Daily* (1 January 1976).
22. 'Reversing Correct Verdicts Goes Against the Will of the People' in *RMRB* (10 March 1976) translated in *PR*, no. 11 (1976) p. 4.
23. 'Beat Back the Right Deviationist Wind to Reverse Correct Verdicts, Promote Industrial Production' in *RMRB* (23 March 1976) translated in *PR*, no. 14 (1976), p. 4. During the Cultural Revolution Deng was criticised for using the phrase 'It does not matter whether the cat is white or black; if it catches mice it is a good cat'.
24. At the time Wu De was the Mayor of Beijing, a post which he later lost and eventually, at the Fifth plenum of the Eleventh CC, he 'resigned' all his Party and state posts.
25. These documents were: On the General Programme for All Work of the Whole Party and the Whole Nation; Some Problems in Speeding-up Industrial Development; and Some Questions Concerning the Work of Science and Technology.
26. *RMRB* (24 and 27 February 1976).
27. See, for example, *RMRB* (30 December 1976) and *Red Flag*, no. 1 (1977).
28. Although born in Shaanxi Hua Guofeng's political career really advanced in Chairman Mao's home province of Hunan. Before the Cultural Revolution Hua had gained top leadership positions in Hunan province and was one of the few provincial leaders to survive the attacks of 1966–7. Despite criticism from the ultra-left he headed the Hunan Revolutionary Committee and was elected to the Ninth Central Committee in 1969. In 1971 Hua began to be engaged in work at the centre (with the staff office of the State Council) and was appointed to the special committee to look into the alleged coup by Lin Biao. In August 1973 Hua was promoted to the Politburo and in 1974 became Minister of Public Security.

Despite these gains his policy pronouncements showed a divergence with those later denounced as the Gang of Four and with those of Deng Xiaoping. This middle position presumably facilitated his choice as a compromise Acting Premier following Zhou Enlai's death in January 1976 and the Tiananmen Riots in April 1976. Following the arrest of the Gang of Four (Wang Hongwen, Zhang Chunqiao, Jiang Qing and Yao Wenyuan), Hua became both Chairman of the Party and Premier of the State Council — a concentration of power which had not occurred even while Mao was alive.

29. See *Issues and Studies*, vol. XV, no. 2 (February 1979), p. 88.
30. 'Practice is the Sole Criterion for Testing Truth' in *Guangming Daily (Guangming Ribao GMRB)* (11 May 1978).
31. See *PR*, no. 52 (1978), pp. 6–16.
32. See *GMRB* (26 and 28 January 1979).
33. This had been referred to as early as April 1979. See, for example, Lishi Yanjiu no. 4, 1979 translated in Summary of World Broadcasts: the Far East (SWB FE) 6147. At the time of this speech the octogenarian Marshal Ye Jiangying was Chairman of the Standing Committee of the National People's Congress and a member of the Standing Committee of the Politburo. It is thought that it was Ye who gave the command to arrest the Gang of Four. Although he was opposed to the Gang of Four he has been unwilling to see an extension of the criticisms against them to include Mao. He appears to have acted as a moderating influence on the extent to which Mao should be publicly criticised.
34. SWB FE/6497.
35. *The Times* (28 July 1980).

Chapter 4

1. K. Wittfogel, 'The Legend of Maoism' in *China Quarterly (CQ)*, nos 1 and 2 (January–March and April–June 1960) pp. 72–86 and 16–34.
2. B. Schwartz, 'The Legend of the "legend of 'Maoism"'' in *CQ* no. 2 (April–June 1960), pp. 35–42.
3. J. Fairbank, *The United States and China* (Harvard University Press, 1948).
4. S. Schram, 'The Marxist' in D. Wilson (ed.), *Mao Tse-tung in the Scales of History* (Cambridge University Press, 1977), p. 67.
5. See, for example, N. Harris, *The Mandate of Heaven: Marx and Mao in Modern China* (Quartet Books, 1978), pp. 283–94.
6. Ibid., p. 287.

7. A. Walder, 'Marxism, Maoism and Social Change' in *Modern China*, vol. 3, nos 1 and 2 (January and April 1977), pp. 101–16 and 125–60.
8. R. Pfeffer, 'Mao and Marx in the Marxist-Leninist Tradition. A Critique of "the China Field" and a Contribution to a Preliminary Reappraisal' in *Modern China*, vol. 2, no. 4 (October 1976), p. 426.
9. S. Schram, 'The Marxist' in D. Wilson (ed.), *Mao Tse-tung in the Scales of History*, p. 35.
10. See F. Schurmann, *Ideology and Organisation in Communist China* (University of California Press, 1968), chapter 1.
11. J. Starr, *Continuing the Revolution, the Political Thought of Mao* (Princeton University Press, 1979), p. 65.
12. Ibid.
13. Ibid., p. 70.
14. S. Schram, 'Chinese and Leninist Components in the Personality of Mao Tse-tung' in *Asian Survey*, vol. 3, no. 6 (June 1963), p. 268.
15. See, for example, S. Schram, *The Political Thought of Mao Tse-tung* (Penguin Books, 1969), pp. 84–110; F. Schurmann, *Ideology and Organisation in Communist China*, pp. 53–7, and J. Starr, *Continuing the Revolution, the Political Thought of Mao*, pp. 3–45.
16. For an interesting analysis of this influence and its differences with the Western philosophical tradition, see J. Starr, *Continuing the Revolution, the Political Thought of Mao*, chapter 1.
17. J. Starr, *Continuing the Revolution, the Political Thought of Mao*, p. 9.
18. S. Schram, 'The Marxist' in D. Wilson (ed.), *Mao Tse-tung in the Scales of History*, p. 60.
19. Mao Zedong, 'On the Correct Handling of Contradictions Among the People' in *Selected Works* (Beijing: Foreign Languages Press, 1977), vol. 5, pp. 384–421.
20. Ibid., p. 384.
21. Mao Zedong, 'On the Ten Major Relationships' in *Selected Works*, vol. 5, pp. 284–307. The ten major contradictions that Mao outlines are those between: heavy industry and light industry and agriculture; coastal industry and inland industry; economic construction and defence construction; the state, the units of production and the producers; central and local authorities; Han nationality and minority nationalities; Party and non-Party; revolution and counter-revolution; right and wrong; and China and other countries.
22. S. Schram, 'The Cultural Revolution in Historical Perspective' in S. Schram (ed.), *Authority Participation and Cultural Change in China* (Cambridge University Press, 1973), p. 41.

23. Mao Zedong, 'Some Questions Concerning Methods of Leadership' in *Selected Works*, vol. 3, p. 119.
24. Mao Zedong, 'The Foolish Old Man Who Removed the Mountains' in *Selected Works*, pp. 271–4.
25. Mao Zedong, 'Talks at Three Meetings with Comrades Chang Ch'un-ch'iao and Yao Wen-yuan' in S. Schram (ed.), *Mao Unrehearsed* (Penguin Books, 1974), p. 277.
26. 'Correctly Understand the Role of the Individual in History' in *People's Daily (Renmin Ribao RMRB)* (4 July 1980).
27. Ibid.
28. J. Starr, *Continuing the Revolution, the Political Thought of Mao*, p. 303.
29. In S. Schram (ed.), *Mao Unrehearsed*, p. 94.
30. *Peking Review (PR)*, no. 9 (1975), p. 5.
31. Yao Wenyuan, 'On the Social Basis of the Lin Piao Anti-Party Clique' in *PR*, no. 10 (1975), p. 6.
32. Zhang Chunqiao, 'On Exercising All-Round Dictatorship Over the Bourgeoisie' in *PR*, no. 14 (1975), p. 7.
33. Ibid.
34. 'Refuting Lin Piao's Claim: Every Sentence is Truth' in *PR*, no. 39 (1978), p. 15.
35. Communique of the Third plenum of the Eleventh CC in *PR*, no. 52 (1978), p. 15.
36. 'Correctly Understand the Role of the Individual in History' in *RMRB* (4 July 1980).
37. Ibid. This reiterates the point made in Ye Jianying's speech on the Thirtieth Anniversary of the Founding of the PRC. In the speech he stated, 'Of course, Mao Zedong Thought is not the product of Mao Zedong's personal wisdom, it is also the product of the wisdom of his comrades-in-arms, the Party and the revolutionary people, and, as he once pointed out, it emerged from the "collective struggles of the Party and the people".' In *BR*, no. 40 (1979), p. 8.
38. 'A Fundamental Principle of Marxism' in *PR*, no. 28 (1978), p. 6.
39. Notice from the First Plenary Session of the Central Committee for Inspecting Discipline Under the Party Central Committee in *Guangming Daily (Guangming Ribao GMRB)* (25 March 1979).
40. 'Fundamental Change in China's Class Situation' in *Beijing Review (BR)*, no. 47 (1979), p. 15.
41. Mao Zedong, 'On the Correct Handling of Contradictions Among the People' in *Selected Works*, vol. 5, p. 397.
42. *BR*, no. 47 (1979), p. 16.
43. Ibid., p. 17.

Chapter 5

1. See Chapter 7 for a fuller discussion of this problem.
2. Summary of World Broadcasts: the Far East (SWB FE) 3400.
3. Peng Zhen, 'Explanation of the Seven Draft Laws' in *Main Documents of the Second Session of the Fifth National People's Congress* (Beijing: Foreign Languages Press, 1979), p. 219.
4. *The Times* (28 July 1980). The five people are: Deng Xiaoping, Chen Yun, Wang Zhen. Xu Xiangqian and Li Xiannian.
5. See Parris Chang, 'Decentralisation of Power' in *Problems of Communism*, vol. XXI, no. 4 (1972), pp. 67–75.
6. V. Falkenheim, 'Continuing Central Predominance' in *Problems of Communism*, vol. XXI, no. 4 (1972), pp. 75–83.
7. David S. G. Goodman, 'The Provincial First Party Secretary in the People's Republic of China 1949–78: A Profile' in *British Journal of Political Science*, no. 10, p. 72.
8. With the revived emphasis on united front work since the fall of the Gang of Four the other eight parties have resumed their work and in October 1979 they held national congresses in Beijing. Their function is limited to that of providing expertise and presumably they will cease to function when the present members die. The parties and their chairmen are listed below:

Revolutionary Committee of the Guomindang	Zhu Yunshan
The Democratic League	Shi Liang
Democratic National Construction Association	Hu Juewen
The Association for Promoting Democracy	Zhou Jianren
The Peasants and Workers Democratic Party	Ji Fang
The Zhi Gong Dang	Huang Dingchen
The Jiasan Society	Xu Deheng
The Taiwan Democratic Self-Government League	Cai Xiao

9. SWB FE/6377.
10. Article 8 of The Constitution of the Communist Party of China (Party constitution) in the *Eleventh National Congress of the Communist Party of China (Documents)* (Beijing: Foreign Language Press, 1977).
11. Article 11 of Party constitution.
12. Article 12 of Party constitution.
13. The Eighth Party Congress is unique in the fact that it called a second session. The purpose of this second session was to approve the plans for the Great Leap Forward.
14. Hua Guofeng, 'Political Report to the Eleventh National Congress

of the Communist Party of China' in the *Eleventh Party Congress of the Communist Party of China (Documents)*, p. 69.

15. An alternate member does not have the right to vote.
16. F. Schurmann, *Ideology and Organisation in Communist China* (University of California Press, 1968), p. 140.
17. According to David S. G. Goodman the average age at the congresses was as follows: Eighth CC (as of 1968) 65.8 years; Ninth CC (1969) 61.4 years; Tenth CC 63.1 years; Eleventh CC (1977) 65.9 years; David S. G. Goodman, 'Changes in Leadership Personnel After September 1976' in J. Domes (ed.), *Chinese Politics After Mao* (University College Cardiff Press, 1979), p. 47.
18. Article 16 of Party constitution.
19. 'Resolution on Establishing the Secretariat of the Central Committee' in *Beijing Review (BR)*, no. 10 (1980), p. 12.
20. Ibid.
21. The present head is Yao Yilin, who replaced Wang Dongxing. Yao is also a member of the Secretariat.
22. These were Li Xiannian, Kang Sheng and Ye Jianying.
23. Huang Kecheng in SWB FE/6333.
24. SWB FE/6375.
25. The principles are: adhere to the Party's political and ideological line; uphold collective leadership and oppose arbitrary decision-making by a single person; safeguard the Party's centralised leadership and strictly observe Party discipline; uphold Party spirit and root out factionalism; speak the truth and match words with deeds; promote inner-Party democracy and take a correct attitude towards dissenting views; protect the rights of Party members against any encroachment; elections should fully express the wishes of the electors; struggle against erroneous tendencies, bad people and bad actions; treat comrades who have made mistakes correctly; accept supervision by the Party and the masses; and study hard and strive to be Red and Expert.
26. SWB FE/6370.
27. *People's Daily (Renmin Ribao RMRB)* (8 May 1977). For a discussion of this see D. Solinger, 'Some Speculations on the Return of the Regions: Parallels with the Past' in *China Quarterly (CQ)*, no. 75 (September 1978), pp. 623–38.
28. 'Baige Jingji Wenti' in *Zhongguo Jingji Wenti (China's Economic Problems)* (January 1978), p. 20.
29. The Provinces are:

Heilongjiang	Zhejiang	Henan	Yunnan
Jilin	Fujian	Shanxi	Jiangxi
Liaoning	Guangdong	Shaanxi	Sichuan

Hebei	Hunan	Guizhou
Shandong	Hubei	Qinghai
Jiangsu	Anhui	Gansu

The term 'autonomous region' signifies that there is a substantial national minority in the region. The autonomous regions and their minorities are:

Xinjiang	Uygur minority
Guangxi	Zhuang minority
Nei Menggu	Mongolian minority
(Inner Mongolia)	
Xizang (Tibet)	Tibetan minority
Ningxia	Hui minority

The special cities or municipalities are: Beijing, Shanghai and Tianjin (Tientsin)

30. Article 18 of Party constitution.
31. Article 1 of Party constitution.
32. Articles 3 and 4 of Party constitution.
33. Article 5 of Party constitution.
34. Article 7 of Party constitution.
35. *Red Flag*, no. 4 (1980).
36. SWB FE/6341. The same figure of 43 per cent was mentioned for Zhejiang province (SWB FE/6347) and Ye Jianying has stated that nearly half the Party members had joined since the Cultural Revolution and that 7 million had joined since the Tenth Party Congress.
37. *RMRB* (15 August 1979).
38. Chen Zihua (Minister of Civil Affairs), 'On China's Electoral Law' in *BR*, no. 37 (1979), p. 18.
39. *Guangming Daily (Guangming Ribao GMRB)* (11 March 1979).
40. *RMRB* (1 February 1979).
41. Ibid.
42. *RMRB* (11 January 1979).

Chapter 6

1. F. Schurmann, *Ideology and Organisation in Communist China* (University of California Press, 1968), pp. 188—94.
2. Originally the period was three years but this was changed in the 1975 constitution.
3. Article 25 of The Constitution of the People's Republic of China (state constitution 1978): *Documents of the First Session of the Fifth National People's Congress of the People's Republic of China* (Beijing: Foreign Languages Press, 1978).

4. F. Schurmann, *Ideology and Organisation in Communist China*, pp. 183–5 and J. Starr, *Ideology and Culture* (Harper & Row, 1973), pp. 201–3.

5. Ye Jianying, 'Report on the Revision of the Constitution' in *Documents of the First Session of the Fifth National People's Congress of the People's Republic of China.*

6. Article 25 of The Constitution of the People's Republic of China in *Documents of the First Session of the Fourth National People's Congress of the People's Republic of China* (Beijing: Foreign Languages Press, 1975).

7. Ye Jianying, 'Report on the Revision of the Constitution' in *Documents of the First Session of the Fifth National People's Congress of the People's Republic of China*, p. 198.

8. Article 55 of state constitution 1978.

9. Article 41 of state constitution 1978.

10. Peng Zhen, 'Explanation of the Seven Draft Laws' in *Main Documents of the Second Session of the Fifth National People's Congress of the People's Republic of China* (Beijing: Foreign Languages Press, 1979), pp. 218–19.

11. *Guangming Daily (Guangming Ribao GMRB)* (17 October 1979).

12. Peng Zhen, 'Explanation of the Seven Draft Laws' in *Main Documents of the Second Session of the Fifth National People's Congress of the People's Republic of China*, p. 201.

13. Information given by Marc Blecher from an interview with the head of the General Office of the Provincial Planning Commission of Jiangsu.

14. People's governments replaced the revolutionary committees following the Second Session of the Fifth NPC (June 1979).

15. Article 35 of the state constitution 1978.

16. Article 37 of the state constitution 1978.

17. Chen Zihua, 'On China's Electoral Law' in *Beijing Review (BR)*, no. 37 (1979).

18. Hua Guofeng, 'Report on the Work of the Government' in *Main Documents of the Second Session of the Fifth National People's Congress of the People's Republic of China*, p. 72.

19. This was first suggested by Zhou Enlai in his 1957 'Report on the Work of the Government'.

20. *BR*, no. 8 (1980), pp. 11–19.

21. Deng Xiaoping, 'Report on the Current Situation' in Summary of World Broadcasts: the Far East (SWB FE) 6363.

22. Ibid.

23. The following incomplete list gives some idea of the scope of the plans. They project: output for the main industrial and agricultural products; the amount of investment in capital construction and its

magnitude; the distribution of important materials; the state budget; the number of new workers and staff to be taken on and the total amount of wages; and the purchases and marketing of main commodities and foreign trade.

24. Xue Muqiao, 'Economic Work Must Grasp the Laws of Economic Development' in *Documents on Communist Affairs*, vol. 2 (Macmillan, 1980).

25. Ren Luosan, 'China's Economic Management', *BR* no. 5 (1980), p. 22.

26. SWB FE/W 1063.

27. Xue Muqiao, 'Economic Work Must Grasp the Laws of Economic Development'.

28. *BR*, no. 12 (1979), p. 7.

29. *BR*, no. 1 (1979).

30. *BR*, no. 12 (1979), p. 7.

31. Ibid.

32. Xue Muqiao, 'Economic Work Must Grasp the Laws of Economic Development'.

33. *BR*, no. 12 (1980), p. 25. In July 1979 the State Council issued five documents including 'Provisions on Expanding the Right of Self-Management of State-Owned Enterprises'. This provides regulations for an enterprise to retain a share of the profit it has made, and to keep most of the depreciation funds for fixed assets, authorising the state to levy taxes on the fixed assets and provide all the working capital in the form of loans.

34. SWB FE/6408.

35. *BR*, no. 2 (1979).

36. *Peking Review (PR)*, no. 49 (1978), p. 9.

Chapter 7

1. Article 14 of The Constitution of the Communist Party of China in *Documents of the Eleventh Party Congress of the Communist Party of China* (Beijing: Foreign Languages Press, 1977).

2. Article 19 of The Constitution of the People's Republic of China in *Documents of the First Session of the Fifth National People's Congress of the People's Republic of China* (Beijing: Foreign Languages Press, 1978).

3. The present Chief of Staff is Yang Dezhi, who replaced Deng Xiaoping in early 1980.

4. Its Director is Wei Guoqing.

5. The first change in Kunming was when Yang Dezhi replaced Wang Bisheng and Yang was replaced by Zhang Zhixiu when Yang was made Chief of Staff.

6. Military districts do not have air force or naval units stationed under them.

7. J. Gittings, *The Role of the Chinese Army* (Oxford University Press, 1967), p. 202.

8. Ibid., p. 211.

9. H. Nelson, *The Chinese Military System* (Westview Press, 1977), p. 184.

10. 'Organise the Militia Well', *People's Daily (Renmin Ribao RMRB)* and *Liberation Army Daily* editorial (29 September 1973).

11. Quoted in H. Nelson, *The Chinese Military System*, p. 184.

12. *RMRB* (3 June 1977).

13. Nie Rongzhen, 'The Militia's Role in a Future War' in *Peking Review (PR)*, no. 35 (1978), pp. 16–19.

14. For example, see J. Domes, *The Internal Politics of China 1949–1972* (C. Hurst & Co., 1973).

15. See W. Whitson, 'The Field Army in Chinese Communist Military Politics' in *China Quarterly (CQ)*, no. 37 (January–March 1969), pp. 1–31.

16. *RMRB* editorial (24 July 1954) quoted in J. Gittings, *The Role of the Chinese Army*, p. 128.

17. See J. Gittings, *The Role of the Chinese Army*, pp. 225–34, for a full discussion of this point.

18. D. Charles, 'The Dismissal of P'eng Te-huai' in *CQ*, no. 8, p. 65.

19. The Five-Good Movement, or the Five-Good Soldier Movement, was launched at the end of 1960 and early 1961. The 'Five-Goods' soldiers were to attain were to be good at: political thought; military training; the 'Three-Eight Work Style'; fulfilment of duties; and physical training. The Three-Eight Work Style' referred to the three phrases of correct political orientation, hard work and simple life, and flexibility in strategy and tactics and to the eight characters for unity, earnestness, energy and vitality. In 1963 Lei Feng was first put forward as a person to be emulated. Before his death, aged 22, Lei Feng had led a life of selfless devotion to his work and comrades as was revealed in his diaries. As a model to be emulated he was used to show that ordinary people carrying out their ordinary lives could contribute to socialism – one did not have carry out spectacular deeds.

20. J. Gittings, *The Role of the Chinese Army*, p. 247.

21. At the Eleventh plenum of the Eighth CC (August 1966) Lin put forward the three criteria for cultivating cadres. They were: (1) Do they hold high the red banner of Mao Zedong's Thought? Those who fail to do so shall be dismissed from office. (2) Do they engage in political and ideological work? Those who disrupt it and the Great Proletarian Cultural Revolution are to be dismissed. (3) Are they enthusiastic about the revolution? Those who are entirely devoid of such enthusiasm are to be dismissed.

22. Quoted by Paul H. B. Goodwin in 'China's Defence Dilemma: The

Modernisation Crisis of 1976—77' in *Contemporary China*, vol. 2, no. 3 (fall 1978), pp. 63—85.

23. Xu Xiangqian, 'Strive for the Realisation of the Modernisation of National Defence', *Red Flag*, no. 10 (1979).
24. D. Tretiak, 'China's Vietnam War and its Consequences' in *CQ*, no. 80 (December 1979), p. 756.
25. New China News Agency (23 October 1979).
26. On the morning of 18 May 1980 China launched its first carrier rocket to a target in the Pacific Ocean. The object of this exercise, according to Li Xiannian, was to develop science and technology and to accelerate the modernisation of the country as well as strengthening its defence capabilities against the threat of 'hegemonist powers'. See *Beijing Review (BR)*, no. 21 (1980).
27. Summary of World Broadcasts: the Far East (SWB FE) 6420.
28. *RMRB* (5 March 1980) and SWB FE/6393.
29. David S. G. Goodman, 'Changes in Leadership Personnel After September 1976' in J. Domes (ed.) *Chinese Politics After Mao* (University College Cardiff Press, 1979), p. 43.

Chapter 8

1. A. Etzioni, *Modern Organisations* (Prentice-Hall, 1964), pp. 58—67, and A. Etzioni, *A Comparative Analysis of Complex Organisations* (Free Press, 1961).
2. Victor H. Li, 'The Role of Law in Communist China' in *China Quarterly (CQ)*, no. 44 (October—December 1970), pp. 66—111.
3. Ibid., p. 73.
4. For a full consideration of this system see J. Cohen, *The Criminal Process in the People's Republic of China, 1949—1963* (Harvard University Press, 1968).
5. *People's Daily (Renmin Ribao RMRB)* (25 February 1980).
6. Xu Lisheng, 'A Talk on the Deprivation of Political Rights in China's Criminal Law' in *RMRB* (14 January 1980).
7. Zhou Enlai, 'Report on the Work of the Government', *The First Session of the First National People's Congress* (Beijing: Foreign Languages Press, 1954), p. 27.
8. M. K. Whyte, 'Inequality and Stratification in China' in *CQ*, no. 66 (December 1975), pp. 684—711.
9. M. Blecher, 'Income Distribution in Small Rural Chinese Communities' in *CQ*, no. 68 (December 1976), pp. 797—816.
10. *Peking Review (PR)*, no. 18 (1978), p. 13.
11. *Beijing Review (BR)*, no. 28 (1979), p. 5.
12. *The Observer* (25 May 1980).
13. Hua Guofeng, 'Report on the Work of the Government' in *Documents of the First Session of the Fifth National People's Congress*

of the People's Republic of China (Beijing: Foreign Languages Press, 1978), p. 63.

14. Ibid., p. 64.

15. See, for example, 'Implementing the Socialist Principle "To Each According to His Work"' in *PR*, nos 31–2 (1978) and 'Integrating Moral Encouragement With Material Reward' in *PR*, no. 16 (1978).

16. Quoted in *BR*, no. 19 (1980).

17. Economic Management no. 1, 1980, translated in Summary of World Broadcasts: the Far East (SWB FE) 6415.

18. Ibid.

19. Ibid.

20. For the most part this results from the decision of the Third plenum of the Eleventh CC to raise the purchase price for agricultural products and the reduction of the price of industrial farm products. This has caused losses for many industrial and business enterprises, leaving them the choice of either reducing standards or increasing the price of their goods.

21. See Deng Xiaoping, 'Report on the Current Situation' in SWB FE/6363.

22. *BR* no. 19 (1980). 'Bonuses in command' is a phrase used to criticise the tendency of relying too heavily on the use of material incentives to stimulate production.

23. For an expression of this view see Deng Xiaoping, 'Report on the Current Situation', SWB FE/6363.

24. The eleven regions are: Kaifeng, Hangzhou, Sichuan, Beijing, Tianjin, Shenyang, Shanghai, Guangzhou, Heilongjiang, Xizang (Tibet) and Xinjiang.

25. M. Meisner, 'The Shenyang Transformer Factory' in *CQ*, no. 52 (December 1972), p. 731.

26. A. Doak Barnett, 'Social Stratification and Aspects of Personnel Management in the Chinese Communist Bureaucracy', *CQ*, no. 28 (October–December 1966), p. 13.

27. M. K. Whyte, 'Inequality and Stratification in China', *CQ* no. 64 (December 1975), p. 732.

28. See 'Let Some Peasants Become Well-Off First' in *BR*, no. 9 (1979), pp. 5–6.

29. D. M. Lampton, 'New "Revolution" in China's Social Policy' in *Problems of Communism*, vol. XXVII, no. 5–6, p. 19.

30. Some peasants in the Shanghai suburbs have incomes of around 1900 yuan.

31. *BR*, no. 28 (1979).

32. *BR*, no. 15 (1980), p. 23.

33. Ibid., pp. 22–3.

34. In the countryside men can earn more work-points than women

because more work-points tend to be given for harder physical work while in the cities the jobs in which women form the majority, such as in the textile industry and as shop assistants, tend to be lower paid.

35. The term 'intellectual' has a broad application in China and includes 'professors, scientists, senior engineers and writers who are commonly known as highly qualified intellectuals as well as ordinary technicians in factories, primary-school teachers and other mental workers with professional knowledge'. At present it is estimated that there are 25 million intellectuals in China.

36. 'Social Sciences: A Hundred Schools of Thought Contend' in *BR*, no. 14 (1979), p. 10.

37. The origins of the phrase of letting a hundred schools of thought contend originated during the Spring and Autumn and the Warring States Period (5th–3rd centuries B.C.) when a range of schools of thought (e.g. Confucianism, Taoism, Mohism, Legalism and the School of Names) competed for prominence.

38. It should be noted that this discussion does not include those writers whose articles appeared in the unofficial press and on Democracy Wall. They are not considered to be intellectuals by the Chinese authorities.

39. *RMRB* (25 February 1980).

40. Ibid.

41. *Liberation Daily* (26 May 1942).

42. See, for example, 'Literature and Art Should Sing the Praises of the Four Modernisations' in *Wen Hui Bao* (23 February 1980) and SWB FE/6369.

43. SWB FE/6361.

44. 'Literature as a Mirror of Life' in *BR*, no. 52 (1979), p. 13.

45. *BR*, no. 13 (1980), p. 24.

46. Over 61 300 teachers in institutions of further education have been given new titles since mid-1978 and new regulations for the awarding of degrees of bachelor, master and doctor come into force from January 1981. See SWB FE/6330 and *RMRB* (14 February 1980).

47. SWB FE/6382.

48. *BR*, no. 13 (1980).

49. Quoted in 'How the Gang of Four Stamped on the Party's Policy on Intellectuals' in *PR*, no. 12 (1977).

50. During the early years of the Cultural Revolution intellectuals were designated the 'stinking ninth category' after landlords, rich peasants, counter-revolutionaries, bad elements, rightists, renegades, enemy agents and capitalist-roaders.
no. 1 (1980).

52. SWB FE/6336.

53. Between 1968 and 1976 different localities were encouraged to work out their own details concerning administration in order to accommodate the needs particular to the area. This was particularly important for the rural areas where many children's education is disrupted by the demands of the farming season. Greater flexibility in terms of hours is beneficial for ensuring that children would not miss important lessons.

54. This is to be achieved by 1985. See Liu Xiyao, the then Minister of Education, 'Report at the National Education Work Conference' in Guangming Daily (Guangming Ribao GMRB) (11 June 1978).

55. BR, no. 20 (1979).

56. SWB FE/6336.

57. See, for example, BR, no. 1 (1980).

58. GMRB (3 December 1977).

59. G. White, 'Higher Education and Social Redistribution in a Socialist Society: The Chinese Case', p. 40.

60. See Vento dell'est (Milan, 1976), pp. 112–23.

61. RMRB (23 October 1977).

62. See, for example, SWB FE/6427. Technical schools are one of the alternatives to university promoted. In 1980 they were to enrol 400 000 students, a figure which compares with a total of 650 000 students in all such schools in October 1979. Entrants must be single, between 15 and 22, have attained junior-secondary or senior-secondary education level and must be permanently registered in the cities or towns.

63. For example, GMRB in January 1978 published a list of 20 primary and secondary schools to be run directly by the Ministry of Education. For higher education 88 institutions have been designated as key points and they will take the best students. These students will not have to return to their original work-units after graduation. Eighty-eight seems an ambitious total given the amount of resources available and it is likely that the number will be trimmed considerably in the future.

64. BR, no. 20 (1979), p. 6.

65. For a full discussion of small groups, see M. K. Whyte, Small Groups and Political Rituals in China (University of California Press, 1974).

66. Ibid., pp. 12–13.

67. These are organisations such as the Communist Youth League, the All-China Federation of Trade Unions, the All-China Women's Federation and the Peasant's Association.

68. J. R. Townsend, Political Participation in Communist China (University of California Press, 1969), p. 157.

Chapter 9

1. M.-C. Bergère, 'China's Urban Society After Mao' in J. Domes (ed.), *Chinese Politics After Mao* (University College Cardiff Press, 1979), p. 156.
2. For a discussion of urban communes, see F. Schurmann, *Ideology and Organisation in Communist China* (University of California Press, 1968), pp. 382–99, and J. W. Salaff, 'The Urban Communes and Anti-City Experiment in Communist China' in *China Quarterly (CQ)*, no. 29 (January–March 1967), pp. 82–110.
3. *Beijing Review (BR)*, no. 35 (1979), p. 12.
4. The thirteen cities are: Harbin, Changchun, Shenyang, Beijing, Tianjin, Taiyuan, Xian, Nanjing, Shanghai, Chengdu, Chongqing, Wuhan and Guangzhou.
5. *BR*, no. 11 (1980), pp. 6–7.
6. On 19 January 1980 *People's Daily (Renmin Ribao RMRB)* published four regulations from the fifties on urban organisation.
7. See 'The Organic Regulations of the Sub-District Office (December 31, 1954)' in *RMRB* (19 January 1980). Sometimes the Chinese phrase for Sub-District Office (jiedao banshichu) is translated as Street Office.
8. The sub-district office has a chairperson and if necessary vice-chairpersons and secretaries. Also, they can have from three to seven full-time cadres, of whom one should be concerned with women's work.
9. *RMRB* (19 January 1980).
10. The original document refers to people's councils not people's governments. I have used the term people's government throughout because they have the same functions as the former people's councils.
11. *RMRB* (19 January 1980). The Provisional Organic Regulations of the People's Mediation Committee were first published on 22 March 1954. The Provisional Organic Regulations of the Social Order and Security Committee were made public on 11 August 1952.
12. These committees also operate in the countryside.
13. See F. Schurmann, *Ideology and Organisation in Communist China*, p. 226.
14. B. M. Richman, *Industrial Society in Communist China* (Vintage Books, 1969), pp. 46–57.
15. J. Gray, 'The Two Roads: Alternative Strategies of Social Change and Economic Growth in China' in S. R. Schram (ed.), *Authority, Participation and Cultural Change in China* (Cambridge University Press, 1973).

16. *RMRB* (8 October 1971).
17. *Peking Review (PR)*, no. 42 (1978).
18. Ibid.
19. The number of members depends on the size of the factory. For example, the Shanghai Bicycle Plant, with 4200 workers, has 2 deputy secretaries and 8 committee members.
20. The Shoudu Iron and Steel Factory and the Shanghai Bicycle Plants have 4 deputy directors.
21. The sizes of these cannot be generalised as they entirely depend on the size of the enterprise itself and this can vary greatly. For example, in smaller factories and offices there may only be groups.
22. In 1979 the Shanghai Film Factory held three such congresses, see *BR*, no. 2 (1980), p. 6. The 1978 workers' congress of the Tianjin Clock and Watch Factory was attended by 246 representatives (8.6 per cent of those on the payroll). Of these 66 per cent were workers, 26 per cent cadres and 8 per cent technicians, see *PR*, no. 49 (1978).
23. *BR*, no. 45 (1979), p. 7.
24. Ibid., pp. 6–7.
25. These workers' congresses should not be confused with the present workers' congresses.
26. *BR*, no. 47 (1979), p. 4.
27. *BR*, no. 11 (1979), p. 4.
28. Ibid.
29. *BR*, no. 18 (1980).
30. *BR*, no. 11 (1979), p. 4.
31. *BR*, no. 23 (1979), p. 19.
32. This kind of contest was held at the Shanghai Bicycle Plant, see *BR*, no. 11 (1980), p. 22.
33. *BR*, no. 23 (1979), p. 18.
34. See, for example, *BR*, no. 35 (1979), p. 9.
35. Ibid.
36. *BR*, no. 6 (1980), p. 19.
37. *BR*, no. 35 (1979), p. 11.
38. Ibid. In Beijing 140 000 of those looking for employment found it in small collectively owned enterprises, *BR*, no. 6 (1980), p. 17.
39. Ibid.
40. Ibid., pp. 18–19. Wages in this collective had been as high as 150 yuan a month but these wages were earned by more skilled workers who have now left.
41. *BR*, no. 38 (1979), pp. 8–9.
42. *BR*, no. 22 (1980), p. 5.
43. *BR*, no. 6 (1980), p. 16.
44. Summary of World Broadcasts: the Far East (SWB FE) W1069.

45. *BR*, no. 48 (1979), p. 18.
46. Ibid.
47. *BR*, no. 32 (1979), p. 21.
48. *BR*, no. 48 (1979), p. 18.
49. Ibid., p. 27.
50. SWB FE/6401.
51. *BR*, no. 32 (1979), p. 23.
52. *BR*, no. 45 (1979), p. 24.

Chapter 10

1. For a detailed description of land reform in one village see W. Hinton, *Fanshen* (Penguin Books, 1972).
2. The Agrarian Reform Law (Beijing: Foreign Languages Press, 1951).
3. The categorisations were: landlord, rich peasant, middle peasant, poor peasant and farm labourer.
4. *New China's Economic Achievements, 1949–1952* (Beijing: Foreign Languages Press, 1952), p. 194. One mu equals one-sixth of an acre.
5. F. Schurmann, *Ideology and Organisation in Communist China* (University of California Press, 1968), p. 442.
6. Mao's speech was not released until October 1955, presumably to avoid risk to the harvest because of the speed-up.
7. Xue Muqiao, 'Economic Work Must Grasp the Laws of Economic Development' in *Documents on Communist Affairs* (Macmillan, 1980).
8. Ibid.
9. Formerly these industries were run by the local government. In 1979 and 1980 there were suggestions that this system should be reverted to.
10. Reported in The *Guardian* (10 June 1980).
11. These regulations were first drawn up under Mao's supervision in 1962.
12. *Beijing Review (BR)*, no. 12 (1980), pp. 14–15.
13. 'Regulations on the Work in the Rural People's Communes (Revised Draft), in *Issues and Studies*, vol. XV, no. 10, p. 93.
14. *Guangming Daily (Guangming Ribao GMRB)* (6 November 1979).
15. *People's Daily (Renmin Ribao RMRB)* (14 May 1980).
16. *BR*, no. 9 (1979), pp. 5–6.
17. *BR*, no. 12 (1980), p. 20.
18. *BR*, no. 4 (1980), p. 21.
19. Xue Muqiao, 'Economic Work Must Grasp the Laws of Economic Development'.
20. *BR*, no. 16 (1979), p. 15.

21. Ibid., p. 19.
22. 'Regulations on the Work in Rural People's Communes (Revised Draft)' in *Issues and Studies*, vol. XV, no. 10, p. 106.
23. Normally 5 to 7 per cent of the Production team's cultivable land is used for private plots.
24. The total area for this varies but at most totals 15 to 17 per cent of the production team's cultivable land.
25. *BR*, no. 16 (1979), p. 24.
26. *BR*, no. 15 (1980), p. 23.
27. Summary of World Broadcasts: the Far East (SWB FE 6374).
28. *BR*, no. 12 (1979), p. 8.
29. Ibid.
30. *BR*, no. 22 (1979), pp. 4–5. The average price of grain dropped by 20 per cent.
31. *BR*, no. 47 (1979), p. 6.
32. *BR*, no. 12 (1979), p. 8.
33. *BR*, no. 5 (1980), p. 7.
34. Ibid.
35. See for example 'The Operation of Commune and Brigade-run Enterprises Must Benefit the Enrichment of the Production Teams' in SWB FE/6337.
36. *BR*, no. 16 (1980), p. 7.
37. *BR*, no. 20 (1979), p. 5.

Chapter 11

1. Other important changes in personnel announced were as follows: Deng Xiaoping, Li Xiannian, Chen Yun, Xu Xiangqian and Wang Zhen retired from their posts as Vice-Premiers because of their age; Wang Renzhong gave up his post of Vice-Premier because of his 'acceptance of an important post in the Party'; and Chen Yonggui (the peasant leader from the now disgraced agricultural model of Dazhai) was relieved of his Vice-Premiership 'on his own request'. Yang Jingren, Zhang Aiping and Huang Hua were appointed Vice-Premiers.
2. Hua Guofeng — speech at the Third Session of the Fifth National People's Congress in *Main Documents of the Third Session of the Fifth National People's Congress of the People's Republic of China* (Foreign Languages Press: Beijing, 1980) p. 196.
3. The trial was conducted in two tribunals, the first trying those concerned with Lin Biao and the second the civilians associated with Jiang Qing. Apart from the ten still alive another six people who had died were charged with crimes in the indictment. They were: Lin Biao (former Minister of National Defence), Kang Sheng (former adviser to the Central Cultural Revolution Group and a

Vice-Chairman of the Tenth CC), Xie Fuzhi (former Minister of Public Security and Ninth CC Politburo member), Ye Qun (former Ninth CC Politburo member and wife of Lin Biao), Lin Liguo (former Deputy Chief of the Operations Department of the PLA Air Force HQ and son of Lin Biao), and Zhou Yuchi (former Deputy Director of the General Office of the PLA Air Force HQ). The sentences passed on the ten who stood trial were as follows:

Jiang Qing — sentenced to death with a two-year reprieve and permanent deprivation of political rights;

Zhang Chunqiao — sentenced to death with a two-year reprieve and permanent deprivation of political rights;

Yao Wenyuan — sentenced to 20 years' imprisonment, deprivation of political rights for five years;

Wang Hongwen — sentenced to life imprisonment, permanent deprivation of political rights;

Chen Boda — sentenced to 18 years' imprisonment, deprivation of political rights for five years;

Huang Yongsheng (former Chief of General Staff) — sentenced to 18 years' imprisonment, deprivation of political rights for five years;

Wu Faxian (former Commander of the Air Force) — sentenced to 17 years' imprisonment, deprivation of political rights for five years;

Li Zuopeng (former First Political Commissar of the Navy) — sentenced to 17 years' imprisonment, deprivation of political rights for five years;

Qiu Zuohui (former Director of PLA General Logistics Department) — sentenced to 16 years' imprisonment, deprivation of political rights for five years;

Jiang Tengjiao (former Air Force Political Commissar of the PLA Nanjing Units) — sentenced to 18 years' imprisonment, deprivation of political rights for five years.

For a translation of the full text of the written judgment see Summary of World Broadcasts: the Far East (SWB FE) 6633.

4. The four major charges were: (1) the frame-up and persecution of Party and state leaders and plotting to overthrow the political power of the dictatorship of the proletariat; (2) the persecution and suppression of large numbers of cadres and masses; (3) plotting to assassinate Chairman Mao Zedong and engineer an armed counter-revolutionary *coup d'état*; (4) plotting armed rebellion in Shanghai. For a full translation of the indictment see *Beijing Review (BR)* no. 48 (1980), pp. 9–29.

5. *BR*, no. 2 (1981), p. 23.

6. SWB FE/6612.

7. 'A Milestone of Socialist Democarcy and the Legal System' in *People's Daily (Renmin Ribao)* (22 Dec. 1980).

8. See for example, 'Only By Consolidating Stability and Unity Shall We Be Able to Carry Out Economic Readjustment Successfully' in *Liberation Daily (Jiefang Ribao)* (10 January 1981) and 'Constantly Consolidate and Develop the Political Situation of Stability' in *Jilin Daily (Jilin Ribao)* (21 January 1981).

9. Hua Guofeng, at the Third Session of the Fifth National People's Congress, announced that the Ten-Year Plan (1976—85) was to be abandoned altogether and that a new plan was to be drawn up for the years 1981—90. Commenting on the old plan Hua stated that 'some targets were inappropriately high, the scale of capital construction was too large, and comprehensive balance was lacking in many projects'. Hua Guofeng, speech at the Third Session of the Fifth National People's Congress in *Main Documents of the Third Session of the Fifth National People's Congress of the People's Republic of China*, op. cit. pp. 155—6.

10. 'Emancipate the Mind, Promote Reform' in *Red Flag (Hongqi)* no. 21 (1980).

11. Reported in the *Manchester Guardian* (30 January 1981). The paper was the *Yangtse Daily (Changjiang Ribao)*.

Selected further reading

General reading

The following books all provide general introductions to various aspects of the politics of the PRC:

B. Brugger, *Contemporary China* (London: Croom Helm, 1977).

P. Chang, *Power and Policy in China* (University Park, Penn.: Pennsylvania State University Press, 1974).

J. Domes, *The Internal Politics of China, 1949–1972* (London: C. Hurst & Co., 1973).

F. Schurmann, *Ideology and Organisation in Communist China* (Berkeley: University of California Press, 1968).

R. Solomon, *Mao's Revolution and the Chinese Political Culture* (Berkeley: University of California Press, 1971).

J. B. Starr, *Ideology and Culture: An Introduction to the Dialectic of Contemporary Chinese Politics* (New York: Harper & Row, 1973).

F. C. Teiwes, *Politics and Purges in China* (New York: M. E. Sharpe Inc., 1979).

J. R. Townsend, *Politics in China* (Toronto: Little, Brown & Co., 1980).

The following journals are useful for research articles, book reviews and contemporary commentary:

Asian Survey
The Australian Journal of Chinese Affairs
Beijing Review
The China Quarterly
Issues and Studies
Modern China
Problems of Communism

The following readings are not meant to provide an exhaustive introduction to the topics covered. They provide a selected cross-section of the literature available. For further detailed study students are advised to follow up the references listed in these works.

Chapter 1

L. Bianco, *Origins of the Chinese Revolution, 1915–1949*, trans. from French by Muriel Bell. (Stanford: Stanford University Press, 1971).

C. Brandt, B. Schwartz and J. Fairbank (eds.), *A Documentary History of Chinese Communism* (New York: Atheneum, 1967).

Chow Tse-tsung, *The May Fourth Movement: Intellectual Revolution in Modern China* (Cambridge, Mass.: Harvard University Press, 1960).

L. Eastman, *The Abortive Revolution, China Under Nationalist Rule, 1929–1937* (Cambridge, Mass.: Harvard University Press, 1974).

J. Guillermaz, *A History of the Chinese Communist Party, 1921–1949* (New York: Random House, 1972).

J. P. Harrison, *The Long March to Power: A History of the Chinese Communist Party, 1921–1972* (New York: Praeger, 1972).

C. Johnson, *Peasant Nationalism and Communist Power: The Emergence of Revolutionary China, 1937–1945* (Stanford: Stanford University Press, 1961).

M. Meisner, *Li Ta-Chao and the Origins of Chinese Marxism* (Cambridge, Mass.: Harvard University Press, 1967).

B. Schwartz, *Chinese Communism and the Rise of Mao* (New York: Harper & Row, 1967).

B. Schwartz, *In Search of Wealth and Power, Yen Fu and the West* (Cambridge, Mass.: Harvard University Press, 1964).

M. Selden, *The Yenan Way in Revolutionary China* (Cambridge, Mass.: Harvard University Press, 1971).

M. C. Wright, *China in Revolution: The First Phase, 1900–1913* (New Haven: Yale University Press, 1968).

Chapter 2

A. Doak Barnett, *Communist China: The Early Years, 1949–55* (New York: Praeger, 1964).

R. Baum, *Prelude to Revolution: Mao, the Party and the Peasant Question, 1962–66* (New York: Columbia University Press, 1975).

R. Baum and F. C. Teiwes, *Ssu-Ching: The Socialist Education Movement of 1962–66* (Berkeley: University of California Press, 1968).

R. Bowie and J. Fairbank, *Communist China 1955–59: Policy Documents with Analysis* (Cambridge, Mass.: Harvard University Press, 1962).

P. Bridgham, 'Mao's Cultural Revolution: Origins and Development' in *China Quarterly*, no. 29, pp. 1–35.

L. Dittmer, 'Line Struggle in Theory and Practice: the Origins of the Cultural Revolution Reconsidered' in *China Quarterly*, no. 72, pp. 675–712.

J. Gray, 'The Two Roads: Alternative Strategies of Social Change and Economic Growth in China' in S. R. Schram (ed.), *Authority, Participation and Cultural Change in China* (Cambridge: Cambridge University Press, 1973), pp. 109–58.

V. Lippit, 'The Great Leap Forward Reconsidered' in *Modern China*, vol. 1, no. 1, pp. 92–115.

R. MacFarquhar, *The Origins of the Cultural Revolution: 1 Contradictions Among the People 1956–57* (New York: Columbia University Press, 1974).

C. Neuhauser, 'The Chinese Communist Party in the 1960s' in *China Quarterly*, no. 32, pp. 3–36.

S. R. Schram, 'The Cultural Revolution in Historical Perspective' in S. R. Schram (ed.), *Authority, Participation and Cultural Change in China* (Cambridge: Cambridge University Press, 1973), pp. 1–108.

R. L. Walker, *China Under Communism: The First Five Years* (London: George Allen & Unwin, 1956).

Chapter 3

B.-J. Ahn, *Chinese Politics and the Cultural Revolution: Dynamics of Policy Processes* (Seattle, Wash.: University of Washington Press, 1976).

R. Baum (ed.), *China in Ferment: Perspectives on the Cultural Revolution* (Englewood Cliffs, N.J.: Prentice-Hall, 1971).

C. Bettleheim and M. Burton, *China Since Mao* (New York: Monthly Review Press, 1978).

P. Bridgham, 'Mao's Cultural Revolution in 1967: The Struggle to Seize Power' in *China Quarterly*, no. 34, pp. 6–37.

P. Bridgham, 'Mao's Cultural Revolution: The Struggle to Consolidate Power' in *China Quarterly*, no. 41, pp. 1–25.

B. Brugger (ed.), *China: The Impact of the Cultural Revolution* (London: Croom Helm, 1978).

B. Brugger (ed.), *China Since the 'Gang of Four'* (London: Croom Helm, 1980).

P. Chang, 'Mao's last Stand?' in *Problems of Communism*, vol. XXV, no. 4.

P. Chang, *Radicals and Radical Ideology in China's Cultural Revolution* (New York: Columbia University Press, 1973).

J. Chen, *Inside the Cultural Revolution* (New York: Macmillan Co., 1975).

L. Dittmer, 'Bases of Power in Chinese Politics: A Theory and Analysis of the Fall of the Gang of Four' in *World Politics*, vol. 31, no. 1.

J. Domes, *China After the Cultural Revolution* (London: C. Hurst & Co., 1977).

J. Domes (ed.), *Chinese Politics After Mao* (Cardiff: University College Cardiff Press, 1979).

D. S. G. Goodman, 'China: The Politics of Succession' in *The Word Today*, April 1977.

T. W. Robinson, *The Cultural Revolution in China* (Berkeley: University of California Press, 1971).

J. B. Starr, 'From the Tenth Party Congress to the Premiership of Hua Kuo-feng' in *China Quarterly*, no. 67, pp. 457—88.

R. Terrill, *The Future of China (After Mao)* (London: André Deutsch, 1978).

Ting Wang, 'The Succession Problem' in *Problems of Communism*, vol. 22, no. 3.

B. Womack, 'Politics and Epistemology in China Since Mao' in *China Quarterly*, no. 80, pp. 768—92.

Chapter 4

The major collections of Mao's writings are as follows:

Selected Works of Mao Zedong (Beijing: Foreign Languages Press), 5 vols.

Selected Readings from the Works of Mao Zedong (Beijing: Foreign Languages Press, 1967).

Selected Military Writings of Mao Zedong (Beijing: Foreign Languages Press, 1963).

Miscellany of Mao Tse-tung Thought 1949—1968 (Arlington, Va: Joint Publications Research Service, 1974).

Unselected Works of Mao Tse-tung 1957 (Hong Kong: Union Research Institute, 1976).

J. Chen, *Mao Papers* (London: Oxford University Press, 1970).

S. R. Schram (ed.), *Mao Tse-tung Unrehearsed* (Harmondsworth: Penguin Books, 1974).

The range of interpretations of Mao's writings is shown by the following.

C. Johnson (ed.), *Ideology and Politics in Contemporary China* (Seattle, Wash.: University of Washington Press, 1973).

M. Meisner, 'Leninism and Maoism: Some Populist Perspectives on Marxism-Leninism in China' in *China Quarterly*, no. 45, pp. 2—36.

R. Pfeffer, 'Mao and Marx in the Marxist-Leninist Tradition' in *Modern China*, vol. 2, no. 4, pp. 421—60.

S. R. Schram, 'Mao Tse-tung and the Theory of Permanent Revolution' in *China Quarterly*, no. 46, pp. 221—44.

S. R. Schram, *The Political Thought of Mao Tse-tung* (Harmondsworth: Penguin Books, 1969).

B. Schwartz, 'The Legend of the "Legend of Marxism"' in *China Quarterly*, no. 2, pp. 35—42.

B. Schwartz, *Communism and China: Ideology in Flux* (New York: Atheneum, 1970).

J. B. Starr, *Continuing the Revolution: the Political Thought of Mao* (Princeton, N.J.: Princeton University Press, 1979).

A. Walder, 'Marxism, Maoism and Social Change' in *Modern China*, vol. 3, nos 1 and 2, pp. 101–16 and 125–80.

K. Wittfogel, 'The Legend of Maoism' in *China Quarterly*, no. 1, pp. 72–86 and no. 2, pp. 16–34.

Chapter 5

The text of the Eighth Party constitution can be found in P. S. M. Tang, *Communist China Today*, vol. 2 (London: Thames & Hudson, 1957). The Ninth, Tenth and Eleventh Party constitutions can be found in the Documents of these Congresses published by Beijing: Foreign Languages Press, 1969, 1973 and 1977 respectively.

A. Doak Barnett, *Chinese Communist Politics in Action* (Seattle, Wash.: University of Washington Press, 1969).

P. Chang, 'Research Notes on the Changing Loci of Decision in the CCP' in *China Quarterly*, no. 44, pp. 169–94.

D. Klein and L. Hager, 'The Ninth Central Committee' in *China Quarterly*, no. 45, pp. 37–56.

J. W. Lewis, *Leadership in Communist China* (Ithaca, New York: Cornell University Press, 1963).

J. W. Lewis (ed.), *Party Leadership and Revolutionary Power in China* (Cambridge: Cambridge University Press, 1970).

K. Lieberthal, *A Research Guide to Central Party and Government Meetings in China, 1949–1975* (White Plains, N.Y.: International Arts and Sciences Press, 1976).

J. Lindbeck (ed.). *China: Management of a Revolutionary Society* (Seattle, Wash.: University of Washington Press, 1969).

S. R. Schram, 'The Party in Chinese Communist Ideology' in *China Quarterly*, no. 38, pp. 1–26.

Chapter 6

The State constitutions adopted at the Fourth and Fifth NPC, were published by the Foreign Languages Press, Beijing, in 1975 and 1978 respectively.

S. Andors, *China's Industrial Revolution: Politics, Planning and Management 1949 to the Present* (London: Martin Robertson, 1977).

A. Doak Barnett, *Cadres, Bureaucracy and Political Power in Communist China* (New York: Columbia University Press, 1967).

J. A. Cohen, *The Criminal Process in the People's Republic of China 1949–1963* (Cambridge, Mass.: Harvard University Press, 1968).

J. A. Cohen, 'The Party and the Courts 1949–1959' in *China Quarterly*, no. 38, pp. 120–57.

D. W. Klein, 'The State Council and the Cultural Revolution in *China Quarterly*, no. 35, pp. 78–95.

V. Li, 'The Evolution and Development of the Chinese Legal System' in J. M. Lindbeck (ed.), *China: Management of a Revolutionary Society* (Seattle, Wash.: Washington University Press, 1971), pp. 221–55.

D. Perkins, *Market Control and Planning in Communist China* (Cambridge, Mass.: Harvard University Press, 1966).

J. Robinson, *Economic Management in China* (London: Anglo-Chinese Educational Institute, 1976).

Chapter 7

P. Bridgham, 'The Fall of Lin Piao' in *China Quarterly*, no. 55, pp. 427–49.

D. A. Charles, 'The Dismissal of Peng Teh-huai' in *China Quarterly*, no. 8, pp. 63–76.

J. Domes, 'The Cultural Revolution and the Army' in *Asian Survey*, vol. VIII, no. 5, pp. 349–63.

J. Domes, 'The Role of the Military in the Formation of Revolutionary Committees' in *China Quarterly*, no. 44, pp. 112–45.

J. Gittings, *The Role of the Chinese Army* (London: Oxford University Press, 1967).

S. B. Griffiths, *The Chinese People's Liberation Army* (New York: McGraw-Hill, 1967).

E. Joffe, *Party and Army: Professionalism and Political Control in the Chinese Officers Corps 1949–64* (Cambridge, Mass.: Harvard University Press, 1965).

E. Joffe, 'The Chinese Army Under Lin Piao: Prelude to Political Intervention' in J. M Lindbeck (ed.), *China: Management of a Revolutionary Society* (Seattle, Wash.: University of Washington Press, 1971).

C. Johnson, 'Lin Piao's Army and its Role in Chinese Society in *Current Scene* (Hong Kong), vol. IV, nos 13 and 14 (1 and 15 July 1966).

Y. M. Kau (ed.), *The Lin Piao Affair: Power Politics and Military Coup* (White Plains, N.Y.: International Arts and Sciences Press, 1975).

H. Nelson, *The Chinese Military System* (Colorado: Westview Press, 1977).

R. L. Powell, 'The Party, the Government and the Gun' in *Asian Survey*, vol. X, no. 6, pp. 441–71.

260   CHINA: POLITICS AND GOVERNMENT

J. D. Simmonds, 'Peng Te-huai: A chronological Re-examination' in *China Quarterly*, no. 37, pp. 120–38.
D. Tretiak, 'China's Vietnam War and its Consequences' in *China Quarterly*, no. 80, pp. 740–67.
W. Whitson, *The Chinese High Command: A History of Communist Military Politics, 1927–1971* (London: Macmillan, 1973).

Chapter 8

M Bastid, 'Economic Necessity and Political Ideal in Educational Reform' in *China Quarterly*, no. 42, pp. 16–45.
G. Bennett, 'Mass Campaigns and Earthquakes: Hai-Ch'eng, 1975' in *China Quarterly*, no. 77, pp. 94–112.
M. Blecher, 'Income Distribution in Small Rural Chinese Communist Communities' in *China Quarterly*, no. 68, pp. 797–816.
T. Bowden and D. S. G. Goodman, 'China: The Politics of Public Security' in *Conflict Study, no. 78*.
J. A. Cohen, 'Chinese Law: At the Crossroad' in *China Quarterly*, no. 53, pp. 139–43.
C. Hoffman, 'Work Incentives in Chinese Industry and Agriculture' in Joint Economic Committee of the U.S. Congress, *An Economic Profile of Mainland China* (New York: Praeger, 1968), pp. 471–498.
V. Li, 'The Role of Law in Communist China' in *China Quarterly*, no. 44, pp. 66–111.
R. Nathan, 'China's Work-Point System: A Study in "Agricultural Splittism" ' in *Current Scene* (Hong Kong), vol. II, no. 31 (15 April 1964).
S. Pepper, 'Chinese Education After Mao: Two Steps Forward, Two Steps Back and Begin Again?' in *China Quarterly*, no. 81, pp. 1–65.
J. R. Townsend, *Political Participation in Communist China* (Berkeley: University of California Press, 1969).
G. White, *The Politics of Class and Class Origin* (Australian National University, 1976).
M. K. Whyte, *Small Groups and Political Rituals in China* (Berkeley: University of California Press, 1974).
M. K. Whyte, 'Inequality and Stratification in China' in *China Quarterly*, no. 64, pp. 654–74.
M. K. Whyte, 'Red vs Expert: Peking's Changing Policy in *Problems of Communism*, vol. 21, no. 6.

Chapter 9

M.-C. Bergère, 'China's Urban Society After Mao in J. Domes (ed.), *Chinese Politics After Mao* (Cardiff: University College Cardiff Press, 1979), pp. 155–74.

B. Brugger, *Democracy and Organisation in the Chinese Industrial Enterprise 1948–1953* (Cambridge: Cambridge University Press, 1976).

J. W. Lewis (ed.), *The City in Communist China* (Stanford: Stanford University Press, 1971).

B. Richman, *Industrial Society in Communist China* (New York: Random House, 1969).

J. W. Salaff, 'The Urban Communes and Anti-City Experiment in Communist China' in *China Quarterly*, no. 29, pp. 82–110.

E. Vogel, *Canton Under Communism* (Cambridge, Mass.: Harvard University Press, 1969).

Chapter 10

S. J. Burki, *A Study of Chinese Communes* (Cambridge, Mass.: Harvard University Press, 1969).

F. W. Crook, 'The Commune System in the People's Republic of China, 1963–74' in Joint Economic Committee, *1974 Congress, First Session, China: A Reassesment of the Economy* (Washington: U.S. Government Printing Office, 1975), pp. 366–410.

W. Hinton, *Fanshen* (Harmondsworth: Penguin Books, 1972).

R. Hofheinz, 'Rural Administration in Communist China in R. MacFarquhar (ed.), *China Under Mao: Politics Takes Command* (Cambridge, Mass.: M.I.T. Press, 1966), pp. 79–118.

J. Myrdal, *Report from a Chinese Village* (New York: Pantheon, 1965).

J. Myrdal and G. Kessle, *China: The Revolution Continued* (New York: Pantheon, 1970).

C. Riskin, 'China's Rural Industries: Self Reliant Systems or Independent Kingdoms' in *China Quarterly*, no. 73, pp. 77–98.

Index

Coláiste Oideachais Mhuire Gan Smal
Luimneach